The Dialogue of the Ancients of Ireland

The Dialogue of the Ancients of Ireland

a new translation of

Acallam na Senórach

Translated with Introduction and Notes by

Maurice Harmon

with a Preface by

Seán Ó Coileáin

Carysfort Press

A Carysfort Press Book in association with Peter Lang

The Dialogue of the Ancients of Ireland

A new translation of

Acallam na Senórach

Translated with an Introduction and Notes by
Maurice Harmon

Portrait of Maurice Harmon © Leonard Photography, Dublin

First published as a paperback in Ireland in 2009
by Carysfort Press Ltd
58 Woodfield, Scholarstown Road, Dublin 16, Ireland

ISBN 978-1-78997-117-0

Cover design by Alan Bennis
Typeset by Carysfort Press Ltd

This book is published with the financial assistance of The Arts Council (An Chomhairle Ealaíon), Dublin, Ireland

Contents

PREFACE

Perhaps the most interesting feature of *Acallam na Senórach* is its perspective on the events it narrates. It is not so much that these events are perceived to lie in the long-distant past but that we are constantly and deliberately reminded of the fact. In this the *Acallam* differs essentially from the earlier saga literature where we find ourselves in the eternal present of the heroic, where no distancing devices intrude by way of extraneous culture or comment, where even the genuinely wondrous is not greatly wondered at, but where, rather than the memory of a marvellous vanished world, we encounter the matter-of-factness of a social setting and of characters felt to be real and immediate.

The late twelfth-century author of the *Acallam* employs the conceit of third-century pagan warriors, who have somehow survived the intervening centuries, meeting with a fifth-century Christianizing St Patrick and bridging the distance between them with their stories and poems, simultaneously authenticating the past and having it included in the new dispensation. In fact the dilemma would have been that of the author himself, though here sublimated in his characters: how to incorporate such material in the literary canon of his own time, where it had yet to be properly established, while attempting to answer the question posed long before by Alcuin of York, with reference to the compatibility of pagan and Christian traditions, *Quid Hinieldus cum Christo*? ('What has Ingeld to do with Christ?').

The earliest surviving manuscript copy of the text is some three centuries later than the first writing, and there would be many other renditions, some of which are still extant, each subject to its own constraints and to the circumstances of its time. It is as though we were to enter a corridor of mirrors, receding into the distance that variously reflect and refract one another according to their nature and disposition. Somewhere beyond stands the author who first shaped the story image, out of what materials we can only guess. While his sources seem to have been largely traditional, and while the form he gave them is also the traditional alternation of prose and verse (although the verse is more prominent than heretofore), the *Acallam* is overwhelmingly a new creation, one worthy to stand comparison with anything that had gone before in the long history of Irish literature.

But any comparison must be a general one, for the heroes of the *Acallam* inhabit a very different world from that of its predecessors: its history and geography are not those of a firmly ordered society; its fluid landscapes, shifting boundaries, anomalous characters and unsure pedigrees lead outwards to a new world of European romance rather than inwards and backwards to a determined, almost claustrophobic 'known' past, that is to say, known and controlled by and in the present.

The ethos of the *Acallam* is one of liberation rather than of control, of nature rather than civil society, of giving rather than acquiring, out of time rather than in time, elegiac and nostalgic rather than functional and prescriptive. The constant interplay of human voices imparts a dramatic quality that partially negates the pretended antiquity of its subject matter and prevents the kind of turgidity that tends to mar other prose works of the period and genre; likewise, its poems have a sense of delicacy and fragility about them quite unlike the professional compositions of the period which usually concern more mundane matters.

The stories and poems of the *Acallam*, which sometimes lie in uneasy relationship with one another, run parallel to and are evoked by various places visited by hero and saint: it is as though a romantic history were being superimposed on an equally romantic geography. Nor would we expect a sense of structure beyond that minimum required to trace their wanderings; such a thing would seem almost out of keeping with the values of the text itself. One is reminded of the little poem spoken by Caílte when asked if his lord, Finn mac Cumaill, had been good to him. His answer is to the effect that, had the yellow leaves that strewed the woods in autumn all been gold, Finn, in his generosity, would have given it all away. In Gaelic society, from beginning to end, there could be no greater praise than this. The *Acallam*, for its part, is a wonderfully generous text, continually heaping riches on us; it would seem churlish to complain that its liberality could have been better arranged.

As with texts so with translations: each must engage the sensibilities of its own time and place. For example, Standish Hayes O'Grady's dignified and solemn rendition in *Silva Gadelica* (1892) is suffused with the warm comforting glow of the late Victorian period when the ancient Celtic world could be recalled with something approaching fondness. Similarly Maurice Harmon brings to his translation a wide experience of modern Irish literature in English, in many areas of which, from O'Faoláin to Beckett, he is an acknowledged expert. He here contends directly with a much earlier expression of Irishness as part of a continuing process of cultural and textual renewal in which we as readers are privileged to participate.

Seán Ó Coileáin, NUI, Cork

INTRODUCTION

The Dialogue of the Ancients of Ireland, a translation of *Acallam na Senórach*, not to be dated earlier than c. 1200, and may be an early thirteenth-century text of about 80,000 words mainly of prose but with many poems interspersed in the prose. A medieval Irish romance, the *Dialogue* tells of the meeting between Oisín and Caílte, two surviving members of the third century Fian, a band of roving warriors who used to guard Ireland, and Saint Patrick, who brought Christianity to Ireland in the fifth century. Caílte and Patrick travel round Ireland together. Patrick is concerned with converting the provincial kings, their nobles and followers, but Caílte wants to revisit places associated with his former comrades. The frame story deals with Patrick's journeys but within that are over two hundred stories told mainly by Caílte about people, places, and events in the legendary past.

The stories reflect many genres: wonder tales, romances, mythological tales, tales of monsters and magic, sea journeys, stories of revenge, transmogrifications and attacks by forces from the Otherworld. Flocks of birds lay waste areas of Munster; a woman from the Island of Women seeks protection from the Fian, but is killed before their eyes by a man from the Island of Men. Three strange men from Norway, each with a particular gift, and their dog protect the Fian but insist on sleeping in their own camp with a wall of fire about them; they do not want anyone to see them at night because every third night one of them is dead and their dog shrinks; that same dog vomits treasure on demand, wine comes from his mouth, his breath turns men's bodies to ashes and he protects Finn mac Cumaill, the leader of the Fian, by walking about him three times each day. The Tuatha Dé Danann in one fairy mound are attacked by Tuatha Dé Danann from another and are saved only by the help of the Fian.

There are also many kinds of poems: poems of praise, nature poems, elegies, genealogical poems, commemorations, eulogies, prophecies. The *Dialogue* is a rich compendium of imaginative literature, a collection of contrasting tales and poems whose diversity and interaction make for a lively imaginative experience. It has been shaped with such intelligence and care and with such a profound understanding of tradition that it is easy to agree with Gerard Murphy that it had a single author. 'Some unknown Irishman of genius,' he said, 'steeped in the ancient lore of Ireland, but inspired also by the innovating tendencies of his time, got the idea of combining all the modes and spirits of various branches of Irish tradition in one vast literary compilation.'[1]

Despite its great variety of stories, poems, incidents and people, the *Dialogue* is coherent and ordered. Formulaic patterns that help to bind the tales together include the manner by which stories are introduced, the formal style of personal address, and the words Patrick and others use to thank Caílte for his stories. Stories are formally introduced by questions about the origin of place-names as, for example, 'Why is this rath called the Rath of the Dog's Head and this mound the Mound of Women?' In response Caílte tells a story that gives the explanation required. At the end of the telling Patrick compliments him courteously with the words, 'Victory and blessing be yours, Caílte, this is entertainment of mind and spirit for us.' At its conclusion all the main participants, Patrick, Caílte, Oisín, the High King of Ireland, the provincial kings, and significant minor figures assemble for the Festival of Tara where narrative strands are brought to conclusion.

The aesthetic interaction of prose narratives with poetic comment or illustration is effective, providing a contrast with the prose and often highlighting particular events, figures, or places. When, for example, Caílte finds a well for Patrick, he recites a sensuous lyric about it:

Well of Tráig Dá Bhan,
lovely your pure-topped cress,
since your verdure has been neglected,
your brooklime cannot spread.

Trout out from your banks,
wild pigs in your wilderness,
deer good to hunt on your crags,
dappled redbreasted fawns.

Mast on the tips of your trees,
fish in your river mouths
lovely colour in your arum shoots,
green brook in the woody hollow.

Caílte's idealized description of Arran is outstanding:

Arran of many stags
The sea beats against her cliffs
Island feeder of hunting bands
Ridges red with steely spears.

[1] 'Acallam na Senórach' in *Irish Sagas*, ed. Myles Dillon (Dublin 1959): 125.

Restless stags on the summits
Ripe bilberries in thickets
Cool water in her streams
Mast in her red oaks.

Hunting dogs and beagles there
Blackberries and blackthorn sloes
Its wall dense with thickets
Deer straying among the oaks.

A purple crop on the rocks
Unblemished grass in the glades
Pleasant cover on the crags
The skipping sound of dappled fawns.

Smooth plains and fat swine
Happy fields, a tale to believe,
Nuts on the tops of her hazels
Long ships sail by.

Pleasant in fine weather
Trout below the river banks
Gulls circling the white cliff
Arran always beautiful.

The contrast between Christianity and paganism permeates the entire work. If there are examples of heroic deeds by the Fian, there are also examples of Patrick's miraculous powers: raising the dead, striking water from a rock, healing the sick, promising salvation and cursing evil-doers so effectively that the ground swallows them. As he zealously pursues his spiritual mission, Patrick is a powerful exponent of Christianity and an impressive advocate for its values. Kings and nobles in each of the provinces readily submit to his spiritual authority. He drives legions of demons from Caílte and Oisín when he first meets them, does the same at Cashel when he ascends the Rock, and in the end will reduce the glorious Tuatha Dé Danann, the gods and goddesses of the Otherworld, to dwellers within hills and mountains. While Patrick's God is not judgemental the unmerited mass destruction of princes at Tara was sufficient proof of His existence to have made Finn mac Cumaill believe in Him. Caílte willingly accepts baptism but laments the disappearance of former comrades and all that they stood for. His stories bear witness to the extraordinary prowess of the pagan Fian in battle, their skill in the use of weapons, their attractiveness to women and their unusual adventures. One of the recurrent themes is the greatness of Finn mac Cumaill and his people, the Clanna Baíscne, and their disruptive rivalry with the other great family, the Clanna Morna.

Patrick, who maintains that Caílte is lucky to have survived long enough to become a Christian, counters these seductive themes. 'You should not feel sad,' he tells him. 'Your condition and your hope are better than all the others, since I have come to you and because the reward of the true God, faith, holiness, and prayer with the arms crossed have come to you and not to any others of the Fian.'

Early on in the work Patrick asks Caílte, 'What values did you live by?' and Caílte makes the famous reply: 'Truth in our hearts, strength in our hands, and fulfilment in our tongues.' In a listing of Fian leaders Caílte associates each with specific qualities such as nobility, knowledge, wisdom. They were brave, loyal, wise. But Finn is the ideal: 'gift-giver to noble hosts, our many-talented wise man./Our chief, leader, seer, judge, magician, and druid.' Fian values include skill in battle, fame, personal honour. The tribute most frequently ascribed to people is that they were hospitable. Generosity is always praised as in this poem about Finn:

> Were but the brown leaf gold
> that the wood sheds,
> were but the white wave silver
> Finn had given all away.

Storytelling itself, however, is an even more important value, transcending all others. Many of the stories compiled and shaped by the nameless author belong to oral tradition and the *Dialogue*'s success depends on the author's effectiveness as a teller of tales. When Patrick questions the propriety of listening to secular stories, his two guardian angels not only approve but urge him to record what Caílte and Oisín say 'for gatherings of people and noblemen in times to come will be delighted to listen to those stories.' Indeed, they say, since the old men only remember a third of what they know, it is imperative to write down what they still recall. Caílte may be proud of the military skills he once had but he is valued by those who listen to him because of what he knows and because he is such a good teller of tales. 'Victory and blessing, Caílte,' says Diarmaid mac Cerbaill, High-King of Ireland, 'where are the poets and storytellers? Let these matters be written in the tablets of the poets, in the records of the learned, in the words of the judges, so that all the knowledge of land and territory may be retained together with all of Caílte's and Oisín's great deeds of valour and prowess, and the place-lore of Ireland.' The *Dialogue* records and affirms the antiquity, strength, endurance and richness of Irish tradition and the poet-minstrel-storyteller is recurrently praised and generously rewarded. In addition to Caílte, the chief storyteller, two of the most attractive figures in the entire work are Cnú Dereóil, the much-loved dwarf minstrel, and Cas Corach, who is surrounded by mystery and who is appointed Poet of Ireland in the final pages.

Heroic and Christian values are finely balanced. Confirming prophecies retrieved from the past validate the coming of saints to sites once associated with the Fian. It is clear, however, that the author favours Connaught where the last portion of the work is set.

While Finn prophesies the coming of particular saints to the monasteries of Ferns, Rosbroc, and Glendalough, his highest praise is for Saint Ciarán, who will come to Clonmacnoise, the most important monastic site on the Shannon.

> A birth will occur there by the will of the Lord of the great clan,
> the worthy son of Heaven's King whom angels serve.
> He will be holy Ciarán, will be born in the royal rath,
>
> will seize half of Ireland, the mason's son from Muirthemne.
> To those who would wreck his church sudden red-speared death,
> hanging, pitiless racking and the lowest pit in hell.

Significantly, Croagh Patrick, also in Connaught, is identified as a place of pilgrimage guaranteed by Saint Patrick. 'I have,' he declares, 'ensured that the place be a place of holiness and truth. Whoever commits evil or wrong there will experience withering of children, kindred and people. My blessing on him who will honour and defend it.' In the next breath he promises that three Connaught kings will rule Ireland and that the country will prosper under them.

The potential conflict between the two cultures is never an issue, the force of paganism never allowed to burst through the author's restraining hand. Caílte laments what has gone but never challenges what has ensued. What he values and represents is subordinated to what he has come to accept. If he regrets and eulogizes the destruction of places where the Fian used to hunt or assemble, their transformation into centres of Christian gathering is celebrated even within the one poem. That process is part of the Christian author's revisionist agenda. Patrick replaces what the Fian represent: Finn is shown to have foreseen and welcomed the coming of Christianity. The story-cycle form itself ensures creative interaction between the various narrative levels and between the pagan, oral world of the Fian and the literate, Christian world of Patrick.

Over and over the *Dialogue* stresses the supremacy of Christianity. No one experiences a crisis of conscience, no one rebels against the teachings of the church. When Aillén Fhialchorcra falls in love with the king of Connaught who already has a wife, Patrick says that such a relationship is forbidden by God and by himself. Both the woman and the king accept this ruling. Only when the first wife dies are they able to marry and that union is one of the threads tied in the conclusion. Significantly this story is told not by Caílte but by the Christian narrator.

The point is also made in the story of Tuathal Techtmar's two daughters, Fithir and Dáirine. Eochaid mac Echach, king of Leinster, wants to marry Fithir but her father will not give her in marriage before her older sister, Dáirine. Eochaid accepts Dáirine, but it is the younger sister he loves. After a year he builds a house in the forest and hides Dáirine there and then goes back to her father. He tells Tuathal that Dáirine has died and that he wants to marry Fithir. Reluctantly the High King agrees. Eochaid takes her back to Leinster but when they arrive they find Dáirine before them. At sight of her sister Fithir dies and then Dáirine also dies. As the poem says: 'Fithir died from shame, Dáirine died from grief.'

The *Dialogue* is a highly allusive text. Behind its evocation of an imaginary landscape lies not only the world of the Fian and of early Christianity but figures and events in Irish sagas, such as the heroic world of the *Táin Bó Cuailnge* (*The Cattle-Raid of Cooley*) and the legend of Suibne Geilt (Mad Sweeney). There are associations with people, places, and events in the *Fianaigecht* (*Adventures of the Fian*), with Patrician hagiography and with European romances. Within the romanticized world of the *Dialogue*, known elements of Irish society exist and help to explain what goes on. Plunderers, for example, are those who do not have ties of kinship with a king or lord; agreements are guaranteed by people of stature; blood-fines are paid for murders; formal gifts are exchanged in accordance with Irish customs. All create a layered landscape and a layered consciousness. The *Dialogue* appears to be grounded in actuality but is free-standing, its imagined reality superimposed on a sketchily outlined real world.

The *Dialogue* gives the impression of being set in a realistic social world through the identification of places and directions to them, through the naming of provincial kings and High King, through the provision of genealogies, through the naming of royal sites and places in which the Tuatha Dé Danann live. But this impression is largely illusory. The names of the kings are almost all fictitious and the place names that seem real are often imaginary. It would be a mistake, however, to think that the *Dialogue* takes place in a political or social vacuum. Ultimately it offers a civilizing ideal at a time of political disruption, c. 1200. Some stories have a moral force: they show how one should behave; they show what kinds of behaviour are deeply, even fatally, shameful. Many deal with relationships between men and women and with marriage, elopements, angry fathers, jealous rivals, sexual arrangements. In early Irish society a man could have more than one wife and so the sharing of his sexual activity could be an issue in marriage arrangements. Some focus on the proper behaviour of retainers. Others illustrate how princes ought to behave. The poem of advice to Mac Lugach is a case in point. Finn mac Cumaill urges him to respect the elderly, to be gentle to women and children, to reward artists, to shun sexual looseness, to be loyal, and prudent.

Do not speak in big words,
or say you will not do what is right.
It is shameful to speak fiercely,
if you cannot match deeds with words.

Do not abandon your lord
while you live in this yellow world.
Nor for any wealth or gold
go back on your support.

One of the most attractive aspects of the *Dialogue* is the connection between the visible and the invisible worlds, between the landscape in which Patrick and Caílte travel and the places under fairy mounds where the Tuatha Dé Danann live. To some degree there is little difference between the people of this world and the people of the Otherworld. They too have elopements and battles, make alliances for purposes of marriage or combat, and have a range of feeling. But they are forever young and beautiful, live in crystal palaces, and enjoy an abundance of food and drink. The *Dialogue* has several descriptions of their houses, such as this sophisticated account of Créde's home under the Paps mountains in north County Kerry.

> A hundred feet in Créde's house
> from one end to the other,
> twenty measured feet the width
> of its splendid doorway.
>
> Its wattling and thatch
> of bird feathers yellow and blue,
> its wall-railing to the east
> of glass and carbuncle.
>
> Four pillars for each bed
> patterned with silver and gold,
> the glass gem on each pillar
> a pleasant crowning.

Créde may be a creature of the Otherworld but her lament for her drowned husband, Cael, at the Battle of Finntrága is as moving as any human elegy:

> The harbour cries out at the red race of Rinn dá Bharc,
> the wave against the shore laments the drowning of the man from
> Loch Dá Chonn.
>
> The crane cries in the marshes of Druim Dá Thrén,
> but cannot guard her young when the fox comes near.
>
> Sad is the cry the thrush makes in Druim Caín,
> no less sad the blackbird's voice in Leitir Laíg.
>
> Sad the sound the stag makes in Druim dá Léis,
> for the dead doe of Druim Sílenn the stag roars.
>
> It grieves me the death of the hero who used to lie with me,
> the son of the woman of Doire Dá Doss with a cross above his head.
>
> It grieves me, Cael, to have you dead by my side,
> the wave-drench over your bright side maddens me.
>
> Sad the sound the wave makes against the shore,
> it drowned a fine handsome man, my grief Cael went near.

Sad the sound the wave makes to the north,
hammering the hard rocks, lamenting Cael's death.

Sad the sound the wave makes to the south,
my time is done as my appearance reveals.

Sad the sound made by Tulcha's dragging wave.
I have no future, since its tidings reached me.

Since Crimthann's son drowned, I will love no one,
his hand felled many, on a hard day his shield never cried out.

The *Dialogue* has a splendid imaginative power. We are persuaded that vast numbers of people, kings, nobles and followers, Christians and pagans travel from place to place and that they enjoy lavish banquets, but no mention is made of the practical difficulties involved. The Tuatha Dé Danann add to this sense of a romantic cavalcade and Caílte's stories of place-identifications with their array of characters and events deepen the atmosphere of romance. The medieval imagination enjoys the crowded canvas, splendid figures, kings, queens, romances, wonders, magic, daring deeds, banquets and feasts.

More generally the atmosphere of medieval romance casts an attractive ambience over the entire work so that accounts of battles, beheadings, fights against monsters, or against the Tuatha Dé Danann all fit into a pleasing style. In telling the story of the journeys made by Patrick, Caílte, and Oisín and providing a geographical context for them, the author at the same time usually achieves a smooth transition to the many different kinds of stories within that frame story. He can sustain a narrative across several stories, introducing characters, leaving them aside, introducing other stories, and then return to the original story and its characters.

The *Dialogue* connects the present with the past and revivifies what once was. Past splendour is confirmed by Caílte's stories and by the evidence he produces in the form of goblet, sword, or treasure. These, he says, belonged to Finn or Oisín; here is where that woman was buried; that hill, that ford, that plain is where these events took place. In the end it is the narrative richness and values of the work that are most important. Second in length only to the *Táin Bó Cuailnge*, the scale, variety and artistic power of the *Dialogue* make it one of the greatest and most entertaining works in Irish literature.

Acallam na Senórach was edited by Standish Hayes O'Grady in *Silva Gadelica*, vols. 1-11, 1892, and by Whitley Stokes in *Irische Texte* in 1900. The version that follows, based on the Stokes edition, is a free rendering and not a work of textual scholarship. My aim is to provide an accessible text for the general reader. In the case of the prose I have changed the original text from long paragraphs incorporating both narrative and dialogue to the conventions of modern fiction which many times separate dialogue from description and narration. In the case of some of the poetry that is written in an older form of the language than the prose I have often provided a literal translation.

I am grateful to Fergus Kelly, Proinsias MacCana, and Gearóid Mac Eoin for guidance in translating some of the poems, but the errors that may remain are mine. I wish to thank Barbara Brown for invaluable editorial assistance and Mary Brennan and Michael Hayden for computer skills. I am grateful to Seán Ó Coileáin, Professor of Modern Irish at University College Cork, for his generous Preface. To Dan Farrelly, Eamonn Jordan, and especially Lilian Chambers at Carysfort Press, I owe a particular debt of gratitude.

THE DIALOGUE OF THE ANCIENTS OF IRELAND

(*Acallam na Senórach*)

Part I

When the battle of Comar, the battle of Gabair, and the battle of Ollarba had been fought and the Fian virtually wiped out, they scattered in groups throughout Ireland until the time of which we speak. Then only two of the leading warriors were still alive, Oisín mac Finn and Caílte mac Crunnchon meic Rónaín, the last of the Fian, with their strength and agility diminished and two bands of nine warriors with them and with these eighteen came from the forested Fews mountains to Lugbarta Bána, now called Louth. There as night fell they were sad and dispirited.

Oisín, my friend, Caílte said, what road will we take to find hospitality for the night?

I do not know, said Oisín, since only three of the old Fian and the followers of Finn mac Cumaill survive, you and I, and Cáma, the woman-chief and woman-provider who minded Finn from when he was a boy to the day he died.

We are entitled to food and lodging from her, said Caílte, since it would be impossible to reckon how much treasure and valuables Finn, the Fian-chief, gave her, including one of the three best treasures that he ever obtained, Angalach, the drinking-horn that Moriath, daughter of the king of the Greeks, gave him.

They found hospitality that night with Cáma. She asked their names and, when they told her, lamented and shed many tears. They asked one another for news. Later they came into the bed-house that had been prepared for them. Cáma gave them the freshest food and the oldest wine. She knew how men like them used to be fed. Although she was very feeble, she spoke of the Fian and Finn mac Cumaill, Oscar mac Oisín, Mac Lugach, and the battle of Gabair and other things. Then a great silence came over them.

Caílte spoke, Nothing could be harder than that we, the twice nine left of that great company, should part from one another.

Oisín replied, Since they are gone, I have neither fight nor strength.

And although they were brave warriors, they and Cáma, the woman-chief, wept sadly and in great sorrow. They were given all the food and drink they needed and stayed for three days and three nights.

Oisín said:

Cáma is weary today her career is ended.
Cáma is an old lady without son or grandson.

Coming out on the grassy green, they decided to separate, parting like the division of soul and body. Oisín went to the fairy mound of Cleittech where his mother, Blaí, daughter of Derg Dianscothach, lived. Caílte continued on to the estuary of Bec Loingsech in Brega, now known as the monastery of Drogheda, called after Bec Loingsech mac Airist, who was drowned there. He was the son of the king of the Romans who came to invade Ireland.

Caílte continued on to Linn Féic on the Boyne and south across the old plain of Brega to the fort of Druim Derg where Patrick, son of Calpurnius, happened to be. Patrick was chanting the divine office, praising the Creator, and blessing the fort where Finn mac Cumaill was, that is, the Rath of Druim Derg.

When the clerics saw the warriors approach they were seized with fear and terror of the huge men and their enormous dogs, for they were not people of the same time as themselves. Then the Salmon of Sovereignty, the Pillar of Lordship and the Angel of the Earth, Patrick mac Calpurnius took a sprinkler to shake holy water over the big men, for there were a thousand legions of devils above their heads until that day. The demons fled on all sides into the hills, the clefts and the borders of that region. Then the huge men sat down.

Patrick spoke to Caílte, What is your full name?

Caílte mac Crunnchon meic Rónaín, he replied.

The clerics wondered greatly and gazed at them for a long time, for the tallest of them when they were seated came only to the waist or the shoulder of any of the warriors.

I'd like to make a request of you, Caílte, said Patrick.

If I have the strength or power it will be given, Caílte replied, just tell me what it is.

To find a well of pure water nearby from which we can baptize the peoples of Brega, Mide [Meath], and Uisnech.

I have it for you.

They went out across the dyke of the fort. Caílte took Patrick by the hand. Seeing a gravelled well-spring in front of them, they were surprised by the size and thickness of the watercress and the brooklime growing there. Caílte began to speak of its fame:

Well of Tráig Dá Bhan,
lovely your pure-topped cress,

since your verdure has been neglected,
your brooklime cannot spread.

Trout out from your banks,
wild pigs in your wilderness,
deer good to hunt on your crags,
dappled redbreasted fawns.

Mast on the tips of your trees,
fish in your river mouths,
lovely colour in your arum shoots,
green brook in the woody hollow.

From you the Fian went,
when loyal Coinchenn died,
after the dreadful slaughter of Finn's Fian,
that morning above Maolglinn.

From you went Fothad of the feasts,
a warrior who suffered hardship,
who gained the bounty of the eastern world,
and died in the battle of Clárach.

There came to the well's side
Blaí, daughter of Derg Dianscothach.
Baying by her side a great hound,
that she loosed in the furious fight.

When men and dogs were slain
and bright warriors torn,
Garad's clear call was heard
at night from the well's side.

Well, asked Patrick, is our meal ready yet?

It is, said Bishop Sechnall.

Divide our food, Patrick said, and give half to these nine fine warriors, survivors of the Fian.

Then the bishops, priests, and psalmists rose, blessed the food, and took their fill of food and drink for the good of their souls.

It was then Patrick asked, Was Finn mac Cumaill, whom you served, a good lord?

Caílte spoke this little praise poem:

Were but the brown leaf gold
that the wood sheds,
were but the white wave silver
Finn had given all away.

What values did you live by? asked Patrick.

Truth in our hearts, strength in our hands, and fulfilment in our tongues.

My good friend, said Patrick, were there drinking-horns, cups, or goblets of crystal and white gold in houses before our time?

Caílte answered, In my chief's house there were indeed drinking vessels:

> Finn had three hundred and twelve golden drinking horns,
> wonderful their liquor, amazing how much they held.

Were it not for us, Patrick said, an impairment of the religious life, a distraction from prayer, and an abandonment of discourse with the King of heaven and earth, talking with you would be a pleasant way to pass the time.

Then Caílte began to sing of the drinking horns and the lords and chiefs who owned them:

> The horns that were at Finn's house, their names we call to mind,
> Macalla, slender Grugán, Women's Horn and Admall.
> Macám, horn of Ailbe, all with large sides,
> are handed round among the hosts, slower ebbing than filling.
> Adharcán the horn Diarmaid had whose lavish drop would be given to women,
> drink for four dozen men, on my life it held that much.
> Mac Lugach's two horns, Golden Light and Golden Odrán,
> brimful Golden Light loved by men, would part them from precise speech.
> We would drink together in the house of famous Finn,
> Echo in my hand, Diarmaid who loved me had Múdán.
> Grugán held by the Fian-chief, their own horns in the hands of women.
> Drinks for forty from Echo, sixty from the Women's Horn.
> Drink for eighty from Múdán, drink for a hundred from pure Grugán.
> Fair-Youthful, the horn that glorious Oscar brought to the assembly.
> It was the cynosure of foreign hosts and women smiled to see it.
> Lescach, a great beauty, horn of glorious Aillenn,
> Finn raised it to his lips from bright-fingered Gothán.
> The Earl which gave merriment as it made its fair rounds
> Finn gave to Dubán mac Dubnóna in the drinking house.
> Finn had Green Man, the cup we brought over every sea,
> if you drank it did not decrease but filled thirty men.
> The smallest in our drinking sessions, son of Calpurn in whose house we are,
> was Fer Tuillid, horn of Glas mac Gathail, you do not have its match.
> A sorrow to brave men the horn of mac Rethe of great horror,
> they were not pleased to be in Finn's house when you were in Cromglenn.
> Speckled Red, great its capacity, the horn of gentle Caílte,
> because of it Finn joined the fierce fight in which Lugaíd Trí Rém fell fighting.
> Head Beautiful the cup of Scotland's king with whom we travelled across woods,
> we drank much mead from the horn of Rónán, the royal warrior.
> No one like Finn will ever come again, does not give cause to plunder,
> king of the world, whatever his fame, never had such horns.

May victory and blessing be yours, Caílte, said Patrick, all this is recreation of mind and spirit for us. Now tell us another story.

I will to be sure, said Caílte, but what story would you like?

Did you have horses or horse-teams in the Fian?

We did indeed, one hundred and fifty foals from one mare and one stallion.

Where did you get them?

I'll tell you how it happened. Finn had a young warrior, Artúr mac Bénne Brit, who had a retinue of twenty-seven men. Finn began hunting on Benn Étair [Hill of Howth] and a fine successful hunt it was. When they let the hounds loose he sat on the Fian's Cairn between Benn Étair and the sea, enjoying the bellowing of the furious stags as they were swiftly slain by the dogs. Artúr mac Bénne Brit was stationed between the hunt and the sea so that deer might not swim away from them.

When he was at the mouth of the harbour he saw three of Finn's hounds, Bran, Sceolaing, and Adnuall, and decided that he and his twenty-seven followers would cross the sea to his own country, bringing the hounds with him. He carried out that plan, crossing the sea with the three dogs until they found haven and harbour at Inber Mara Gaimiach in Britain. They came ashore, went to Mount Lodán, and began hunting. Meanwhile the Fian stopped hunting. They camped at Benn Étair and as usual counted the dogs in Finn's company. He had many hounds.

Caílte sang:

> I count Finn's hounds numerous as branches
> a pack of fine, sweet-tongued animals
> three hundred fully-grown dogs
> and two hundred pups.

Many men must have owned them, Patrick observed.

That is true, this is how it was.

Caílte spoke:

> There were a hundred and fifty in Finn's retinue,
> shrewd leaders of the Fian,
> three hundred beloved youths,
> two hundred worthy fosterlings.

When the hounds were counted they discovered a great lack: Bran, Sceolaing, and Adnuall. Finn was told.

Have the three battalions search for them, he said. They searched but the hounds were not found.

Then they gave Finn a golden basin. He washed his kingly face, placed his thumb under his tooth of knowledge, and the truth was revealed to him: The son of the king of Britain has taken your hounds, he said. Choose nine men to go in search of them.

The men were chosen: Diarmaid mac Duinn meic Donnchada meic Dubáin of the Érainn of Munster and Goll mac Morna.

Was Goll the son of a king, asked Patrick, or the son of a warrior?

The son of a king.

Caílte said:

> Son of Tadg, son of Morna of the plain,
> Son of Faelán, son of Feradach,
> Son of Fiacha, son of Art of the plain,
> Son of Muiredach, son of Eógan.

There was also Caol Cróda, grandson of Nemnann, slayer of a hundred, rich in venom who had this gift: his arm never fired a cast that missed its mark, his hand never wounded someone who did not die within nine days. There was Oisín, Finn's son, who never refused anyone who had a head to eat with and legs to carry him.

That is a great tribute, Patrick remarked.

And a true one.

Caílte said:

> Oisín never denied anyone gold, silver, or food.
> Nor demanded anything from anybody though his generosity be king-like.

There was Oisín's son, Oscar, the king's son, who surpassed everyone in Ireland in strength and agility; and Ferdoman, son of Bodb Derg, son of the Dagda; Finn's son, wide-eyed Raigne; Finn's son, purple-red Cainche; Glas mac Aencherda Bérra; Mac Lugach, and myself. We felt sure that from Taprobané to the Garden of the Hesperides in the western world there were not four hundred warriors who could match us in battle or in hand-to-hand combat. No shoulder was without a bright shining shield, no head without a helmet, no right fist without two long broad spears. We set off on this course until we came to Mount Lodán mac Lir and were not long there before we heard close-by the voices of men hunting on the plain. At that time Artúr mac Bénne Brit was sitting on his hunting mound with his people. We attacked them quickly, killing all of Artúr's followers, but Oscar put his arms around Artúr and protected him. We took our three hounds away with us.

When Goll mac Morna looked about him, he saw a brindled grey stallion that had a bridle ornamented with gold. On his left he saw a bay mare that would not be hard to catch. She had a reticulated silver bridle fitted with a golden bit. Goll caught this horse and gave her to Oisín, who gave her to Diarmaid Ó Duibne. We came away from our successful slaughter, bringing with us the heads of the thrice nine, our dogs, the horses and Artúr himself as a prisoner. We came to where

Finn was at the old plain in the district of Étar. When we reached the chief's tent, I spoke:

> We have brought Artúr with us
> that he may be one of Finn's warriors
> from now till the day of his death.

We gave the horses to Finn, a stallion and a mare. From their seed came all the horses of the Fian, who previously had not been accustomed to horses. The mare foaled eight times, eight foals each time, which were given to the companies. Afterwards they made chariots.

Victory and blessing, Caílte, said Patrick. Tell us the names of the chiefs and champions who owned the horses.

Caílte replied as follows:

> I know the horses of the Fian whoever might speak to one another,
> whenever the slender host came to the fair of slender-sided Tailtiu.
> Coinchenn of Eochaid Mac Lir, Aignech of dear Diarmaid,
> Coscrach of Finnchad of battles, Mac Lugach's Gormlasrach.
> Bodb owned by Mac Lugach, Conán's shapely Érim.
> The Mare from Man from overseas, owned by Finn Bán ua Bresail.
> Oscar's lucky Échtach, Dubán's Dubluirgnech,
> Midach, Scál's unhappy loss, and Fer Baeth of Mac Sidhmaill.
> Francán and Lúth in harness, princely steeds the Fian unyoked,
> Lúth for Scuirín, brave master, and Francán for Dubdruman.
> Golden Gerr, Silver Gerr, together before the chariot,
> The two steeds of Ailme, daughter of Ireland's High King.
> Dub of the Rapid, Dub of the Wave, steeds of Aengus Angluinne,
> Caílte and Oisín together used go to every gathering.
> The horse of Goll mac Morna, a watchman in Maenmag,
> when released on mountain or plain as swift as a spring wind.
> The horse that was never outstripped by anything, dog, animal, deer,
> Coinchenn, Finn of the feast had, brought from Saxon lands.
> Glas Gaillme, great in deed, better on its own than a hundred horses,
> Finn had in fine condition at the head of every host
> Four score and two hundred and a thousand, no lie,
> splendid for heroes of substance the cavalry of Finn of Alma.

Victory and blessing, Caílte, said Patrick, all this would be a relaxation of mind and spirit for us were it not a distraction from devotion and a diversion from prayer.

They were there until the following morning when Patrick put on his vestments and came out onto the green with three score priests, three score psalm-singers, and three score holy bishops who were spreading faith and holiness throughout Ireland with him.

Patrick's two guardian angels, Aibelán and Solasbreathach, appeared. Patrick asked if the King of heaven and earth wished him to listen to the stories of the Fian.

Beloved, holy cleric, the angels said, because of forgetfulness and loss of memory these old warriors can only tell you a third of their stories. Make sure that what they say is written on poets' tablets and in the words of the learned for gatherings of people and noblemen in times to come will be delighted to listen to those stories. Then the angels left.

Patrick sent messages to Caílte. He was brought to the saint together with his nine warriors. These were their names: Failbe mac Flainn; Eógan Airmderg, son of the king of Ulster; Flann mac Fergusa, son of the king of Cenél Conaill; Conall Coscarach, son of Aengus, king of Connaught; Scannlán mac Ailella, son of the king of Ossory; Baedán mac Gairb, son of the king of Corca Duibne; Luaimnech mac Linn, son of the king of Érainn of Munster; Aed Lethderg mac Eógain, son of the king of north Munster; Failbe and Uanchenn, the two sons of the king of Dál nAraide in the north; and Fulartach mac Fingin, son of the king of Brega and Mide.

Do you know, Patrick inquired, why you have been brought to speak with me?

We do not, Caílte replied.

So that you may submit yourselves to the gospel of the King of heaven and earth, that is, to the Supreme God.

Then Patrick poured the water of Christ's baptism on them.

Caílte stretched his right hand to the box of his shield and for the baptism of the nine who were with him gave Patrick a ridgy mass of red gold that weighed thrice fifty ounces.

That was the last wage I got from the chief, Finn, said Caílte. I want you to have it, Patrick, for my soul's sake and for the sake of the Fian-chief's soul.

The piece of gold stretched from the tip of his middle finger to the top of his shoulder and had the width and depth of a man's wrist. This gold was used for the Táilchenn's blessed handbells of the canonical hours and for the psalters and mass books.

Tell me, my friend, Patrick said, what was the best hunting the Fian ever had, in Ireland or Scotland?

The hunting in Arran, said Caílte.

Where's that? asked Patrick.

Between Scotland and the land of the Picts. We, the three battalions of the Fian, would go there on the first day of Lammastide, now called Lughnasad, to have our fill of hunting until the cuckoo would call from the tree-tops in Ireland. On that island the voices of the birds as they flew up from the waves and from the shore were sweeter than any music. There were a hundred and fifty flocks there, of every colour – blue, green, grey, yellow.

Caílte spoke this poem:

Arran of many stags
The sea beats against her cliffs
Island feeder of hunting bands
Ridges red with steely spears.

Restless stags on the summits
Ripe bilberries in thickets
Cool water in her streams
Mast in her red oaks.

Hunting dogs and beagles there
Blackberries and blackthorn sloes
Its wall dense with thickets
Deer straying among the oaks.

A purple crop on the rocks
Unblemished grass in the glades
Pleasant cover on the crags
The skipping sound of dappled fawns.

Smooth plains and fat swine
Happy fields, a tale to believe,
Nuts on the tops of her hazels
Long ships sail by.

Pleasant in fine weather
Trout below the river banks
Gulls circling the white cliff
Arran always beautiful.

Victory and blessing be yours, Caílte, my friend, said Patrick, you and your stories will please us forever.

At that moment Patrick saw a fort, a fine dwelling, due south from him. What place is that? he asked.

The proudest place in the whole of Ireland or Scotland, Caílte replied.

Who lived there? asked Patrick.

The three sons of Lugaid Menn mac Aengusa, that is, the king of Ireland's three sons: Ruide, Fiacha, and Eochaid.

How did they get their great wealth?

One time they went to talk with their father at the Grave of the Druids to the northwest of Tara. Where have you come from? he asked them. From Echlais Banguba in the south, they replied, from the home of our nurse and guardian. They were dressed in beautiful cloaks, a green cloak on the eldest, Ruide, a fringed woollen cloak from the Land of Promise on Fiacha, and a blue one on Eochaid, who had a band of shining silver fastened across his chest with a golden pin.

Young men, asked the king of Ireland, why have you come? To ask you for land and territory, they replied. The king was silent for a while before he answered: No father gave me land and territory, but my own ability and determination. I will not give you land. You must earn it yourselves.

They rose up as one and went to the green of Bruig na Bóinne where they sat with nobody near them.

What is your advice this night? asked Ruide.

Our advice, said his brothers, is that we fast against the Tuatha Dé Danann to be granted a kingdom, estates, land, and great wealth from them.

They were not long there before they saw a pleasant, cheerful-looking young man coming towards them. He had a forked brown beard and his beautiful soft, plaited yellow hair hanging over his shoulders was tied with a slender fillet of gold so that the tempestuous wind might not impede sight or vision. He had silver sandals on his feet but when his foot touched the ground it did not shake the dewdrop from the blade of grass. He greeted the king of Ireland's sons and they responded in kind.

Where do you come from? they asked him.

From that sunlit hostel in front of you?

What is your name? they asked.

Bodb Derg, son of the Dagda.

It was made known to the Tuatha Dé Danann that you would come here tonight to fast for lands and great wealth. Come with me.

They all rose and went into the hostel where they were seated on chairs of clear glass in the middle of the fairy mound. They were served food but did not eat.

Bodb asked why they did not eat. The king of Ireland, they explained, our own father, has refused us territories and land. In Ireland there are only two assemblies that are equal: the sons of Mil and the Tuatha Dé Danann. We have come now to one of them.

Then Bodb approached with a fine delicate goblet in his hand. Be quiet everyone, he said, and the entire fairy people became silent. Holding their drinking horns, their cups, and their golden and silver goblets, the Tuatha Dé Danann entered into consultation. He who was the noblest and most eminent, Midir of the Yellow Hair, spoke to them: Give these men three wives, he said, for it is from women that good and bad luck comes. They gave the three daughters of Midir: Doirenn, Aífe, and Ailbe.

Tell me, Bodb, said Midir, what gifts will we give them?

We are in this fairy dwelling with one hundred and fifty kings' sons. Give one hundred and fifty ounces of gold from each son and one hundred and fifty suits of clothes of every colour.

My gift for them, said Aed, son of Aed, one of the Tuatha Dé Danann from Cnoc Ardmulla, now known as Rathlin, is a drinking-horn and a vat. When you fill this vat to the brim with water it makes sweetly intoxicating mead. Even if you put bitter deep seawater into it, it will turn immediately into wine.

My gift, said Lir from the fairy mound of Finnachad, one hundred and fifty swords and a hundred and fifty tall, well-riveted spears.

My gift, said Aengus Óg, son of the Dagda, a fort, a fortress, and a great kingly place with high palisades, clear bright sun-rooms, roomy houses with attractive outlook, and all of this where they will most desire between Rathcoffey and Tara.

My gift, said Áine, daughter of Modarn, my cook who by *geis* is forbidden to refuse food to anyone, for whatever she gives comes back to her.

My gift, said Bodb Derg, my fine minstrel, Fer Tuinne mac Trogain. Even if brave men were being whipped, women were labouring in childbirth, and champions after being defeated, they would be put to sleep by the soothing music he makes. He is not more of a minstrel for this fort than for the people of the whole country.

They stayed in that fairy mound for three days and three nights. Aengus told them to take the three apple trees of Fid Omna with them: a tree in bloom, a tree shedding blossom, a tree with ripe fruit. They went to the fort and lived there for one hundred and fifty years but then returned to live permanently with the Tuatha Dé Danann because of their marriages and friendship with them. And that, Patrick, Caílte concluded, is the fort you asked about.

Caílte sang:

Three floods
from Ruide's high fort:
a flood of youths, a flood of horses,
the flood of Lugaid's sons' hunting dogs.

Three kinds of music
that noble kings enjoy:
harp song, lute sound,
the bass of Fer Tuinne, Trogan's son.

Three cries
never scarce there:
Sheep bleating on the green,
horses neighing, cattle lowing.

Three cries:
from Daig's great-chined fat pigs,
voices of hosts on the palace green,
the sound of love and mead.

Three crops
on its branches:
nuts falling day by day,
a tree in flower, fruit that's ripe.

Three sons
sired by Lugaid
though their fame has passed:
Eochaid, mighty Fiacha, Ruide.

I will vouch for Eochaid,
who never ebbed in rout,
nor ever lacked for music,
and never short of drink.

I will vouch for Fiacha,
though his raids have ceased,
he never said too much,
no one was more brave.

I will vouch for Ruide,
who had the three that poured,
he never refused anyone,
nor begged from anyone.

Thirty lords, thirty chiefs,
thirty warriors fit for a king,
hundreds in his hosts,
three times three hundreds.

Victory and blessing be yours, Caílte, said Patrick, all this eases our mind and spirit.

Before long they saw a resplendent young man coming straight towards them from the south. He wore a purple cloak with a pin of gold, a sun-yellow silk shirt next to his skin, and he had a bag-apron full of round nuts and beautiful golden apples. These he placed in front of Patrick.

Where do you bring this fruit from? Patrick asked.

From Fid Gaible's [Feeguile] beautiful boughs, he said.

Who are you? asked Patrick.

I'm Fulartach mac Fergusa, he said.

Where do you come from?

We rule over the lands of Brega and Mide, and the Déise of Tara is also ours, replied the young man, but I am a marauder and plunderer.

Whom do you plunder? asked Patrick.

Becán mac Fergusa, my own brother.

May you get your inheritance soon, Patrick said.

Tell me when, holy cleric, asked the young man.

Within this year, said Patrick. But where do you bring this fruit from?

I know where you brought it from, Caílte said, from Ros meic Treoin [New Ross] in Fid Gaible, a hunting preserve that belonged to Mac Lugach the Strong, a great slaughterer and one of Finn mac Cumaill's favourite warriors.

May he rest in peace, said Patrick. There's a favourite member of my family there also, Cesán, son of the king of Scotland, a champion of mine.

It was a hunting preserve of the Fian, said Caílte. Whenever they ran short of hunting in Ireland and Scotland they got plenty of it for three days and three nights in Ros meic Treoin.

Caílte sang:

Before the Táilchenn came Cluain Cesáin was well known
as Ros meic Treoin, the exact place, where Mac Lugach used to go.
Although clerics intone psalms in turn at Cluain Cesáin,
I saw its gentian plain alive with playful red deer.
Although there is learning above the sea one time it was not a hollow church
its stream a place for apples and for swimming, the fertile gentian plain.
The happy prophecy came about, the clerics tilled Cluain Cesáin,
Finn, generous giver, said it would be a sacred place for holy angels.
Often we roamed with hounds after lively young deer
warriors and dogs relaxed, hunting the smooth plain.
In truth three score queens were mine at one time,
I used to do favours for all, I was a deceitful trickster.

What time is it? Patrick asked.

Almost night, said Benignus.

Has our meal been served yet? asked Patrick.

Not yet, said Benignus.

Holy Patrick, said Fulartach mac Fergusa, I could tell you of a place where you would get food and sustenance tonight.

Where's that? asked Patrick.

In the house of my brother, Becán, in the lands of Brega and Mide.

Some clerics went to Becán's house ahead of Patrick. Although Becán had twenty-eight herds of fair milch cows he refused them food. Benignus and the other clergy reported back to Patrick.

I wish, he said, that none of his people and cattle be alive tomorrow.

That came true, as Patrick said:

> Becán: may his cattle be few,
> as long as the sun shall go right
> may there not be six of his descendants.

The earth swallowed Becán and his people all at once, together with his animal and human possessions, said Caílte.

Holy cleric, said Fulartach mac Fergusa, I will give you food and lodging tonight: twenty-nine cows that feed my warriors while marauding and plundering.

From midday tomorrow I give to you and your descendants the power of a lord unless you turn against the church, said Patrick.

Becán was buried and Patrick gave his kingship to Fulartach. This story is called The Destruction of Becán.

It was then Patrick asked Caílte, How many brothers had Finn?

Two. Fíthal and Cithramach.

Caílte said:

> Our historians are not clear about this:
> who were the three sons of Cumall:
> Finn, Cithramach,
> and Fíthal of the poets.

Whose son was Mac Lugach, whom I asked you about last night? said Patrick.

That would be a hard question for someone else, but not for me, replied Caílte. He was the son of Finn's son, Dáire Derg, and of Lugach, Finn's daughter, that is, a daughter, proper or improper, that Finn had. All the women swore that she was Finn's own daughter. But her own brother after drinking ale in Temair Luachra [Tara in Luachair] had slept with her and begotten that son, Mac Lugach. At the end of nine months she went into labour and gave birth to a son. The night the child was born Finn, the three battalions of the Fian, and the child's father, Dáire Derg, came to Temair Luachra and were told about it. It is good for us, said Finn, that a son is born. If it had been a daughter born from her brother that would have been bad. Victory and blessing be yours, king of the Fian, everyone said. You have given him a good name, Gaíne, meaning Blessing:

> Gaíne is the name of the valiant Mac Lugach,
> Dáire, his father before everyone.
> Cú Maige is the name of Rethe's son,
> Brian is the father of Dáire.

They placed the boy, continued Caílte, in Finn's arms, who placed him in the arms of Mongfhinn, daughter of Dubán, Finn's wife. It was she who raised eight hundred shield-bearers of the Fian. She took care of the boy until he was twelve years old. Then she gave him the clothes and arms he needed. He came to Carrac Conluain on the top of Sliab Smóil meic Edlecair, known as Sliab Bladma [Slieve Bloom] today, where Finn and the Fian were. He came before the Fian-chief who welcomed him with genuine tenderness. Shaking hands with Finn, the young lad made an agreement of friendship and was with him for a year. But during that year he showed himself to be very slow with the result that not more than nine of the Fian in his charge had succeeded in killing either boar or deer. In addition he used to beat their dogs and their servants.

When the Fian came to Ros in Fhéinneda [Fian Point] on the shores of the brimming Loch Léin [Lakes of Killarney] and when the three battalions of the Fian had assembled they made Finn aware of their complaint. This is what they said: The choice is yours: either us or Mac Lugach on his own.

Then Mac Lugach was brought to speak with Finn, who asked him, What harm have you done to the Fian, since all of them complain about you?

I give you my word, he replied, I am unable to understand why they think badly of me, unless it be that they do not like my skill in athletics and spear-throwing.

The Fian-chief, said Caílte, gave Mac Lugach advice, good advice that remained with Mac Lugach ever after.

Finn said:

Mac Lugach, let me tell you,
if you want to achieve status,
be peaceful in a strong man's house,
but vigorous in the wild.

Do not strike your dog without cause
nor blame your wife without proof.
Do not strike a fool in battle
No matter how crazy he may be.

Do not mock a holy man.
Do not get drawn into strife.
Do not get involved with a witch
or an evil creature.

Two thirds of your gentleness to women
and those who crawl on the floor.
Be good to artists making poems.
Respect ordinary people.

Do not be first into bed
before your familiars.
Avoid incest and sodomy.
Do not welcome everyone.

Do not speak in big words
or say you will not do what is right.
It is shameful to speak fiercely,
if you cannot match deeds with words.

Do not abandon your lord
while you live in this yellow world.
Nor for any wealth or gold
go back on your support.

Do not strongly criticize
his people to their lord.
A decent man should not
complain to a chief about his people.

Do not bear false tales
nor be rashly censorious.
Though your virtues be many
do not antagonize the assembly.

Do not frequent houses of drink
nor be given to mocking the old.
What you are hearing is proper.
Do not strike the insignificant.

Listen well in the wood,
be alert on the plain,
for you do not know
if the enemy is tracking you.

Do not refuse to give food.
Shun the selfish person.
Do not thrust yourself on a chief
nor be reproached by any lord.

Keep your weapons, keep your clothes
until the rough fight has passed.
Do not be mean when you give.
Follow good manners, Mac Lugach.

Victory and blessing, said Patrick, that's a good story you've told us. Where is Broccán, the scribe?

Here, Broccán said.

Take your book, your ink-horn and your pen, and write that story down.

Then Patrick asked Caílte, Did you have musicians in the Fian?

We had the finest musician in Ireland or Scotland.

What was his name? asked Patrick.

Cnú Dereóil, said Caílte.

Where was he from? asked Patrick.

Between Crotta Cliach [the Galtee Mountains] and Síd Ban Finn [Slievenamon] in the south.

What did he look like?

He was as tall as four of Finn's fists, the instrument he played measured three fists, and the musicians of the Tuatha Dé Danann envied him. One day Finn went west to Síd Ban Finn to hunt deer. He sat on the hump of a sod-built grave and, looking around, saw a little man playing and performing on the harp. The man's yellow hair reached down to his loins. Seeing Finn, the first person he met since he left the fairy mound, he placed his hand in his. He played for Finn and when the Fian arrived they heard a wonderfully pleasing music. My word, Finn, they said, that's one of the three best windfalls you've ever had. The musician stayed with Finn until he died.

Caílte spoke this poem:

Brave Finn found a dwarf
whose memory was great,
whatever he heard east and west
he kept in his head.

Cnú Dereóil the man's name
not unknown in Ireland,
a much-loved lad with clever speech
called Cnú Dereóil, tiny Cnú.

I will tell you, happy chance,
how Finn got the dwarf.
His was a lucky birth
Lug mac Eithlenn's son.

We were in Finn's band
between the Galtees and Slievenamon,
when we heard faultless music
on the mound beside us.

We were listening to it
music that had to be heard,
putting us all to sleep
wonderful pleasing sound.

Then Finn mac Cumaill,
king of Alma, said,
'Little man, where are you from
you play the harp with such skill?'

'I come from Slievenamon
where mead and ale are drunk.

I have come on purpose
to spend time in your company.'

'You will get jewels and wealth,
red gold and good people.
I like your manner,
will give you true affection.'

He shook hands with Finn.
That pleased all of us.
We brought him with us,
our wonderful windfall.

The man was four fists high
three fists in his gentle harp.
A great sound, soft and delicate,
the sweet music of his harp.

They brought out to him
five musicians of the Fian
to learn the fairy sound
directly from gentle Cnú.

Senach's son was one of them.
Senach and the two Daigres
learnt well from him
and so did Cúán.

It troubled Finn of the Fian
that his dwarf had no wife.
The little man did not like
large fat women.

Finn, the wise chief, said
he would give gold and silver
to find a woman for him
in the whole of Ireland.

Scí mac Eógain declared,
a warrior resembling a lion,
'I will tell a fitting tale
a place to find his match.'

'My blessing on your house,
son of Eógan of Munster,
tell us in friendship
where she may be found.'

'Seek the House of Donn,
Finn, brave and trophied,
the woman you seek is there,
a daughter called Bláthnait.'

We went there at once
with Finn the sharp swordsman
to the House of Donn to find her
with our spirits greatly raised.

We found Bláthnait in the mound
and took her with us for sure.
In that great house over there
Bláthnait and Cnú were married.

An ounce of gold from every man
as many as were in the Fian,
dowry for the woman without fault
all given there to the little man.

Four fists the man's height
three fists in his sweet harp
the woman taller than him
that dear soft-mannered pair.

Hers the world's skilled embroidery
plying silver and gold with ease.
As for him, his greatest skill,
entertaining the hosts of the world.

There was no queen in the Fian
nor leader nor chief
did not give love and gifts
to that sweet pair.

Whenever bad weather came
on the hardy chiefs of the Fian,
Finn sheltered under his cloak
Bláthnait and her little man.

When good was to come to the Fian
Bláthnait did not hide that she knew;
when bad was to come to them
the dwarf did not conceal it.

Any music in the world
that a man might long to hear
or might find in the house of drink
could be played better by Cnú.

Three windfalls, the best ever got
by Finn the true Fian-chief:
Bran, faultless Sceólaing,
Bláthnait and her dwarf.

Munster

Not long after Patrick and Caílte saw seven big men approaching. Where have you come from, Patrick asked, and who are you?

From Eógan Lethderg mac Aengusa, king of the two provinces of Munster, and we have come to get you, holy Patrick.

We will go there, said Patrick, for we must travel wherever endowments are to be found.

What will I and my nine warriors do? Caílte asked.

You are welcome to stay for a month, a quarter or a year, Patrick replied.

Then Patrick went through Fid Gaible, Druim Criad, now called Kildare; over the pool at Dermag [Durrow]; across Berba [the Barrow]; over Tóchar Léige, the causeway of Liag, daughter of Cuarnatán where Liag fell; into the old plain of Roiche, daughter of Dian mac Dílenn, now called Morett; into old Moynoe, now called the Plain of Laois; across In Fheoir [the Nore] full of spawning salmon; by Achad Bó [Aghaboe] of the strong blows, now called Achad; into the path of Dal mac Úmór; past Ros an Churad, now known as beautiful Roscrea; by the right towards the marsh of Lodán mac Lir's cattle, now called Clár Daire Móir [Derrymore]; past Corrócaib Cnámchoille [Cloghile]; past Cuillenn ua Cuanach [Coonagh] to the west where Cuillenn mac Morna was killed by Finn; past the Fian's Leap; past the Fair of Cúile, wife of Nechtan, now called the heifer-bearing Fair of old Clochar; past Cenn Febrat of Sliab Cáin to the south; past the Hill of the Fian, now known as Ardpatrick where Eógan Lethderg mac Aengusa, king of the two provinces of Munster, and its leaders were.

They put up a tent for Patrick. The king of Munster and the nobles came before him. The king placed his head on Patrick's chest and bowed down before him. The saint remained there for a week, raising the dead, and healing those who were sick or infirm. Patrick got his own reward there. Eógan Lethderg returned to Rosach na Rí to his own fort, and the nobles went to their own forts and strongholds.

Tell me, Caílte, Patrick said, why was the name Finntulach given to this height?

I will tell you, Caílte replied. From here the three companies of the Fian set off to fight the battle of Finntrága [Ventry]. Our spears were brought to us here and polished rings for the shafts. Here Finn looked about and said, This hill is white. What better name for it than Finntulach?

Caílte sang:

Beautiful high hill to which the fair Fian came,
you were used to a teeming camp of chosen men.
Here we counted, coming to the high level plain,
lovely blackberries, haws, nuts from the woods of Cinntíre [Cantyre].
Tender twigs of thorn, sprig of healthy garlic,
each May we ate the tips and fine shoots of cress.
Birds from the wild woods came to the Fian's cooking pots,
speckled squirrels from Berramain, nests from mountain peaks.
Swift salmon from Linnmuine, eels from noble Shannon,
woodcock from Fidrenn, otters from the depths of the Deel.
Fish from the salt seas off the shores of Baí [Dursey] and Béire [Beare],
seaweed from purest Faíde [Whiddy], dulse from the inlets of Clear.
Mac Lugach often swam Loinges of many lakes,
crowds and hosts would gather on your slopes.
Famous Oisín and I often set off in our currachs,
I risked green seas about the hills of the waves.

We set off from here to the battle of Finntrága, Caílte continued. We saw one of Finn's people approaching, namely, Cael the valiant, slayer of hundreds, grandson of Nemnann.

Where have you come from? Finn asked him.

From bright Bruig na Boínne in the north, replied Cael.

Why did you go there? asked Finn.

To consult my foster-mother Muireann, daughter of the Derg, said Cael.

For what reason? asked Finn.

Because of a fairy lover, a noble spouse who appeared to me in a vision, namely, Créde, daughter of white-skinned Cairbre, king of Ciarraige Luachra.

Do you know, Cael, asked Finn, that she is the most devious woman in Ireland? There are few valuables that she has not lured into her fort and her fine house.

And do you know, asked Cael, what condition she imposes on each of her suitors?

Yes, I do. He must compose a song or poem portraying her goblets and drinking horns, her cups and mugs, her great possessions and great palaces, said Finn.

I have it ready, given to me by Muireann, Derg's daughter, my muse, said Cael.

We neglected the battle for the time being, continued Caílte, and made our way by hillside, rocks, and heights to Loch Cuire in the west. We came to the door of the fairy mound and sounded the chant of the Fian with the shafts of our long, gold-socketed shields. Marriageable yellow-haired girls appeared on the balconies of the sun-room. Créde came to talk with us with three fifties of the women.

The Fian-chief said to her, We have come here to choose and to woo you.

The woman asked who wished to woo her.

Cael, the valiant, slayer of hundreds, grandson of Nemnann, mac ríg Laigen, said Finn.

We have heard of him, said the woman, but have never seen him. Does he have my poem for me?

I have indeed, Cael replied.

He stood up, said Caílte, and sang his song.

Cael sang:

A journey I have on Friday,
to go as a true guest
to Créde's house, no small task,
under the mountain northeast

I am determined to go there
to Créde at the paps of Ana
to face risks there
four days and half a week.

Her house is beautiful
with men, women and boys,
magicians and musicians,
cupbearers and doormen.

Trusty horseboys,
carvers and servers,
with yellow-haired Créde
in charge of them all.

It would be pleasant there
with mattress and down.
Were Créde pleased to hear
my journey would be pleasant.

A bowl she has of sweet juice
that makes her eyebrows black,
crystal vats of grain without lees,
cups and smooth goblets.

Her colour the hue of lime,
quilts between her and the outer rushes,
silk and blue cloaks,

red gold between her and her gleaming drinking-horn.

Her sun-room at Loch Cuire
of silver and yellow gold,
sloped thatch without blemish
of the wings of redbreasted birds.

Two greenish door-posts
the panels without defect,
plundered silver, widely known
the yellow beam of its lintel.

Créde's chair on my left
even more beautiful
its tapestry of gold from Elpa
below her soft bed.

A shining bed stretched out
at the head of the chairs
made at Tuile in the east
yellow gold in its precious base.

Another bed to my right
of gold and faultless silver
a canopy of bright hyacinth
held up on slender rods.

Attendants in that house,
most happily born,
their cloaks neither faded nor worn
abundant fair hair and curled.

Wounded men would sleep there
though badly shedding blood
with fairy birds in song
within her bright sun-room.

If I have reason to be thankful
to Créde a short suggestion,
her many songs will live
if she rewards devotion.

If it pleases Cairbre's daughter
she will not delay our joy,
but may say to me at once
'Your journey pleases me.'

A hundred feet in Créde's house
from one end to the other,
twenty measured feet the width
of its splendid doorway.

Its wattling and thatch
of bird feathers yellow and blue,
its wall railing to the east
of glass and carbuncle.

Four pillars for each bed
patterned with silver and gold,

the glass gem on each pillar
a pleasant crowning.

A vat of princely enamel
to which a malt juice pours,
above the vat an apple tree
laden with heavy fruit.

As Créde's horn fills
with mead from the stout vat,
four apples fall at once
right into the horn.

She who owns all this
from end to end,
Créde from Tulcha's three-peaked hills
Ireland's best by a spear's cast

This poem, her formless bride-gift,
a rash, inept epithalamium
for shapely Créde over there,
may my journey please her.

The couple, Cael and Créde, said Caílte, were placed in the hand-made marriage-bed. The Fian spent seven days there, eating and enjoying themselves, with no shortage of food, drink, or any good thing. But Finn had another concern: the strangers at Finntrága. The woman gave each of us appropriate clothes for battle and we took our leave.

Let the woman come with us, said Finn, that we may find out if good or ill attend this venture.

The woman took a great many cattle with her for the sick and the wounded. She fed them fresh milk while they faced death in battle. The invalids and wounded were brought to her house. Just as she surpassed the women of the Fian in bestowing jewels and treasure, her husband surpassed the three battalions of the Fian in valour and military prowess. Cael's drowning on the last day of the battle was a tragedy and there were other creatures whose lives ended at the same time. A wave brought him in after he had been drowned. The woman and the leaders of the Fian went to find him. They raised him up and carried him to the strand south of Finntrága, known since then as Cael's Strand, or Cael's Grave.

The woman came, stretched herself by his side and wailed out loud in great grief, Why should I not die of grief for my husband, seeing that the restless wild creatures are dying of grief for him?

Créde said:

The harbour cries out at the red race of Rinn dá Bhárc,
the wave against the shore laments the drowning of the man from
Loch Dá Chonn.

The crane cries in the marshes of Druim Dá Thrén,
it cannot guard her young when the fox comes near.

Sad is the cry the thrush makes in Druim Caín,
no less sad the blackbird's voice in Leitir Laíg.

Sad the sound the stag makes in Druim dá Léis,
for the dead doe of Druim Sílenn the stag roars.

It grieves me the death of the hero who used to lie with me,
the son of the woman of Doire Dá Doss with a cross above his head.

It grieves me, Cael, to have you dead by my side,
the wave-drench over your bright side maddens me.

Sad the sound the wave makes against the shore,
it drowned a fine handsome man, my grief Cael went near.

Sad the sound the wave makes to the north,
hammering hard rocks, lamenting Cael's death.

Sad the sound the wave makes to the south,
my time is done as my appearance reveals.

Sad the sound made by Tulcha's dragging wave,
I have no future, since its tidings reached me.

Since Crimthann's son drowned, I will love no one,
his hand felled many, on a hard day his shield never cried out.

The woman lay by Cael's side and died of grief. They were buried there in a single tomb.

I myself, said Caílte, raised the stone over their grave, known as the Tomb of Cael and Créde.

Victory and blessing be yours, said Patrick, you have told a good story. Where is Broccán the scribe?

Here, said Broccán.

Write down all that Caílte has told, said Patrick.

Before long they saw a large troop of men coming towards them, surrounded by a bulwark of locked shields with a protection of gold-socketed spears over their shoulders. Entering Patrick's tent, their leader placed his head on Patrick's chest and bowed before him.

Who are you? asked Patrick.

I am Bran mac Deirg, said the young man, son of the king of Munster.

Why have you come here? asked Patrick

I want to learn fianship, holy cleric. I have heard that one of Finn's warriors is with you and I would like to study the ways of the Fian with him, said Bran.

Do you hear that, Caílte? asked Patrick.

I do. Tell me, Bran, asked Caílte, how do you go about hunting?

We surround a height or a cairn or a mountain wood with dogs, servants, and men. Then we hunt for a full day. At times we kill some game, at other times it escapes.

Caílte wept sadly in front of Patrick so that his shirt and chest were wet.

Then Patrick, Caílte, and their company went to Cenn Febrat of Sliab Caín. There were three glens around the mountain with a lake between them called Loch Bó. The mountain's name was Osmetal, with Cnoc na hAeire to the west of the lake and Finnbél, the mountain to the east, where Fergus Finnbél mac Finn, Ferdoman mac Bodb Derg, and the Fian warriors used to be.

The name of this hill is Cnoc Maine, said Caílte, where there was a rogue stag known as the three-antlered Liath that had escaped from the Fian, their dogs, and their people for twenty-seven years. It was a Fian warrior who killed him. I was that warrior. I do not boast when I tell you.

Caílte placed his people east, west, north, and south of the lake. Patrick sat down. Hence the name of that place, Cenn Febrat of Sliab Caín, is Patrick's Seat.

Caílte raised the cry for the hunt, the chase, and the deer-killing. He gave three fierce war-cries so that there was not next or near him a deer ranging freely on the plain, the moor, the mountain or the wood that did not join in the headlong race. To cool themselves after their flight they plunged into Loch Bó in sight of the warriors. Horror, fear, and dread seized the men at the great, rushing noise of wild stags, agitated roe deer, and heavy-sided boar who almost died from loss of breath and the long race. The crowd of men surrounded the lake so that none of those hunted escaped alive. When they shared out the animals they came to eight hundred.

Give us a tithe of the hunt, said Benignus.

Bran mac Deirg, the king of Munster's son who did not find it easy to divide his share with anyone, was seized by a sickness in his stomach.

Holy cleric, he begged, put your hand on it.

On my word, said Caílte, he will not help you until you pay his fee.

What fee is that? asked Bran.

Since the illness is in your belly, bring every cow, every pig, and every sheep to Patrick and his holy church forever.

I will, said Bran, as will my son after me.

From then on that became a custom in Ireland. Patrick put his hand on Bran mac Deirg's stomach and he was cured.

We must go, said Caílte.

In what direction? asked Patrick.

I remember people used not sit on these three hills for fear of the Tuatha Dé Danann, said Caílte, and sang:

> I remember three hills that do not age nor waste,
> the three-antlered Liath ran from rim to rim.
> I remember three churches once forts for a great lord,
> no bell's call inside but the wizard's knot outside.
>
> Caílte indeed my name, leader of the honest Fian,
> we did not make a halt going through the glen.
> Finn, the Fian-chief, when he lived, did not suffer
> the antlered buck's belling above his broad camp.
>
> I and Flann mac Failbe reddened many Leinster heroes,
> I have good reason to remember many great fights.

Victory and blessing be yours, said Patrick, this is entertainment of mind and spirit for us.

The company went away taking the spoils of the hunt with them to the mountain of Cenn Febrat where the Fian used to camp. Once when Caílte looked to the left of the mountain he saw a fort, a fine place.

On my word, he said, we did not know there was a fort there. Let us go over to it.

They went there and were surprised to see neither hosts nor gatherings but nine women-slaves and three men-slaves. They came to a private sun-room in the town with two women in it, sighing and weeping. One wore a purple-fringed cloak with a silver pin and a glittering crown of yellow gold on her forehead, the other wore a green gown fastened across her breast with a golden pin. They were fed and attended, the trappings of their travels and journeys removed.

Whose fort am I in? asked Caílte.

The fort of Lochán and Eógan, the two sons of the king of Fir Maige [Fermoy], the women replied.

Why are you sad and distressed? asked Caílte.

We have good reason, they said. We two sisters belong to those two brothers, but our husbands have gone this night to get two other wives and we can stay here only until they return with the new women.

When Caílte looked about him he saw a huge stone at the back of the fort that had been erected for Senach mac Maelchró, one of Finn's original people and one of his favourite warriors. That pillar was so designed that what Finn had given him, one hundred and fifty ounces of gold, one hundred and fifty ounces of silver, and one hundred and fifty of white bronze, was enclosed within it.

What reward will you give me, Caílte asked the women, if I help you and get your husbands back for you?

We would give you any reward in the world that you wanted, they replied.

There is, he said, that big stone at the side of the hostel.

What a hard thing to ask, they said, for it required a big number of people to put it there. It was hard work for them fixing it there, but you want to move it on your own.

If I cannot do it, said Caílte, I am much mistaken.

You can have it with our blessing, they said.

When Caílte came out of the town he filled his right hand with especial fairy herbs that belonged to queens and noble women of the Fian. He gave them to the two women who washed themselves with them. This caused their husbands to love them and to send away the women they had brought with them. The huge stone was given to him.

Caílte said:

Stone of Belach Átha Í often we gathered there,
the wealth of Senach mac Maelchró was found here in fact.
There are herbs here for you, will not be without effect,
in this whole world no women will be more pleasing to men.
I will say to you, and what I affirm is true,
all those who know me know I love this stone.

Caílte was fed and attended well there. He got up next morning and pulled the stone out of the ground.

CONNAUGHT

They were not long there when they saw men arriving. Where have you come from? Patrick asked.

From the province of Connaught in the north, they said.

Why did you travel?

We have come, holy cleric, from the nobles of Connaught to bring you with us so that you may convert us, men and women, to your Gospel.

It would not be right, said Patrick, not to spread the Gospel.

Patrick and his followers set off. They travelled from the south through mid-Munster to Limerick; to Fid na Cuan which is called In Chetalach; to Sliab Oidid of the king;

to Sliab Echtge [Aughty], daughter of Nuada of the Silver Arm; to Cuaill Cepáin near Sliab Echtge where Cepán mac Morna was killed; to Loch na Bó Girre, known as Loch Gréine, daughter of Finn; to the Brecthír, known at this time as Tír Maine; and to Loch Linngaeth, known as Loch Cróine. There, waiting for Patrick, was Muiredach Mór mac Finnachta, king of Connaught.

A tent was raised over Patrick and his clergy. The chiefs of Connaught came to him and placed their heads on his chest.

Patrick emerged from the tent and sat on a grave mound. Caílte sat with him, and said, Here, holy Patrick, Oscar fought his first battle.

What reason had he? asked Patrick.

As a matter of fact, Caílte replied, it was about Niam, daughter of Aed Donn mac Fergusa Finn, king of Ulster, who was engaged to Aed mac Fiadaig meic Finntain and had been given to the king of Connaught. They did not have enough men to fight with Oscar or the Fian until they requested support troops from Cormac, grandson of Conn and king of Ireland. Cormac brought warriors from the four provinces of Ireland to fight with the Fian. The battle over that girl was fought on that plain. These were Oscar's first exploits in battle.

Finn said:

Rise up, Oscar, know you belong to the old stock,
though their good men have much fame, kill a hundred.
Go through them and over them, sever heads from necks,
take the broad green shield, take the sharpest sword.
Take the shield, seize spears from the warrior you have slain,
seize mail, may it aid you, let them not boast trophies of yours.
It is a great event for me, in the sight of the Fian,
the initiation of my child, his nine years completed.
There has not come, will not come a better in deed and word,
there is no spearhead will pierce further into a man.
Pity the man he charges with his sharp sword,
when anger enters his hand, a truly fierce surge.

Caílte said:

Victorious Oscar's first exploits over Ulster's haughty king,
over Leinster's king as well, and the brave king of Connaught.
Aed mac Fiadaig meic Finntain came at him after that,
he left him headless, seldom a fight matched so hard.
Aed Donn mac Fergusa Finn, Ulster's king with the deadly point,
Oscar killed using shield and hard sword at the same time.
Not with poison Baedán mac Firnairb, a fierce king of Leinster,
he killed on the spur of the moment though he was hard to beat.
His foster brother, wise and gentle, Oscar's princely companion,
Linne mac Ligne, with deeds to his name, Oscar slew in error.
Niam of the many-coloured clothes came to see the battle,
the fight raged about her, the tenacious queen was slain.
I give praise for the champion, warrior of swift blows,

> there never mounted a horse one superior in skill and honour.
> I tell you this, Patrick, and I tell you the truth,
> his fury was truly royal, his first exploits were not slight.

Victory and blessing be yours, Caílte, said Patrick. Where is Broccán? Write that story down so that it may entertain chieftains to the end of time.

Tell me Caílte, said Patrick, who is buried in the mound on which we are?

In fact, Caílte replied, a warrior of the Fian of Ireland who died here, Airnélach mac Adhmalláin, son of the king of Leinster. A minstrel came here with a poem for him and delivered it.

Airnélach said, Poet, in the name of friendship, grant me time to have my jewels and valuables brought here.

On my word, said the poet, I will not allow it without shaming and satirizing you today if you do not reward me.

When he heard that, Airnélach put his face to the ground and did not raise it until he had died from shame. They built a green mound over him and placed a stone above his head, against which, Patrick, you have leaned your back.

Caílte said:

> The grave under Lodán's stone, is the grave of a man of proud origin,
> a small grave for a warrior of splendid nobility, Airnélach mac Adhmalláin.

May he find Heaven through me, said Patrick, to counter his shame and to release him from pain. At that very moment his soul escaped from suffering and was a white dove on the standing stone above Patrick's head.

Caílte, Patrick asked, who is in the southern end of this mound?

Sálbuide mac Feidlecair, son of the king of Munster, together with thirty hounds, thirty boys, and thirty warriors who died here while chasing a fairy deer.

Caílte said:

> At the southern end lies Sálbuide of the poets
> with fifty chains, no small amount.

What we would like, said Benén, is to get possession of his treasure.

You will get it, said Caílte. He opened the grave. To the depth of his spear it was full of arm-rings.

You granted Heaven a while ago to a man because of his shame, said Benén. Give Heaven to this other because of his treasure.

I will grant that, said Patrick.

It was then Patrick asked Caílte, What was it that destroyed all of the Fian?

Two battles we fought at the end: the battle of Gabair and the battle of Ollarba. We went in three battalions to fight at the estuary of Ollarba and only six hundred of us came back. Finn had never doubted the Fian before in battle or contest, but this time he took account of the loss of chiefs, warriors, champions, and senior people who fell in these battles.

Caílte said:

> Count how many we were, no harm for you to know
> however we reckoned, in luck and valour, we did not outnumber them
> in battle.
> It was not right for Fothad to attack me, a great day, when he makes peace,
> not by the wish of Luigdech meic Con does Fothad go against me.
> I am reluctant to go into combat, although I must do it,
> Brilliant each step I take to Dubthor in Dál nAraide.
> Eight and six score men, each of them my equal
> were killed at Ard Alba by Donngas mac Lánamna.
> Three hundred battles the Fian fought from north to south to west
> but up to this never had any fight with as much sorrow.
> The people who came to us, did not hold their two lines
> if they took the field today, it is not Fothad who would shine.

May victory and blessing be yours, Caílte. You have spoken great goodness in that poem. Write it down, Broccán, said Patrick, and he did.

Then Cainén mac Faible meic Fergusa meic Eógain Móir asked Caílte, Where did Ailill Ólom mac Moga Nuadat die?

Caílte replied, He died from a great letting of blood on the top of Sliab Cláire in the south.

And where did Sadb, daughter of Comán, die?

She died from the loss of her greatly-loved son, Mac Con from Temair of the Kings.

And where did the poet Ferchis mac Canan die?

By the cast of a hard point of a holly-tree that Ael mac Derg Dub gave him on the top of Sliab Crot when he aimed at a stag.

And the seven fine sons of Ailill, where did they die?

Benne Brit killed them in the great battle of Mag Mucrama as they were fleeing from the large forces of Mac Con.

How did the large, smooth Ford of the Fall get its name?

Connla Derg from the Hill wounded Fiacha Muillethan mac Eógain there and since then it is known as the Ford of the Fall.

Caílte said:

> Ford of the Fall the name of the ford to all who know why
> When Connla from Cnoc Dian brought down good Fiacha Muillethan.

Who fought in the battle of Samain and who were laid low? asked Eógain Mór.

Cormac Cas, son of Ailell Ólom, attacked Eochaid Abratrúad, king of Ulster in the north, who fell there. Cormac Cas was struck and was sick for thirteen years. His brains were spilling at a time when he was king of Munster. They made a fort and fortress for him at Dún ar Sléib. At its centre was a clear, fresh spring-well. They built a great royal house about it for him, put up three stone pillars, and placed the king's bed there between them with his head to the east. A favourite warrior from his household poured water over his head from a bowl or basin. He died there and was buried underneath within the fort. For this reason it is called the Fort of the Three Pillars.

Caílte said:

> There is a fine fort to the east now known as Dún Eochair,
> even more attractive at daybreak the graves of Sadb and Ailill.
> Sadb died grieving for Mac Con, killed by Ferchis's single cast
> from the host attending him, Ailill died from a wasting illness.
> Faultless Eógan Mór died in the battle of Mucrama, a bad event,
> struck by a blade in combat, Cormac Cas had a bloody death.
> Fiacha Muillethan, fine son of Eógan, had very many wounds,
> they were sufficient then, struck by Connla at Áth Lethan.
> The Battle of Samain was fought where the men of Ulster were routed,
> Cormac was struck in the fight, the king of Ulster was killed.
> Many wounds were delivered on the son of the king of Fid Findlais
> a man whose fame will not be short, cold water relieved him.
> Every day he went to the falls, Cormac Cas, son of Ailill,
> the pleasing treatment was near him, as he went to the cleansing of Es Maigi.
> He went from there to Dún ar Sléib, to the fort of his own father,
> there they raised three columns for him to cool his gentle head.
> From these three stones that you see Dún Trí Liac gets its name,
> this is its name even since after Cormac Cinn Cláire.
> The son of Munster's king died after that from his bloody wounds
> in that clean, pleasant fort they made his fine cooling bed.

As for Muiredach, king of Connaught, Caílte continued, he had a favourite son, Aed mac Muiredaig. One time when the boys of the province organized a game of hurling, he scored six goals against them on his own, but when he sat down he was seized by a fatal illness and died. When they told his mother, Aífe, daughter of the king of Ulster, and his people, the women made a great wail for the death of that young boy. His mother asked that he be brought to the Táilchenn to whom God had entrusted the whole of Ireland and the healing of everyone within it.

I would regard it as great shame, said the king, should he not be willing.

They sent word to Patrick but the king and his people stayed in the tent where the dead youth lay covered by a purple cloak with a soft hood. His mother, three fellow-students, and his sister said they would die of grief.

When Patrick heard that, his heart went out to them. They brought a golden basin full of water to him. He blessed the water, poured some into a fine silver cup, raised the purple hood, and put three drops of water in Aed's mouth. At the third drop the boy rose, completely cured, rubbed his hands across his face, and went out. The people were delighted. They believed in God, laid their heads on Patrick's chest, and gave him power over them in big things and in little.

Patrick and Caílte remained there that night and left next day. The entire gathering went to Gannmagh, now known as Mag Finn; to Tóchar of the Troop of Women, now known as Tóchar Finn; and right to Ros na Fingaile, now known as Ros Comáin [Roscommon], which was called Ros na Fingaile, that is, the Wood of Kin-Slaying, because it was there the nine sons of Uar mac Innaist killed one another. They went to Ráth Glais, now called Ráth Brenáin, where the king of Connaught pitched his tent. Patrick and Caílte sat on the grassy mound around the rath and the king of Connaught together with his entire gathering sat with them.

Muiredach mac Finnachta then asked Caílte, Why is this rath called Ráth Glais?

I'll tell you, Caílte replied. Glas mac Drecáin, son of the king of Lochlann, came with twenty-five battalions to seize the kingship of Ireland. They arrived at the stone fort of Dám Dílenn, now called Dún Rosarach. At that time Finn mac Cumaill happened to be at Alma, that is, at the Hill of Allen in Leinster.

Muiredach asked Caílte, Why was it called Alma?

There was a warrior of the Tuatha Dé Danann in the Bruig whose name was Bracan and whose daughter Alma was a virgin. Cumall mac Trénmóir married her but she died giving birth to his son and was buried in this green grassy mound. From her the mound got its name. Before this it had been called Tulach na Fairscena [Lookout Hill]. Or Alma was the name given to it in the time of Nemed. Or Nuada, the magician, burnt alum on the fort which was called Alma afterwards.

Caílte sang:

Alma of Leinster, a Fian fort, frequented by generous Finn,
this, as all the ancients say, is how it got its name:
Alma, who took it by force in Nemed's time,
died on the green hill from sudden deadly plague.
A warrior of the Fir Bolg called Iuchna, no lightweight,

east-west filled the fort with his clothes and herds.
Driven by thirst his cattle went to a well to drink,
so bad their need they locked and broke their horns.
From the horns of the speckled white cattle left there
comes the well's name—'the horns of Iuchna's many cows.'
Mighty Iuchna, the fierce fighter, had five daughters,
the lands they seized spread far and wide.
In Carman, rough Carman, where bards used to live,
Trega's wife had a well-run house, no woman more enjoyed.
Mag Life [Plain of Liffey], this fair young woman's share,
a true record in my opinion, the fifth daughter, Alma.
Nuada, the wizard, a harsh man, built a strong fort in Alma
with sparkling glass for the palisades of his stronghold.
The entire fort a sparkling white from Ireland's best lime,
from the herd brought from his house comes the name Alma.

You've told that story well, Caílte, said Muiredach mac Finnachta.

We were in Alma in Leinster, said Caílte, when we heard that ships had arrived. Spréd Aithinne [the Firebrand], daughter of Mugna Mianchraesach and the king of Ireland's woman-messenger, brought the news to us. Finn called his woman-messenger to muster and assemble the Fian of Ireland and Scotland. Cormac, grandson of Conn, gathered the people of Tara, the troops of Brega, and a great army of the men of Ireland. Twenty-five battalions assembled on this plain. The Fian and the farming people cast lots to see which of them would first fight with the invaders. It fell to the Fian to engage them first. They fought every day for a week. Fifteen hundred of the Fian and of the invaders were slain. Then the main battle took place. Glas fell by Finn mac Cumaill and his seven sons by the Fian. Three times fifty of us young men set out to fight that battle and we each killed fifty warriors. Three of us went with Finn to the tent where Glas mac Drecáin lay. We found nine piles of gold there, the smallest of them equal in weight to what an ox might draw. We hid them in the red bog on the north side of the fort.

Caílte spoke this poem:

O Ráth Glais, which we frequented many a time,
I concealed nine pillars of gold in the bog at your northern wall.
Three of us concealed it, that was our total number,
Finn and Oisín, hardy Caílte, we hid it in one hour.
Thrice fifty we went with greatly handsome Finn.
We killed fifty every time around the mound of the green rath.

They buried Glas mac Drecáin in this ground; this rath is called Ráth Glais after him.

Victory and blessing, Caílte, said Patrick, you have told us a good story. Write it down, Broccán.

They spent the night there and getting up early next day moved on to the Field of Fergus's Chariot, now called Mac Conrach's Ridge, and to the Hill of Kings, now called Garad's Well, where they rested and camped. They erected a tent for Patrick, who sang his hours.

Blessing the hill's beautiful slope, he said, This burial ground is one of the eighteen which will be dearest to me in Ireland.

We regret, said the king of Connaught, that it has no water.

If it be God's will, said Patrick, may it have water.

He went to a pointed rock that he saw near the town, stuck his staff into its base, and three streams of pure water poured forth.

Your blessing on the well, holy Patrick, said Benignus.

Protection on everyone who drinks the water, said Patrick, and may God grant Heaven to anyone who dies after that. When through the will of the Creator the waters of Ireland fail at the end of the world Ireland shall be sustained by this well. If this water is given three times to a sick person it will ease every distress.

Caílte, said Patrick, tell us a story.

I will tell you how the Fian of Ireland, both dogs and people, almost perished on this hill on which you stand. Guaire Goll and Flaithius Faebrach carried Finn's chessboard. Finn Bán mac Bresail, son of the king of Leinster, came to play chess here with Guaire.

I will play you for a bet, said Guaire Goll.

What is the bet? Finn Bán asked.

Three ounces of gold each for three days and three nights, said Guaire.

As it happened, said Caílte, Finn Bán was one of the best chess-players in the Fian, after Finn mac Cumaill, Diarmaid Ó Duibne, and Flaithius Faebrach.

Oisín sang:

> Finn's servant, Flaithius Faebrach, was the best chess-player,
> there came not to the gaming board a hand more skilled at playing.

The pair played for three days. Guaire did not win any game and his stake was forfeited. He heaped scorn and abuse on the other young man saying that he was deficient as a servant, useless as a soldier, and unskilled in feats of arms. Finn Bán raised his hand, struck Guaire with his fist, knocked three teeth from his upper jaw and caused him to fall on the chessboard.

This was reported to the Fian-chief, who said Finn Bán and his people should be killed.

On my word, said Oisín, he will not be killed but sent for judgement to Diarmaid Ó Duibne, Fergus Finnbél, and to me, judges of the Fian, and to you, Finn.

These three gave their judgement: Wherever you meet Finn Bán's servant, you will strike him. In addition you will be given a gift – an ounce of gold from each leader of the Fian of Ireland.

That was how we made peace between them.

Twenty years later we came to Caill Coiméta in the territory of the Tairsig of Leinster, now called Drumcree. The Fian went hunting and left a warrior, Garad mac Morna, to mind the women. At that time Garad was well on in years and his kinsmen were dead.

But the women said, Garad, would you like to play chess with us?

I would not, said Garad.

Why not?

Because of what happened one day when we were at the Hill of Kings near Loch in Eoín [Lake of the Bird] in the province of Connaught.

And Garad told them the story.

But one of the women asked, Was Garad not left behind with us to light the fire and to play chess with us, since he has lost his vigour and dexterity and is an old man.

By my word, said Garad, that's the voice of slanderous women. No matter how long I might have served in the Fian they were not true friends in the end.

He lit a big fire in the hostel, continued Caílte, closed its seven doors on them, came outside, taking his arms with him, and spoke an old stave at them:

> Lovely women of Finn's Fian, play chess on your own,
> you, the wise king's young ones, I am old, my game is old.
> The weight of age leans on me, I am old as your fathers,
> every young thorn is sharper playing together as equals.
> I remember a day at the Lake of the Bird, an old man has an old tale,
> where almost all were slain because of a row over a game.
>
> Finn's servant, Guaire, was playing with skill
> with Finn Bán mac Bresail when a row broke out.
> Finn Bán, a better player than Guaire of Glais Berrann,
> Finn Bán won four games, Guaire but one.
> Guaire grew angry at mac Bresail of the green cloak,
> spoke nasty words at him because of his honest moves.
> In deep shame Finn Bán quickly raised his hand,
> Breasal's son, winning, struck Guaire on the mouth.
> The fierce Fian rose, most renowned and truly brave,
> angry their chief's servant is struck for a bad reason.
> The Fian of Finn Bán rose up, mac Cumaill's Fian, as one,

the Fian of Caílte, of famous Conán, of Oisín, of Ferdoman.
All the warriors rose, Finn's Fian, the Fian of generous Mael,
of Dub Drumann from Ros Cuill, of Goll, and of Irgoll.
Then Finn himself spoke: Look outside, my strong son.
Why are the Fian angry, what has caused them to rise up?
Finn, Guaire, your servant, who carries your chessboard,
should not for any reason be killed by mac Bresail.
Seize mac Bresail, said Finn. Accept no indemnity for him,
nor may Diarmaid, Oisín, or Caílte, act as protectors.
By your hand, good Finn, by your honour and nobility,
mac Bresail will not be killed for his part in this conflict.
Father, son of Cumall, Oisín said, wisdom becomes you,
honest judging suits a prince, not hasty blustering words.
Were we unrestrained, our restraining should come from you.
Place your finger under your tooth, judge not on half-truth.
Seize Faelchú, Fer Crom's son, who serves thick-haired mac
Bresail, if he has killed Guaire, you yourself should kill Faelchú.

We went after Finn Bán from high-minded Cumall
and brought Bresal's son to the chief of Ireland's Fian.
Finn Bán mac Bresail of Alma, asked the other Finn,
why did you attack Guaire, now gone, now no more?
Finn, Guaire, your servant, the lout who carries your board,
came one morning early and challenged me to a game.
I won four games against Guaire mac Beobertaig,
this made him burn hotly in anger and rage.
He abused me fiercely before the Fian of Ireland.
I was not a servant, nor a warrior, nor indeed young.
I lifted my right hand straight up, I do not deny it,
struck him across the mouth, I tell only the truth.
A blessing on the hand that struck, Oisín said, at once,
your servant, Finn of the feasts, was not struck without cause.
Unless you excuse the fist, you will be paid in the wrong,
a tribute of gold from every man of us, unless you pay heed.
If you accept what I show, it will keep your servants from wrong,
Guaire, Comán, slender Saltrán, from shaming the Fian.
Guaire abused Finn Bán, Comán reviled Gles,
worst of all Saltrán spoke evil about Ferdoman.
Finn mac Bresail from Ráth Cró, if he struck your servant,
strike, chief of many horns, mac Bresail's servant.

Take my blessing, go to your house, said Finn to Finn mac Bresail,
the fact is, as Guaire said, bad words earn bad blows.
I request you, chief of the keen-edged Fian, let it be
from today and forever, a servant may not judge a warrior.
We pledged hand to hand, Fian of the honourable mac Cumaill,
he would not keep in the Fian a servant withholding respect.
I am your servant this night and, ladies, you have my respect,
but I gave my word as a true warrior that I would not contend with women

No matter how long we may be together, women of Finn of Alma
as long as I live and remember, I will not play chess with you.

Victory and blessing, Caílte, said Patrick, you have given us both wisdom and knowledge.

Then the gathering went to Carn Fraích mac Fidaig and Patrick ascended the hill.

Tell me, Caílte, he said, did you believe in the King of heaven and earth or did you know that He existed at all?

The Fian-chief knew it, Caílte replied, because he was a magician, a seer, and a chief. We all came to know there was a God because of what we saw on the night of the perishing.

What perishing was that? asked Patrick.

Cormac mac Airt, king of Ireland, had a big household at Ros na Ríg [Rosnaree] northeast of Temair [Tara]: ten times twenty sons of kings, every one of them the son of a king and a queen.

What Ros is that?

Ros Cailled, the Wood of the Forest, answered Caílte. It had thousands of trees of every kind. The king's sons had a large hall there but their food was always brought to them from Tara. One night they had finished feasting and enjoying themselves and their beds were prepared and they remained there for the rest of the night. Binne, the chief steward at Tara, came to talk with the son of the king of Ireland who was in the hall. He looked about the house and they were all dead. We knew then that there was a true and glorious God who had power and dominion over us all.

Caílte sang:

Ros Temrach, place of kings, often a great household,
hosts of people and horses on its green grassy slopes.
Ten score fine sons of kings in that honourable house,
an equal number of women on that bright-surfaced mound.

I never saw such a perishing, noble Saint Patrick,
all dying together, those gathered in that one place.

They buried the ten score men and the ten score women in that mound and since then it is known as Cnoc an Áir [Hill of Slaughter]. And because the earth swallowed the wood in which they were, we realized that the King of heaven and earth existed.

Victory and blessing be yours, Caílte, said Patrick.

Then Caílte said, Patrick, I have to leave tomorrow.

Why must you go? asked Patrick.

To find the hills, cliffs, and fortified places where my companies, foster-brothers, chiefs of the Fian, and the great Fian of Ireland were with me. I have been too long in one place.

They remained there for that night. The entire gathering arose and Caílte placed his head on Patrick's chest.

I give you Heaven, Patrick said, God will put His hand on you wherever you are, outside of a house or inside.

At that time Muiredach mac Finnachta, king of Connaught, began to exercise his kingship and sovereignty. Patrick came to him to sow faith and piety, to expel demons and wizards, to raise up saints, good men, station-stones and altars, and to overthrow idols, images, and druid arts.

Caílte, meanwhile, went north to the wide Magh Luirg [plain of Lorg]; by Corrléim na Fian, now called the Cataract of the Sons of Erc; and north to Sliab Segsa ua Eibric [mountain of Segais]; to Berna na Cét [Gap of the Hundreds], Céis Chorainn [Keshcorran], and out upon the plain of Corran.

They, Caílte and his warriors, heard a great rushing noise coming towards them. Looking about, Caílte saw nine wild stags. He threw nine javelins at them, killed the nine of them, and had food for the night. They packed and took it with them to the Waterfall of Modarn's son, Es Dara, [Ballysodare]; to Crích in Chosnama, now called the Land of Carbury; to Rind Eba, daughter of Geibtine mac Morna, where a tidal wave drowned her; to Druim Derg, now called Druim Cliab [Drumcliff]; to Áth Chomraic [Ford of Conflict], now called Áth Daim Glais [Grey Stag's Ford].

They went on to the pig's grave where the wild boar killed Diarmaid Ó Duibne and to the top of Benbulben where Diarmaid's Bed is.

Caílte put his arms on the ground and lay on the tomb of his foster-brother, Diarmaid Ó Duibne. Weeping copious tears so that his shirt and chest were wet, he said, I am sad that my foster-brother has gone.

They stayed there from midday to the end of the day.

It grieves me, Caílte said, that I should ever go away from this stone that holds Diarmaid and his family.

Did he have sons? Flann mac Failbe asked.

He did.

Caílte said:

The names of noble Diarmaid's sons
by the daughter of Cormac, Conn's grandson:
Donncha, Ilann, and Uath,
Selbach, Sercach, and Iruath.

It was at the Grey Stag's Ford, which we mentioned, that Caílte, the killer of kings, fought with Díthramach mac Scáil meic Eógain, son of the king of Munster and son of Finn's mother.

Caílte said this poem:

They had a hard fight before a great crowd of nobles,
tore up trees in rage on the slope above the Grey Stag's Ford.
First Caílte hurled his spear in the thick of brave deeds,
no sooner had it left his hand than a spear struck him.
The right hand and the left foot he cut from strong Díthramach,
then brave Caílte left the head on the north side of Drumcliff.

They proceeded to Coill na mBuiden [the Wood of the Troops], now called Muadnait's wood; across Benbulben to Garbross, now called Daire na Damraide [Oakgrove of the Deer]; and made a large booth for cooking. They covered and secured it with green-topped, fresh-bottomed sedge. They did their broiling and seething there.

Is there water near us? a man asked.

Certainly, Caílte replied, Oisín's well.

The night is dark, said the warriors.

Not to me, said Caílte. There is no place in the five great provinces of Ireland that gives even a cup-full of water, from river or cliff, that I cannot find by night or day.

He took a silver cup in one hand, his thick-shafted, hard-socketed spears in the other and walked directly to a well. He heard the sound of water being tasted and disturbed and came upon a long-sided boar drinking. He put his finger into the cord of his riveted well-weighted spear and cast a shot at the boar that killed him. He carried him away on his back, holding the goblet in one hand.

They stayed there for the night but next morning went across to Es Ruaid meic Mhodairn [Falls of Assaroe] to the fairy mound of Aed Esa Ruaid [Assaroe]. When they got there, they saw a young man waiting for them on the green grassy slope. He had a purple-red cloak wrapped about him, fastened across his chest with a silver brooch. He carried a bright shield ornamented in red gold with interlaced creatures. There was a cup-knot in his hair. He had two hunting dogs on a twisted leash of old silver in one hand. He held strong deep-blue weapons in the other.

When Caílte came up to him, the young man kissed him three times with love and affection and sat beside him on the mound.

Who are you? Caílte asked.

Derg Dianscothach mac Eógain of the people of Uisnech, your own foster-brother.

How is life for your mother's people? asked Caílte.

We do not lack food or clothing, yet those three, Ligarne Licon, Semenn Sacaire, and Bec, servant of Bromac, have the worst life of any in the Fian. Nevertheless I would prefer their life to the life I have in the fairy mound, answered Derg.

Although you hunted alone today, said Caílte, I have seen you with a large company, fifteen hundred men, fifteen hundred women, and fifteen hundred servants in the valley of the three waters where the Siuir [Suir], the Beoir [Nore], and the Berba [Barrow] meet.

Caílte sang:

Yours a lonely hunting, Derg, parted from Fian and friends,
but do you know in full the tragic story of the Fian?

I know full well every place they fell,
although my hound and I are in the mound, my mind is with the Fian.
I have never been anywhere, north, south, east, or west,
where days were shorter than in their company, however few.

Tell me, Derg, Caílte asked, which of the Fian lies in this earth-mound?

Since you and I buried him, said Derg, you ought to know.

Derg said:

The servant Cuinnscleo, Ainnscleo's son,
fought nine men under a leafy oak.
A man of deeds not words, a fight to the death,
where bright shields were pierced he was not timorous.

It is he, Caílte, who is in this turf-built grave and we are the two who put him there.

Derg, with whom did you have the hard race?

With a black horse owned by Díl mac Dá Chreac.

Derg spoke this poem:

Díl mac Dá Chreac's black horse entered in every race,
won three prizes at the fair at the rock above Loch Gur.

What house were we in that night? asked Derg.

The house of Cathaír mac Ailella, who invited Finn and the Fian. We stayed there for three days and three nights with no shortage of food or drink or any nourishment for our people, answered Caílte.

Did we give him something?

Finn gave him three hundred cattle, three hundred cloaks, and three hundred ounces of gold.

Caílte said:

> Three hundred cows, three hundred cloaks,
> three hundred well-tempered swords,
> Finn gave in recompense
> for Cathaír mac Ailella's hospitality.

Who gave Finn the black horse? Derg asked. Was it Díl mac Dá Chreac or Cathair mac Ailella?

It was Fiacha Muillethan mac Eógain.

Caílte said:

> For you the swift black horse, said Fiacha to the Fian-chief,
> for you my famous sword and a horse for your charioteer.
>
> Finn tested the black horse on the strand beyond Berramain,
> three times I drew away from him for I was faster than anything.

The horse raced to the far end of the strand and died from too much running. Since then it is called the Strand of the Black Horse, not Berramain's Beach, said Caílte. It's the end of the day, the lovely clouds have gone and the shadows of night have come.

Derg Dianscothach went into the mound to speak about Caílte to Ilbrec of Assaroe and Aed Minbrec, son of the Dagda. He told them Caílte was outside.

Bring him in, they said, for we have heard of his fame and prowess.

Derg brought him in together with his nine followers and they sat inside the fairy mound on chairs of crystal.

At that time there was a great war between the fairy mound of Lir Finnachad and Ilbrec of Assaroe. A bird with iron beak and fiery tail used come to the golden window of the mound. He shook himself there every evening so that he did not leave a sword in its scabbard, a shield on its hook, or a spear in its rack without knocking it on the heads of those inside. The inhabitants were annoyed but everything they threw at him fell on the head of a son or a woman or one of their fosterlings. The banquet house was put in order for Caílte's visit but the bird arrived and did the same thing. Those inside threw objects at him but without success.

How long has the bird been doing this? Caílte asked.

For the past year, said Derg, since we and those in the other fairy mound began fighting.

Then Caílte put his hand into the hollow of his shield and took out a bronze dart. He threw it at the bird and killed it. It fell onto the floor of the mound.

Was there ever a better cast than that? said Ilbrec.

Was there anyone in the Fian, asked Aed Minbrec of Assaroe, who could throw as well as you?

I tell you, Caílte answered, no one had the right to boast over anyone else. Each one had the prowess and dexterity he needed, as I had.

Ilbrec took a sharp blue-angled javelin from its rack and gave it to Caílte.

What spear was that, he asked, and which of the Fian owned it?

When Caílte removed the javelin's sheath and covering, there were thirty rivets of Arabian gold in its socket.

I recognize it, he said, the spear of Fiacha mac Conga. It was with this spear that Finn mac Cumaill got the chieftainship of the Fian of Ireland and Scotland in the beginning. It was brought from Finnachad's green grassy mound. Aillén mac Midna of the Tuatha Dé Danann used to come north from Carn Finnachad to Tara. He would come with a musical lute in his hand that put anyone who heard it to sleep. Then he would blow a fiery breath from his mouth. He came to Tara every year for a period of twenty-three years during the Festival of Samain. He played his lute, put everyone to sleep with its fairy sound, blew his fiery plume and burnt Tara and everything in it. That was the time when the battle of Cnoca was fought when Cumall mac Trénmóir fell, leaving his pregnant wife, Muireann Muinchaem, daughter of Tadg mac Nuadat.

After Cumall's death they gave the chieftainship of the Fian of Ireland to great-deeded Goll mac Morna, who held it for ten years. But Cumall had a son, Finn, a pillager and plunderer until he was ten years of age. In his tenth year Conn of the Hundred Battles held the Festival of Tara and when the men of Ireland were feasting and enjoying themselves in the great Banquet Hall they did not notice anything until an attractive young warrior came amongst them and sat in front of Conn of the Hundred Battles and Goll mac Morna with the nobles of the Fian of Ireland about him. During the Festival's six weeks of feasting and celebration no one dared to feud or take vengeance. The king of Ireland looked at the young man but did not recognize him nor was he known to anyone else. His horn of state was brought to the king of Ireland, who put it into the young man's hand.

Whose son are you? he asked.

I am Finn mac Cumaill, son of the warrior who was king of the Fian in the past, and I have come, king of Ireland, to make friends with you.

You are the son of a friend and a man I trusted.

The young man rose and made a pact of friendship with the king. Conn took him by the hand and placed him beside his son Art and for a while they were feasting and enjoying themselves together.

The king of Ireland stood up and with a smoothly polished drinking-horn in his hand, said, If I could find someone among you, men of Ireland, who would save Tara from now until the morning from being destroyed by Aillén mac Midna, I would give him his inheritance, whether large or small.

They listened to him without stir or sound for even women in labour and wounded warriors used fall asleep to the sound of the bewitching music and the sweet song played by the invincible fairy who destroyed Tara every year.

Finn rose up and said to the king of Ireland, Who will give assurances and guarantees on your behalf if I undertake this?

The provincial kings of Ireland and Cithruad and his druids.

All of them gave guarantees. Finn undertook to save Tara from destruction throughout the night.

Fiacha mac Conga, a warrior trusted by Cumall, was in the king of Ireland's company. How would you reward me, he asked, if I gave you a deadly spear never thrown in vain?

What payment do you want? asked Finn.

Whatever your right hand wins, a third for me, a third of your private conversation, and a third of your counsel.

Agreed, said Finn, and gave his word as his bond.

Then Fiacha said, When you hear the fairy music, the sweet-stringed lute, and the soft whistling sound remove the casing from the head of the javelin, put the weapon to your forehead or any other part of your body and the envenomed point will prevent you from falling asleep.

Finn got up then before the men of Ireland to protect Tara. Unknown to Clanna Morna or anyone else in the house Fiacha mac Conga gave him shield and spear. Before long he heard the bewitching music and put the point of the poisonous spear against his forehead. As usual Aillén played his lute to put everyone to sleep and then released the plume of fire from his mouth. Finn unfurled a bright-red fringed cloak between himself and the plume, which fell through the air and was taken twenty-six hands into the earth inside the four-folded cloak. The name of that hill is the Height of Finn and the name of the valley is the Valley of the Cloak.

When Aillén mac Midna realized that his magic had been thwarted, he went back to the fairy mound of Finnachad on top of the Fews. Finn followed and as Aillén was going through the entrance put his finger into the cord of the spear and sent a lucky accurate cast that struck Aillén in the upper part of his back and drove his heart out through his mouth in a flood of black blood. Finn cut off his head, took it back to Tara, placed it on a death-stake where it remained until the sun rose over the heights and harbours of the land. His mother came to Aillén, poured out her grief, and sought a healer for him, said Caílte.

Aillén mac Midna's mother sang:

Come, woman-healer of Amarrthe,
Aillén mac Midna has been pierced
by the spear of Fiacha mac Conga,
by the war-cloak, by the split-spear.
Alas, Aillén is slain, the blood from his heart
released in three waves, when they pierced his back.
Alas, Aillén is slain, fairy-chief from the peak of Boirche,
now that the slow mists have come,
draw near, woman-healer of Boirche.
He was happy, Aillén mac Midna of the Fews,
destroyed Tara nine times, seeking fame at all times.

All the men of Ireland together with the king, said Caílte, came to Tara's green where Finn was.

You see, Finn said to the king, the head of the man who used to destroy Tara together with his pipe, lute, and musical instrument. Tara and its contents are safe. The place was full of people who decided to make Finn chief of the Fian of Ireland.

Tell me, Goll mac Morna, said Conn Cétchathach [of the Hundred Battles], what is your choice, to leave Ireland or to shake hands with Finn.

On my word, Goll replied, I will shake hands with him.

The charms, said Caílte, used to procure luck and good fortune had worked. The Fian rose and placed their hands in Finn's hand. So that none of the others would feel ashamed to do so, Goll was the first. Finn held the kingship until he died and was buried at the Badger's Cliff in Luachair Degaid. It was with this spear you gave me, Ilbrec, that the profitable deed for Ireland was done. With this spear Finn always had good luck from that time on. Its name was Birga.

Keep the spear, Caílte, said Ilbrec, till we see if he will come to avenge his bird.

Raising cups and drinking-horns, they were feasting and enjoying themselves and finding delight for mind and spirit.

Tell me, Caílte, asked Ilbrec, if he comes with his kinsmen to avenge his bird to whom will you give command of the battle?

To Derg Dianscothach to whom Finn used to assign it.

Do you accept the task, Derg? the fairy people asked.

I accept it with its gains and losses, answered Derg.

That night passed quietly but early next morning they heard the snorting of steeds, the clashing of shields and the tramping of a great crowd approaching. Some went out to see how many there were. There were three strong battalions of equal size.

I am ashamed, said Aed Minbrec, by what must happen now, death and destruction for us, and our fairy mound occupied by the people of Lir from the fairy mound of Finnachad.

Do you not know, said Caílte, that the strong wild boar escapes from the pack and that when the bellowing stag charges he, too, escapes the hounds.

Caílte sang:

> The wild boar gains the hill
> fights against the fierce hounds
> when fury enters his response
> to the carnage of the red-toothed pack.

Which fight is the hardest for you in this battle? asked Caílte.

The most skilful man of the Tuatha Dé Danann is Lir from the Sid of Finnachad, they answered.

What I have always done in the past, said Caílte, is fight with the best. I will not shirk today.

Derg, what fight do you have for us? they asked.

What fight is the next hardest for you? answered Derg.

Donn and Dub, they said.

I will fight them both, said Derg.

The hosts of the fairies emerged at the same time to engage in battle. They threw long blue javelins, small spit-sharp darts, and broad green spears at one another and fought from dawn to midday. Caílte and Lir met in fierce bloody combat. In the end Lir fell at Caílte's hand.

Then that pair of great warriors, Dub and Donn, the two sons of Éirge Anglonnach from Insi Gaid, observed the battle. They joined the fight in this manner: Dub in the van of the troops with Donn strongly defending the rear. When Derg Dianscothach saw that, he put his finger into the cord of his spear, fired a lucky shot at the one closest to him, and broke his back in two. It also happened to enter the side of the one farthest from him so that both were killed by the one cast.

Ilbrec said:

> Lir fell by Caílte, no deed more worthy of praise,
> Donn and Dub fell by a single cast from Eógan's son.
> Northwards the battle decreased against Lir's mighty force
> of whom from this lovely plain only three cleverly escaped.

They returned to the fairy mound after that winning slaughter and breaking and had authority over the fairy mound of Finnachad from then on.

Ilbrec, said Caílte, here is your spear.

You should not say that, Ilbrec replied, for although Lir was struck by that spear, it rightly belongs to you because of your outstanding ability.

They remained in the mound for three days and three nights.

Tell me, Caílte, asked Ilbrec, what caused Finn to believe or did he ever believe?

Yes, he did, said Caílte.

Where did it happen and what brought it about?

At Druim Diamair on the Shannon, now called Druim Dá Én. The reason he believed was that Findine, daughter of Bodb, killed her husband, Conán, but in fact Conán and Ferdoman had killed each other. When the Fian reached Fid Énaig they brought a golden basin to Finn. He washed his fair hands, poured the blue-edged water over his face, and put his thumb under the tooth of knowledge. The truth was revealed to him and the lie concealed. He foresaw that the generous Táilchenn would come before the end of the world and that Ciarán mac an tSaoir, the mason's son, would establish a house for half of Ireland.

Caílte said:

> Dear is the renowned church on the river's edge.
> Dear the serene tomb will be a great redemption of souls.

We heard about the conflict there. Finn made this act of faith and found heaven because of it:

> Woe to the warrior who heard the news when we got to Snámh dá Én,
> the death of Conán Mael from Moy, the death of Ferdoman.
> Druim Diamair its name before the time of the Fian,
> Druim Énaig since then from the fowling of Finn and the Fian.
> A birth will occur there by the will of the Lord of the great clan,
> the worthy son of He aven's King whom angels serve.
> He will be holy Ciarán, will be born in the royal rath,
> will seize half of Ireland, the mason's son from Muirthemne.
> To those who would wreck his church sudden red-speared death,
> hanging, pitiless racking and the lowest pit in hell.
> I myself tell you, and what I say is true,
> I believe in the Father, Son, and the Holy Spirit all in One.
> I hope for the kingdom of Heaven's king which is better than any on earth,
> the King, who gave me respite, will not give me eternal woe.

They remained in the fairy mound for six weeks.

It is time for us to go, said Caílte, for we have been a long time here.

The blessing of God and our people be yours, said the people of the mound. Had you wished to stay forever you would have been welcome.

Since you will leave, said Ilbrec, we give you nine complete suits with beautiful cloaks, nine shields, nine spears, nine swords with golden inlay, and nine hunting dogs.

They took leave of one another, gave their blessings and thanks. Although that battle may have been hard for each of them, Derg Dianscothach found it harder to part from his comrade and his foster-brother. Even the day he separated from Finn and the Fian was not harder.

Caílte and the nine warriors went north to Sliab Cuire, Sliab Cairbre, Sliab Céide and Cathair Daimh Deirg [Fort of the Red Stag].

They were not long there when they saw a resplendent beautiful couple waiting for them on the cairn: a beautiful young man and a lady of the same age. The young man asked about Caílte, and Caílte told him who he was, I belong to the people of Finn mac Cumaill. My name is Caílte mac Rónaín. What is yours?

I am Eógan, the noble hospitaller, and I belong to the ancient people of Cairbre Lifechair mac Cormac. This lady is called Becnait, the woman-hospitaller. She is the same age as me. We have lived ten score years.

Did you not have great wealth? Caílte asked.

Yes, I did, for from Assaroe of Modarn northwards to Torach, now known as Tory Island to the west, there was no herd of milch-cows in every second or third territory that I did not own.

What destroyed it? asked Caílte.

A thieving monster, an ugly pirate, and a son of bad luck ruined us. He has totally consumed seven baronies so that there is no one to manage the grasslands, which he has made devoid of growth. He has harrassed and plundered me also so that I have only twenty-eight milch-herds, the end of my wealth.

Where is this man? Caílte asked.

At an impregnable rock at the wide harbour north of where we are. He and his two followers carry off the full of a ship, for he himself is a match for four hundred, his dog for three hundred, his daughter for three hundred, and nobody can injure them.

Where does he enter the harbour?

From the area to the northwest, said Eógan.

They stayed there that night, were waited on, and had all their needs attended to.

Next morning Caílte got up on his own, took his sword, shield, and two spears, and went to the indestructible rock beside the harbour. After a while he saw a currach approaching with three in it: a rough-haired, pale-grey dog with a crude iron chain tied about his neck, a lump of a bald black woman in the prow who from a distance looked like the top of a rock and in her hand a strong iron spit-spear. In the stern was the boor. They found haven and landing-place close to Caílte, who was gripped by horror and dread.

The large man spoke to his daughter, Loose the dog at that tall solitary man so that he may eat his fill of him before sailing on an expedition and a journey.

The daughter released the dog. Caílte felt fear and terror such as had never seized him in the past before battle or single combat.

May my Maker and the Táilchenn be on my side, he said, casting a small copper dart at the dog. One end of the dart pierced the dog's upper jaw, the other its lower jaw shutting the mouth. It fell out of the currach and died in the depths of the sea. After that a wave carried it into the land.

The other two came ashore after Caílte. They fought him bravely and fiercely, the daughter wounding him thirty times from the toes of his feet to the hair of his head. Caílte gave her a blow of his sword that let out her guts and her entrails. He fought more bravely and fiercely against the huge man, making three horrible slices of him, the third one being his head. He cut off their three heads and brought them back to the hostel. Eógan's and Caílte's people rose up. They recognized the three heads and gave thanks for the deed. Caílte sat down in a feeble condition.

Caílte sang:

Before your house, Eógan, my heart is sorely wounded,
I left Maelán and his dog on the strand, well-matched.
I killed Maelán, his dog and his ill-famed daughter,
From morning to daybreak our fight was hard.
On any journey south and north in a world with hardy hosts,
I have not found at any hour pain as bad as this night.

Weakness and faintness came over him. For six weeks they brought healing herbs to him so that he was cured and made whole again.

We will set off tomorrow, said Caílte, leaving our blessing with you.

Victory and blessing be yours, said Eógan.

ULSTER

They said farewell to him and went to Tulach na Céd [Hill of the Hundreds], now called Tulach dá Ech [Hill of Two Horses]; north to Cuillios na Féinne [Hollywood of the Fian], to Currach na Mílchon [Curragh of the Hunting Dogs], now called Currach Cuan [Curragh of the Harbour]; northward to Both Chnó [Bothy of the Nuts] where the horses' heads appeared to Lug Lámfhada mac Eithlenn; to the place where Colmcille was born; and northward to Dhoire Guill [Oakwood of Goll].

When they came to the side of the oakwood they saw a young man leaning his back against a sturdy rock. He wore a crimson-fringed cloak fastened across his chest with a golden pin and a tunic of soft satin. He had two hunting dogs on a leash and a pack of hounds about him.

Caílte greeted him. The young man returned the greeting and asked, Whose people do you belong to?

Our lord and chief, Finn mac Cumaill, Caílte replied, is no longer alive. The young warrior shed copious tears wetting his shirt and chest.

Who are you? Caílte asked.

I am Donn mac Aeda meic Garaid meic Morna.

Your father was a good man.

Caílte sang:

> Vigorous, of lasting fame, a truly brave fian,
> a famous fruitful branch, winner of the world's rewards.

Tell me, Caílte, do you have my father's spear? asked Donn.

I have his shield and his sword.

By virtue of your courage and prowess, tell me the prime cause of his death.

I will, for I remember it well. Dub Díthre, chief of Ossory's Fian was killed by your grandfather, Garad mac Morna, and Goll mac Morna was attacked at Carrac Goill to the west. The three battalions of the Fian laid siege to him for six weeks and he had no food for the last nine days and nights. His strength and his spear throwing went from him. Dub Díthre's son, Muc Smáile, entered the rock and beheaded Goll in the presence of the Fian of Ireland and brought it to Finn. Your father requested law and justice from Muc Smáile, that what was appropriate for a king and a warrior be given to him.

Caílte said:

> He said he would not give justice
> to the fair and famous Aed
> but would set body to body
> for every evil done by his hand.

Your father said that a mutually agreeable settlement should be made with Muc Smáile, continued Caílte.

I will give you terms, Aed, said Muc Smáile.

What terms? Aed asked.

I will give you the two spears that belonged to Goll mac Morna; the shield of Conbron's son, Cairell; Dub Díthre's horn; Muirenn of Macha's sword that Goll had; and Sigmall's hunting collar.

It was I, said Caílte, who went with this message, as is recorded in the poem:

Send messengers from us to Aed, let them tell the chief
that what was promised will never be fulfilled.
Give him the hunting collar Finn got from Nennta's Mound,
from which no deer jumping a ditch can get away.
Give him Cairell's famous shield worn in every fray,
happy treasure this tough shield, its lord, dread of a hundred.
Give him the battle-sword Muirenn Macha had,
Give him Dub Díthre's horn which I have minded,
its rim of gold a ransom for fifty slaves abroad.
Give him two spears with shafts of deep yellow wood,
no matter how little blood or wound, whomever they strike dies.

Although I offered these, Garad's family would not accept,
trusting their force's size, tall, haughty, bloody sons.
There fell by Clanna Morna brave Fintan from the hazel woods,
Banb Sinna of the spotted shield and Finn Mór, son of Cúán.
They demand an eric from Mac Lugach for killing Goll,
and from Caílte the sharp weapon of the man from Luachair.
A warrior from north of Tara who dared fight mighty Goll,
Flaithius, bald, blood-red, fine-cutting, a handsome man.

Had the brave, handsome Goll three hundred sons, he would not
have been more loved by his family than my father by me.
My father, hardy Dub Díthre, generous, fair-minded man of the Fian,
never complained in battle, his casting-skill beyond compare.
Tell the nine hundred with their backs to the mound
they will get no more from me in the mound to which they come.

By the truth of your courage and prowess, Caílte, said Donn, give me my father's weapons.

I will for I know that he himself was generous when asked.

Caílte gave him his father's arms and said, Show us the way, Donn.

Where do you wish to go? asked Donn.

To the house of Conall mac Néill, king of Cenél Conaill.

Caílte said:

Donn, show us the way in peace and goodwill,
for you are alone after your Fian and your company.
The sons of Morna are gone, a sad, a bitter story,
a thousand warriors, in all, a gathering without care.
I tell you, and everything I say is true,
you will get your request, much gold and silver, Donn.

I'll go before you, said Donn, for he's my mother's brother and has reared me and although he holds the kingship I am in charge. Taking his weapons, Donn went to Dún na mBárc to Conall's house.

Tell me your news, Donn, Conall mac Néill said.

Donn told him how Caílte gave him the weapons and that he was coming to see the king.

I will grant that because he is from Conn's Half and because he has done much good, said Conall.

Donn showed Conall the many sharp weapons that Caílte had given him.

These gifts, the gathering declared, come from a good man.

From a good man indeed, said Conall, for the title of warrior was never given to a better man.

Caílte approached from Sruth na Féinde to the north and by Árd na Maccraide, now called Árd Glas, and to Fid Mór where they waited at the fort. They saw him coming. Conall, the nobles, and the people rose up to make him welcome. Caílte sat on a cairn at the entrance to the fort and the crowd sat about him.

Conall asked Caílte, Why do they call this cairn Carn Garb Daire?

Caílte replied, Garb Daire mac Aengusa, son of the king of Munster and a favourite warrior of Finn mac Cumaill, was there. One day when he was hunting he killed one hundred and fifty stags, one hundred and fifty does, and one hundred and fifty boars. The people of the area saw him. They attacked him and took the deer and the other game although he killed three hundred of their warriors and took their swords. They surrounded him and killed him, turning him into a round apple of spearpoints. The three battalions of the Fian came to avenge him. We devastated the whole region, killing its three kings. Some escaped to the island and that left only a few alive.

Caílte sang:

> Garb Daire was killed on the strand
> by the numerous people of Eógan.
> We killed fifty warriors in all
> in revenge for Garb Daire.

He is in this cairn with his weapons and with him Lug mac Eithlenn's chain that he used to tie the captives of the sons of Mil and of the Tuatha Dé Danann, said Caílte.

We would like to have those sharp weapons, said Conall.

If you wish, said Caílte, we will excavate the cairn to-night.

No, let's dig it tomorrow, for it is night and we will feast and enjoy ourselves.

They went into the big hostel. Caílte and his people were taken to a secluded part of the house and were attended to.

Conall's wife was Bé Binn, daughter of Muiredach mac Finnachta, king of Connaught.

Whether Caílte is with us for a short or a long time, Conall said to her, provide him with nourishment for a thousand every day, put eight score cows into a grassy fenced field for him, have them milked for him every night, and whatever he asks and whatever he presumes from you, give it to him.

They stayed there that night until dawn next day when they went to Garb Daire's cairn. They dug up the cairn and Garb Daire was found inside with his arms. Lug mac Eithlenn's chain was also found. His sword had been placed by his side. The weapons were taken up and his head which was so big that the tallest man among them could have sat inside it.

On my word, Caílte, said Conall, that is a large head.

It is and it belonged to a good man. Caílte gave the weapons to Conall but kept the chain to give to Patrick. They closed up the mound.

Then Conall Mór mac Néill spoke to Caílte. There is, he said, an island out to sea here which has a fort on it. Is this also a great sepulchre that we do not know about?

Caílte wept when he heard this.

By virtue of your courage and prowess, said Conall, let us go to see it.

On my word, said Caílte, that is the third place in Ireland that I do not want to see because of the good noble people who were there. Nevertheless, I will go with you tomorrow.

They remained there until the next day when Conall, his wife, and all the people approached, for listening to Caílte raised their minds and spirits. They gathered round the fort while Caílte sat on the grave inside. The grave was seven score feet in length and twenty-eight in width.

By my soul, said Conall, I have never seen a more marvellous tomb. Tell us whose it is.

I'll tell you the truth, said Caílte. It is the grave of one of the four best women that ever lay with a man in her time.

Who are those four?

Sadb, daughter of Conn of the Hundred Battles; Eithne Ollamda, daughter of Cathaír Mór; Cormac's daughter, freckle-faced Aillbe; and the woman in this grave, Berrach Brec, daughter of Cas Cuailnge, king of Ulster, and Finn mac Cumaill's dearly-loved wife. If the goodness of any one of them exceeded that of the others it was hers. In her house the guest stayed from the first Monday of Samain to the first of spring with his choice to leave or stay. Anyone who did not have enough arms or clothing got enough of both from her to cover him from head to toe.

How did she die?

I can tell you. She was raised by Goll mac Morna's mother and father, their only fosterchild. Finn asked for her from her father, Cas Cuailnge, who said he would not give her without Goll mac Morna's consent.

Finn then asked Goll for his foster-child and Goll replied, I will give her to you on certain conditions: that she will never be sent away, that she will be your third wife, and that you will give her whatever she asks.

All that will be granted, said Finn, for she is a good woman.

Who will provide sureties for us? asked Goll.

You have your choice, said Finn, and gave his own three foster-sons as guarantors: Daigre, Garad, and Conán.

She lived with Finn and bore him three sons: Faelán, Aed Bec, and Uillenn Faeburderg. She was Finn's loving wife until her foster-people, the Clanna Morna, numbering three thousand warriors, became Finn's spoilers and plunderers.

Caílte said:

> I know the families of proud Morna of the great houses,
> without counting the men, over each rampart, over each plain,
> ten hundred and twenty hundred the number of Clanna Morna,
> fifteen hundred in addition the number of chiefs and leaders.

Clanna Morna proceeded to Daire Tarbga [Oakwood of the Bull] in the province of Connaught. The three battalions of the Fian came upon them before they had arisen from their camp. Fifteen capable well-armed sons of Morna fell in the Oakwood. Then Goll mac Morna, that brave soldier, approached and protected their rear so that we were unable to do them the slightest harm. Clanna Morna decided that they would kill anyone who was friendly with Finn and the Fian. Conán Maol mac Morna, the quarrelsome one in assembly, the troublemaker among people, the malicious disturber of hosts and armies gave them that advice. Clanna Morna came to this green and considered what they should do to Berrach Brec, daughter of Cas Cuailnge, their own foster-child. They decided to give her a choice: to take her jewels, valuables, and wealth with her and to leave Finn. Then she need not fear anything as long as they were alive.

It is a pity, said Berrach, would my beloved foster-people want to harm me?

We would, they told her and she replied, I will not leave my husband, Finn mac Cumaill, chief of the Fian of Ireland, my gentle love, and my first family because of you.

Clanna Morna came in battle-array to the place where she was. Each joined hands with his neighbour and surrounded it. They lit fires all about it. The wide-eyed queen came out with thirty of her serving women. Art mac Morna saw her from the balcony of the fort going towards the white sandy beach to her ship. He put his finger into the cord of his spear and fired it at her. Hearing its whistling, the queen turned her face towards the spear which struck her in the breast, broke her back in two and she died. After the fort had been plundered she was raised up by her own people and buried there. She is in this grave.

Caílte sang:

Berrach Brec, Cas Cuailnge's daughter, without a doubt,
queen with yellow hair, outstanding among many.
She was killed on the strand, a far from gentle deed,
they set fire to her fort, it was a malicious pillaging.
Three hundred shields in her house, three hundred sets of chess,
three hundred drinking goblets with which red gold was given.
She never refused anyone, good in body and mind,
the place of her famous grave is called Berrach's tomb.

Here beneath you, said Caílte, is the woman whose grave this is and whose stories these are.

After this Caílte rose and went round to the north and they all followed after him. He laid his hand on a large stone that projected from the side of the fort.

Men, he said, take hold of this stone and leave the other side to me.

The crowd came close to it but could not budge it.

Where, Caílte asked, is Donn mac Aeda meic Garaid?

Here, said Donn.

Get in front of me for you are the son of a warrior and a champion. If I find treasure under the stone I will give you a third.

Both got close to the stone and pulled with such fierceness and strength that they lowered it to the ground.

Victory and blessing, Donn, said Caílte, your help alone is better to me than the help of all Conall's people. Where are Conall, the queen, and Donn?

Here we are, they answered.

Go into this cave, said Caílte, which has three vats in it, one full of gold, another full of goblets, drinking horns, and cups, another full of silver. Just bring me Cráeb Glasach, sword of Finn's side, and his goblet that I may give them to Patrick. The goblet is decorated with one hundred and fifty ounces of gold, one hundred and fifty ounces of silver, and one hundred and fifty crystal gems laid cunningly together.

The three went into the cave and each carried out what he could of that wealth. The entire host went in and brought out an abundance with the result that each band of nine had plenty of gold and silver.

At that time Conall's chariot came for him.

Get into the chariot, Caílte, said Conall.

I need to, said Caílte, because I am weary in this assembly.

They went away in the chariot. Conall urged on the horses with the goad. They went west to Conbec's Strand, where he asked, Why is this strand called Tráig Conbec?

Finn had a favourite hound whose name was Conbec. No deer that he chased would find sanctuary in the whole of Ireland until it was brought to the hounds and servants of the Fian of Ireland. He was the only hound to lie in Finn's bed. Goll mac Morna drowned him here and a big wave washed him into the land. He is under that green cairn at the end of the strand.

Caílte sang:

I am sad at Conbec's death, Conbec, whose jaw was strong,
I never saw a cleverer foot after pig or deer.
I am sad at Conbec's death, Conbec of the deep voice,
I never saw a cleverer foot killing the tall stag.
I am sad at his quick death on the green high waves,
his death a calamity, his dying a great sorrow.

That night they reached Dún na mBárc and next day Conall said to Caílte, There is a ridge here called Nár's Ridge. There is a sow there against which neither dogs nor people can do anything.

I used to be a good hunter of pigs, said Caílte. Where is Donn mac Aeda meic Garaid?

Here, said Donn.

Take your weapons, said Caílte, so that as many of the Fian as we are may hunt this pig. They went up to the mound where they saw a sow with nine tusks in her lower jaw. The sow squealed when she saw the dogs and the big men and horror and fear seized them.

Leave it between me and the pig, said Donn, life or death is all the same to me.

You claim a hero's stay, said Caílte.

Donn approached the sow and as she closed on him Caílte thrust his spear into her from shoulder to shoulder. The sow died. They were unable to carry her until Conall's host arrived and they brought her before Conall.

It is a huge pig, said Conall.

That's true, said Caílte. This is the Muc Slánda and from her kind came the bad blood between Clanna Morna and Clanna Baíscne.

Before long they saw seven men approaching.

Where have you come from? asked Conall mac Néill.

We came, they replied, from Pádraic mac Calpuirn, from Oisín mac Finn and from Diarmaid mac Cerbaill to get you and Caílte.

I cannot go today after that hunting, said Caílte. Go you, Conall, bring those gifts with you: Finn's vessel, Cráeb Glasach, to Patrick; Finn's sword to Diarmaid mac Cerbaill; and the Muc Slánda to the king of Ireland so that everyone may see it and that the king may distribute to them all, both nobles and ordinary people.

All that was done. The sword was given to Donn mac Aeda meic Garaid meic Morna.

What you win or lose by the sword is in your hands, Caílte said, until it reaches the king of Ireland.

Conall himself brought the vessel to Patrick, the slaves carried the sow and went as far as the Upper Hill of Erc, now called Uisnech.

When they arrived Patrick was on the Hill with Diarmaid mac Cerbaill on his right hand, Oisín mac Finn on his left, Eochaid Lethderg, king of Leinster, on the same side, and Eógan Derg mac Aengusa, king of the two parts of Munster, beside the king of Ireland. Conall mac Néill arrived, placed his head on Patrick's chest, and bowed before him.

Come here, Conall, said Diarmaid to the king but he replied, I want to be with Patrick so that he will be over me in Heaven as on earth.

I give you a kingdom, said Patrick, thirty of your sons shall reign. My monastic city and my abbacy I give you and whatever I get from the five provinces of Ireland.

Conall gave the golden vessel to Patrick.

Your friend Caílte mac Rónaín gives this vessel to you, said Conall.

On my word he is a friend, said Patrick, and handed the vessel to the king of Ireland.

The king looked at it for a long time and said, I have never seen a treasure better than this vessel and, Oisín, consider well whose it may have been.

It was my father's, said Oisín, Finn mac Cumaill's. His wife, Berrach Brec, daughter of Cas Cuailnge, who was killed by Clanna Morna, gave it to him. I am sure that he who found this also found the other treasure, the best in Ireland or Scotland, Finn's sword, Cráeb Glasach.

I have it here, said Conall, for the king of Ireland. How well you recognized it. Donn, give this sword to the king of Ireland for Caílte has given it to him.

The young man took the sword from Oisín. The hilt of the sword filled his hand.

I am amazed, said Oisín, that this sword is the full of your hand for it has never filled anyone's grip except someone from the family of Baíscne or Morna.

What is your lineage, young man? asked the king of Ireland.

I am Donn meic Aeda meic Garaid meic Morna.

On my word, said Oisín, your father and grandfather were noble.

He put the sword into the hand of Ireland's king.

What reward for the sword? asked Donn.

What reward do you want? asked the king.

To be leader of the Fian of Ireland even as my grandfather's brother was, answered Donn.

If Oisín and Caílte allow it that will be yours, said the king.

We do, said Oisín, for my permission includes Caílte's. It is Donn's inheritance for seven of his lineage have had the kingship of the Fian of Ireland and Scotland.

Therefore I give it to you, said the king, without tax or tribute from it of gold or silver to be given to you as was given to every chief of the Fian before you but with power over all of Ireland's hunting and game.

Donn received pledges and guarantees on that and for twenty-seven years was chief of the Fian of Ireland and Scotland until Dub mac Dolair killed him in Scotland at the Battle of Cuires.

Next they brought the sow to the king of Ireland.

This, Conall said, is the sow killed by Caílte and Donn and that Caílte gave to you to be shared among the people of Ireland in the belief that they will find healing from a piece of the Muc Slánda.

The king divided the sow between the twenty-five battalions of the men of Ireland who were gathered at Uisnech, which made all of them cheerful and happy.

That was the last Muc Slánda to be divided among the men of Ireland.

Then Conall Mór mac Néill said to the king of Ireland, What provision will you make for Caílte, who is coming to visit you?

The provision of a thousand warriors: eight score milch cows will be driven into a grassy fertile field and their milk will be given to him and to Oisín, his foster-brother, every night.

They remained there until morning.

Conall's horses were caught for Caílte and a chariot prepared. He came across the top of Sliab Fuait [the Fews]; to Caerthann Ban Fionn [Rowan Tree of Fair Women], now called Rowan of the Two-stag Meadow; northward to the Height of the Great Feat, now called Faughart Muirthemne where Cú Chulainn performed his heroic fight against the hosts of the Táin Bó Cuailnge; northward to the Ford of the Chariots, now called Áth Goill; by the Horse-Goad of Cú Chulainn, now called the Grave of the Grey of Macha between Dundalk and the sea; and south to Sliab Con [Mount of the Dogs], now called Sliab Brega.

During that same time Diarmaid mac Cerbaill together with the nobles of Ireland were on the hill of Uisnech.

Diarmaid was seized by thirst. He asked if there was water near them. There is not, they all replied.

Oisín heard that and said, Give me a pail that I may search for water.

Bring a servant with you, said Diarmaid.

I will bring neither servant nor warrior, said Oisín.

He set off and assumed the charm of invisibilty so that no one from the camp would see him. He approached the well, the white-edged well of Uisnech which no one had found since the Battle of Gabair was fought. Oisín came to its gravelled brink and saw eight beautiful varied-coloured salmon in it for the place was so secluded there was no need for them to be afraid. He took eight pieces of watercress and eight of brooklime, dipped the pail into the pool, and brought the eight salmon with him jumping recklessly inside the vessel with the sprigs of cress and brooklime over them. He returned and put the pail before the king of Ireland. They were all amazed.

They must be divided in two, said Diarmaid, one half to Patrick, one half to us.

No, indeed, said Patrick, since you are the more numerous let them be divided in three and give a third to the church for that is her rightful portion.

That was done.

It is well, king of Ireland, said Patrick, that you do not allow that pair to take your share of Heaven from you. What does that mean? asked Diarmaid.

The share you have turned them from.

LEINSTER

Caílte arrived at the plain of Bruig to the north across Linn Féic on the bright streaming Boyne; by the right hand to the Hill of Ward; by the left hand to Cnoc Tailtenn [Hill of Teltown]; and up the Road of the Chariots to the top of Uisnech where the men of Ireland were. He got down, came before Patrick, bowed and put his head on Patrick's chest. An ex-layman of Patrick's people, Mochua mac Lonáin, came before him.

Well, said Patrick, tell us who Mochua is.

Caílte said:

Mochua mac Lonáin of the Shirts, son of Senach, at whom we will not cast,
mac Aengusa of the Grey Stud, son of Mugna, son of freckle-fisted Blat.
Mac Aedáin, son of Blá-Aed, son of Fergus, son of Cinaed,
mac Fiachach, son of Art of the plain, son of Muiredach meic Eógain.

All I can do, said Mochua, is pray for you in the eight canonical hours of the Church.

Sit by my side, Caílte, said Patrick.

I should not sit at a king's shoulder, said Caílte, but in a king's presence for I am the son of a warrior and he who is beside you is a better man.'

I give you my word, said Oisín, no woman anywhere in Ireland in your time gave birth to anyone who could rightly claim to be a better man than you.

Then the men of Ireland welcomed Caílte and the king gave him a triple welcome.

Caílte kissed Oisín three times and sat beside him. Oisín gave Caílte the fistful of cress and brooklime that he had in his hand.

This cress and brooklime are from the Flescach, said Caílte. Did you catch any fish in it?

I got eight salmon, said Oisín. We will share them.

On my word, said Caílte, never have I shared anything more welcome with man or woman. Caílte then put his hand in the box of his shield and laid the chain of Lug mac Ethlenn on the ground before them.

You found the chain, Caílte, said Oisín, in the cairn of Garb Daire.

There for sure, said Caílte and gave the chain to the king of Ireland. If there were twenty-five battalions in a host it would go round them. Eight hundred warriors could fit inside it and if it were closed on the first man of them it could not be opened until he was released.

Then the king said, Caílte, there were four noble men in Ireland at the one time: Cormac mac Airt, Finn, Cairbre Lifechair, and Oisín.

The warrior Cormac was noble, said Caílte, and Finn's nobility was known to everyone.

Caílte said:

> Were his son and his enemy come to seek judgement,
> his goodness was such he could not be unjust to either.

Caílte, asked Diarmaid, was Cormac better than Finn and Cairbre better than Oisín? Caílte replied:

> By the King who rules me Cormac was not better than Finn,
> nor was renowned Oisín less than Cairbre Lifechair.

Then Eochaid Lethderg, king of Leinster, asked Caílte, Why was it that Finn and his Fian did not kill the huge reptile that we have in Glen Rois Énaig when you drove every other monster out of Ireland?

Because, said Caílte, he was the fourth part of Mesgegra's brain that the ground swallowed and changed into a great snake. We were not meant to kill it before the arrival of the Táilchenn. In time one of his disciples will tie it with a single rush-stem and it will be bound like that forever.

How did it happen, asked the king, that the Fian and their dogs were killed by the reptile in that lake?

Finn had a fairy lover, Oisín answered, Úna, daughter of Modarn. Finn stopped loving her because of the many shapes she assumed. There was no animal whose shape she would not take. One day when the Fian came to the cairn above the lake a deer went into it and we followed but the reptile rose up against us, killing a hundred men and a hundred dogs. Then I asked Finn if the creature would fall by us and, if so, would we go after it and avenge our people. Finn put his thumb beneath his tooth of wisdom and the truth was revealed to him as he spoke in this poem.

Finn said:

Glenn Rois Énaig, this will be true, the bell's sweet voice heard forever there.
Though it be home to red deer, its splendid gifts were plentiful.
Loch Énaig, abode of swans, sad the Fian are no longer there.
The clerics will come, will chant with sweet melody.
Loch Énaig between two mountains, the most beautiful I ever saw,
a river with two lakes in the centre filling from the west
An abode for cold pilgrims, an abode for the strong and the weak,
burial place for kings, side by side, when Kevin comes to the glen.

It is impossible to relate the great deeds of valour and prowess that they and the other nobles of the Fian performed in addition to the place lore of every hill and region that the men of Ireland asked about.

Next day they erected a tent over the king of Ireland on the grassy hill and only allowed royal heirs into the tent. Patrick and his clerics were inside the second half of the tent and only a bishop, priest, or those particularly devoted to the King of heaven and earth were allowed access to Patrick. Oisín sat before Patrick and Caílte before the king of Ireland.

Which of you is the oldest? asked Patrick.

I am, said Caílte, for I was already thirty years old when Oisín was born and for the past seventeen years he has shared my bed. It was after he left my house that he got a Fian and a company.

Then the king of Ireland asked, How many kings of Ireland gave territory to the Fian?

Caílte answered, The king of Ireland, Feradach Fechtnach, had two sons called Tuathal and Fiacha. When Feradach died, they divided Ireland between them. One got her jewels, wealth, treasures, cattle, herds, bracelets, clasps, forts, fortresses, and sturdy homesteads. The other got her cliffs, estuaries, mast, and great fruits, her varied hued salmon, and her game.

Where did they make that decision? asked the king of Ireland.

On the hill on which we are sitting, answered Caílte.

It was not a fair division, said the nobles of Ireland.

Which of the two portions would you have preferred? asked Oisín.

Her feasts, houses, and the rest of her treasures are the best division, not her lands, wilderness, hunting, game, and all the rest, they answered.

The portion that is worse in your eyes, said Caílte, is the one we like best.

Oisín sang:

Tell, Caílte, how it is, great knowledge is to be sought,
the first division of Ireland, half and half, of all the lands around Uisnech.
Can you tell me, Caílte, who gave lands to the Fian?
Who gave up minding the dogs, who paid him?

Caílte sang:

I remember what caused it, son of steadfast Derg's daughter,
when Fiacha helped the Fian until you, Oisin, deposed him.
You had ten years of good leadership, Oisín, as high chief,
until Fothad deceived the Fian and you, Oisín, were left.
Feradach had a good son whose name was Fiacha Finn,
his mother, a great queen, was Eithne, daughter of Dáire Dub.
Feradach and Fiacha Find divided Ireland part by part,
they were happy in an Ireland without war and rivalry.
The younger son made the choice to be with the Fian,
in the thickets, wilderness, woods, rivers, cliffs and estuaries.
Feradach chose high kingship over the men of Ireland,
its feasts, fruits, houses, herds and husbandry.
Feradach ruled well until he fell by Mál, the son-chief,
the news of a king of warlike fame, his death that night.
Fiacha came prosperously to Tara once Feradach had fallen,
wrested power over all Ireland from the great Mál mac Rochraide.
Fiacha entrusted the Fian to the great-minded Morna,
after him four members of his tribe, worthy men, led them.
Vigorous Morna mac Cairbre was chief for ten years,
Garad also had ten until they took off his fine head.
Vigorous Daigre mac Garaid was chief for five years.

I count seven years the span of Donn mac Morna, the last of them.
Eochaid mac Nárchada from the east was king of Ireland's Fian from Ulster,
his reign a year and a half as supreme leader of the Fian.
Cas mac Cannáin, strong and fierce, from Ulster had one year,
Dubán, his son, a pleasing event, by my reckoning had two.
Liath Luachra and Labraid Lámderg from Munster through guile were next,
each had ten years, no little time, though sons of vassal peoples from Ara.
Trénmór ua Baíscne, grandson of Sétna Sithbac, was hard,
grandfather to Finn, giver of gifts, father of Cumall and Crimaill.
Trénmór, greatly loved, controlled the Fian of Ireland as one,
they made him king from the south, seventeen years his reign.
Cumall took power, strong and fierce, by sword and shield,
from which he fought three battles, warlike, combative, tough.
Cumall took power, fierce and strong, by sword and shield,
ten years his reign until his death in Cath Cnucha [Battle of Castleknock].
Then grief and sharp sorrow seized the sons of Morna,
thirty warriors of great renown, with Daigre, Goll, and Garad,
Goll Mór, a soldier in battle, last son of Morna,
ten years he had, no small number, chief leader of the Fian of Ireland.
Then came the golden salmon, Finn mac Cumaill meic Trénmóir,
gift-giver to noble hosts, our many-talented wise man.
Our chief, leader, seer, judge, magician and druid,
head of the groups, reliable one, Finn mac Cumaill meic Trénmóir.

It was Finn and fifty warriors, noble, knowledgeable, wise,
none better in shape and form or better in weapons or clothes.
Two hundred renowned years and thirty without weakness,
Finn's life, a long period, until he died in his leap of folly.
Seventeen kings, I know, ruled the Fian of Ireland,
Finn the best of them all, the warrior from high Alma.

Five druids, a choice company, the best in the country of the west,
I remember precisely how to recall them and their druidic art.
There was Badgna from Badgna's Mound, Cathbad, wonderful druid,
Fair Stocán mac Cuirc, adept at wounding, Mog Ruith and Finn of Formail.

Five healers, a fine group, the best in the country of Banba,
although I live long after them I am knowledgeable in telling of them.
Miach and Oirmed from the start and their father, Dian Cécht,
Gabrán, the healer from overseas, Finn, fair-haired grandson of Baíscne.

Five poets, a noble group, the best ever came to Ireland.
I remember them well, their knowledge, their poetry:
Cairbre, the poet Amairgen of the Gael's island found overseas,
Ferchertne and Labraid Lorc, Mog Ruith and Finn of the bare blade.

Five whose sharp minds were the best in any house in Ireland:
Fíthel, his son Flaithrí, Cairbre, Ailbe, and Cormac.
Any question they had in mind, Finn would quickly solve,
a question he raised at a feast none of them could answer.

Five warriors quickly angered, the best ever came to the land of Elga,
the most violent in action and deed, toughest in battle and fight:
Lug mac Céin meic Cáinte from abroad, Cú Chulainn and Conall,

Lugaid Lága, the valorous hand, and fair-haired Finn.
Five the most generous ever, the best for cloaks and food,
of the race of shining Gaels, well they shared their wealth:
Lug, son of Eithne, renowned Aengus, Cú of the feats, hard to quench,
gentle Conaire, fair of form, similarly Finn and Mac Luchta.
Five of the best chiefs with me, the best ever in Ireland,
I remember them exactly, their retelling in their lordship:
Éremón, son of the great Mil, Iugaine after Éremón,
greater their valour, Aengus Tuirbech, Conn Cétchatach, hardy Finn.
A fierce fighter to do deeds, a warrior for companionship,
a cleric to preach the Son of God, a chief for truth.
I cannot fault Finn's Fian, by the King above my head,
except God, who came to earth, not adoring your Son.
The good people live no longer, Finn, true chief, does not live,
the troop without concealment nor royal princes together with the
Fian-chief.
Better their ranks than all others, better their leader than all kings,
such great men, such great shields, such great, agile, rough-grey warriors.
King, sage, poet, chief with a great family,
our wise man, magician, prophet, sweet to us was everything he said.
For all that I say in praise of him, by the King above me,
he was three times better than all that I can say.
Seven times the chief believed, Finn mac Cumaill of Alma,
the seventh time at the limit of his growth, thence his final end.
Eógan had the southern half, Trénmór was his helper,
son of Caireall of Cnoc in Scáil, sweet everything he said.

Victory and blessing, Caílte, said Diarmaid mac Cerbaill, where are the poets and historians? Let these matters be written in the tablets of the poets, in the records of the learned, in the words of the judges so that everyone may take with him to his own land his portion of all that Caílte and Oisín have told us of great deeds of valour and prowess and of the place lore of Ireland.

Then Finn mac Faebardeirg, son of the king of Uí-Cheinnselaig asked, Caílte, why is it that saints and wisemen worship the Giúsach Finn more than any other place in the area?

It was, Caílte replied, a hunting-preserve Finn had and when the Fian could not find enough hunting in the fifth province of Leinster from Inneoin Maige Femen [Anvil of the Plain of Femen] to Benn Étair, they would find it in Giúsach Finn [Pine Forest of Finn].

Caílte, asked Finn mac Faebair, why do they call the ford in the middle of the Giúsach Áth Ferna?

Oisín answered: Goll mac Morna killed Fern mac Cairill there during a raid by Clanna Morna. He was the son of the king of the Déisi in the south and a favourite warrior of Finn's. When he had been buried, Finn put his thumb under his tooth of knowledge and the truth was made known to him. Fern mac Cairill, he said it is good that you are buried where you are. Over your head Mass bells will ring, the white books of the Hours will be read and the body of the Saviour will be adored.

Finn said:

Áth Ferna, where virtuous Maedóg will be,
though now its wolves are many, its heavenly songs will be many.
Ford of Ferns of the grassy banks, excellent will be the man who will own it,
when soul-friends come there they will be very close to God.
Maedóg and his people will cross by the fair stream,
heads will bend low worshipping God.
Maedóg and his people will come, sunlight through showers,
the son of the star will come, a victorious star forever.
It will be the chosen place where the Fian cooked,
Maedóg and his people will come, welcome the king whose mighty grave it is.
He will be the strong fairest-browed boar, he will be a fierce barb of doom,
Maedóg and his people will come, he will be a wave over many a ford.

All this is good, said Finn mac Faebair. I have another question for you, Caílte.

What is it?

Who owns the fort here called Ros Broc on the boundary of the two provinces, where the three rivers, the Suir, Nore, and Barrow, meet?

Two of Finn mac Cumaill's favourite warriors, Cellach Braenbile and Moling Luath, were from Leinster, said Caílte. Each had two hundred soldiers, two hundred servants, and two hundred dogs, and if you searched the three battalions of the Fian you would not find two better men for vigour or prowess. They had another quality: the Fian might stay in their house for a year without going short of food or ale.

We are surprised, said Finn mac Faebair, by the water on this high ground. The stream flowing down the side relieves every disease it encounters.

I can tell you the reason for that bounty, said Caílte. That's the first water in Ireland to have been blessed by God's angels, also the last, and the river's name is Taeidiu. Finn's two warriors remained here until the Clanna Morna came to plunder the Fian. One night before they noticed anything Clanna Morna attacked front and rear and surrounded the dwelling. For three days and three nights they attacked but were unable to make headway until they set it on fire. They plundered it and no one, man, woman, or child, escaped being burnt. When they finished plundering and wrecking they retired across the ford at Inber Dubglaisse, west across the Barrow.

At that time we, the three battalions of the Fian, reached the dwelling but were of no help to the inhabitants. Finn and the three battalions sat on the fort's green. He wept tears of great grief for it was seldom that such a grievous deed had been done to him. They brought a basin of pale gold to him. He washed his hands, applied water to his kingly face, put his thumb under his tooth of knowledge, and made one of the three greatest revelations ever made known to him: Four chosen seers who come after me will reveal their knowledge of the King of heaven and earth. One of the four is Moling mac Faeláin meic Feradaig meic Fidgae. In time a battle will take place in Ireland, Cath Maige Ráth [the Battle of Moira]. Suibne Geilt will come from the battle, will be killed, and buried here. His mother will be a Munster woman and no Munster man will ever dare harm this dwelling.

Finn spoke this poem:

Ros Broc today is a track for wolves, a great red sea between two cliffs,
be it long or short till saints arrive, Moling the name of its church.
Eddying in the creeks the restless Taeidiu fills along the rocks,
multitudes will come, journeying here for God.
The hovering man will come there from Moira in the north,
with rejoicing for the cleric, a morning with abundance of gifts.

The house of Moling mac Faeláin meic Feradaig meic Fidgae,
an ounce of gold from each one for a home in the church.
The Bell of saintly Moling which will be struck at the hours,
Limerick warriors will not attack, his mother being from Munster.
The men of Cualu from the north will come, advancing to St Moling's,
from then to Judgement Day better and better St Moling's.
I tell you in advance, my prophecy will be true,
it will draw Finn's soul, this promise about Moling at Ross.

And that, Finn mac Faebair, said Caílte, answers the question you asked me.

Then the king of Ireland said to Patrick, It is time I went to Tara.

Will you come with me to Tara? Diarmaid asked the old men.

Not until the end of the year, they said.

Then Eochaid Lethderg, king of Leinster, said, I'll take Oisín with me to spend the year at the fort of Liaman Lennchaem, daughter of Dobrán Dubthaire.

I'll take Caílte with me, said Conall mac Néill, to spend the year at Dún na mBarc in the north.

I'll take Patrick with me to Tara, said Diarmaid mac Cerbaill, to baptize, bless, and organize the men of Ireland in his own rule and discipline.

The men of Ireland were released to their own territories and would come together again at Tara in a year's time.

What you have heard is *Acallam na Senórach* at the standing stone on the hill of Uisnech and the wisdom and knowledge they spoke to the men of Ireland.

Part II

Ulster

Caílte went with Conall mac Néill to Ráth Artrach in the north in the territories of Cenél Conaill. Gentle, mature, yellow-haired girls, small boys in green cloaks, and the young men of the fort came out to welcome him. They were drinking and enjoying themselves together on the night of that beautiful day until rising from its fiery zone the sun filled the cliffs, waterfalls, and estuaries of the country with shining light.

After that, Conall, Caílte, and the nobles came from the homestead.

Why, the king asked, is this rath called Ráth Artrach and why is the mound to the south called the Mound of the Poets?

Bodb Derg, son of the Dagda, answered Caílte, had three sons in the glittering Bruig, Artrach, Aed Álaind, and Aengus, who had a quarrel with their father. Now, my sons, said Bodb Derg, leave the realm of the Tuatha Dé Danann to me and go to the king of Ireland to Cormac grandson of Conn. There is good reason you should leave. The Tuatha Dé Danann do not have enough lands to support themselves, not to mention the wealth that Artrach has. Between warriors and servants Aengus, son of Bodb, has more than the Tuatha Dé Danann and Aed Álaind has more poets here than there are in the kingdoms of Ireland and Scotland.

The three sons of Bodb went to Cormac, who asked them why they had come.

Our own father has ordered us to leave the Tuatha Dé Danann and we have come to seek lands from you, they answered.

You will get them, said Cormac, I will give you four cantreds of the rough land known today as Tirconnell.

The eldest son, Artrach, had a hostel with seven doors and a welcome for everyone. The much-talented Aengus was in Ráth Mongaig and had with him the sons of the king of Ireland and of Scotland learning skill in handling. Aed was in the Mound of the Poets with the bards of Ireland and Scotland. They stayed there during the thirty years reign of Cormac, grandson of Conn, who died at Ráth Speláin in Brega. Then they returned to the Tuatha Dé Danann. Although it is a wild rath today this was a pleasant red-speckled mound with smooth red-headed nuts on the woods and golden-yellow apples.

Caílte sang:

> Though once a many-armed rath, Ráth Artrach is wild today,
> this happy well-stocked rath is sunny north and south.
> The stone on the mound's north side, many do not know,
> thrice one hundred and fifty ounces lie under its breast
> The rath to the north is named from Mongach of the hosts,
> a short distance south is Ráth nAeda of the poets.

Where is that stone, asked Conall, under which the gold and silver lie?

Finding it is not difficult, said Caílte.

He rose up with four hundred strong-armed men. They put their hands to the stone at the same time to drag it from the ground but had no success. They could not shift it even a little.

We have no one with us now to help or to lift, they said.

Caílte thrust the head of his spear under the stone and raised it up. He inserted his hand and brought out Finn mac Cumaill's stone chest in which there were one hundred and fifty ounces of silver, one hundred and fifty ounces of gold, one hundred and fifty gold chains and battle-swords. Then Caílte closed the box.

Caílte, said Conall, divide the treasure.

The swords and chains for you, said Caílte, the chest of gold and silver for Saint Patrick since he is the repository of faith and belief for the Irish.

Then Conall Derg mac Néill said to Caílte, There are three hills about us here but we do not know how they got their names. One is called Lecht na Laechraide [Grave of the Warriors], another is named Tulach in Bhanchuire [Hill of the Troop of Women], the third Lecht na Macraide [Grave of the Boys], which has a well and a river flowing out of it. Why is the river called Glaise na bFer [Stream of the Men]?

I can explain, said Caílte. Finn took Sadb, daughter of Bodb Derg, son of the Dagda, as his wife and she asked as a bride-gift that half of his sexual intercourse and of his wealth be given to her. The reason for this request was that there was hardly a better woman from Taprobané to the Garden of the Hesperides. She was married to Finn at the fairy mound of Femen known at that time as the fairy mound of the Fairhaired Women. After the wedding Finn went on the trail of Clanna Morna, who were marauding and pillaging until he came to this rath, Ráth Artrach. He rested and pitched camp here.

As far as Sadb, daughter of the Dagda, is concerned, Finn said to Ferdoman, son of Bodb Derg, his wife's brother, I've been away a long time. She will say it is a shame and a disgrace for her that I have been absent for a year. I ought to send messengers to bring her here but who are the most appropriate?

Her four foster-brothers, Conaing and Cathal, the two sons of Dub mac Aengusa Tírig, king of Munster and her other foster-brothers, Cathal and Crimthann, the two sons of Conn of the Hundred Battles, who are the four she cherishes most in Ireland, answered Bodb Derg. When there was no woman in Finn's bed it was they who kept him company, said Caílte.

Which of you will go? asked Finn.

We will, said Conaing and Cathal, for she is in our country and our territory and of all the women of Ireland she is to us the dearest and most admired.

They went to the fairy mound of the Fairhaired Women with four hundred warriors, four hundred servants and their dogs, and entered the large shining mound. They received a song of genuine welcome without deceit or guile and good food and wine of all kinds. They spent three days and three nights there.

We've come to bring you to Finn mac Cumaill, they said.

What else is to be done, said the woman, but go to him.

Her women, one hundred daughters of kings and rulers, gathered travelling clothes of every colour and possessions for the journey, and came to this hill. They released their horses and gave them grass on stakes driven into the ground. It was then that Sadb, daughter of Bodh, and all the women became very thirsty.

I do not know of any water nearby, said Conaing.

There was a king-sized stone on top of the hill. With a great effort all the men together turned and shifted the stone from its position. A clear cool well of crystalline water flowed from the spot. This water has been excavated in a manly fashion, said the woman, and what better name to give it than the Men's Stream?

They drank their fill of it.

You promised that Finn would be here, said the woman.

On our word he promised to be here, said Cathal.

We know he pursued the Clanna Morna to the Mournes in the greatly-renowned province of Ulster, they answered.

Before long they saw a swift phalanx of fighters in battle-array coming towards them from the north, numbering eight hundred warriors.

Do you know them? asked Sadb.

I know them, said Conaing, renowned Goll mac Morna and he is coming at us.

The men rose, prepared the chariot, and put the woman into it.

Then Goll asked, Do you know these men?

We do, said Conán mac Morna, the two sons of Dub mac Aengusa Tírig, king of Munster, men loved by Finn mac Cumaill.

Finn's people put their knees to the fight and their faces to the danger, said Caílte. They hurled spears at one another. Four hundred of Clanna Morna's fighting-men were killed, they fell without any chance of escaping with their lives. The women put their faces to the ground and died of terror. That's why they call this hill The Hill of the Women. Finn arrived with the three battalions of the Fian and saw the slaughter. The two sons of the king of Leinster came to the hill, put their mouths to the ground, and died of grief for their two foster-brothers. Seeing that, Finn's arms fell from his hands and he shed copious tears that wet his shirt and his chest. All the Fian wept.

It is a pity, Finn said, this story will reach the house of Conn of the Hundred Battles at the fairy mound of Liaman Lennchaem. It is a bad story to be told to Dub mac Aengusa Tírig, king of the two parts of Munster at the fort of Sliab Cláire in the south and to the borders of Sliab Gua in the south. It is a bad story to reach Bodb Derg at the fairy mound of the Fairhaired Women: the death of his daughter.

Finn went and searched through the slaughter but could not find Sadb. The Fian buried the four hundred of Finn's people. They discovered each man with one of the Clanna Morna dead under him. They wrote their names in ogham over them and held the funeral games. Since that time this hill is called The Grave of the Warriors, since then the other hill is called The Hill of the Troop of Women, and the hill to the north is called The Grave of the Boys for the sons of the king of Leinster who were buried there.

This, Conall, said Caílte, is what you asked me about and what happened.

Conall then asked Caílte if Finn was bound by any taboos.

There were many, said Caílte, but they did not affect him. He was seized with trembling and great fear at the burial of those people:

> A sad event, two sons of Dub, the king's two sons,
> a hundred servants, a hundred dogs, slain without doubt.
> A tragic tale, many tears in Ráth Artrach,
> the deaths of Conaing and Cathal, both at the head of one field.
> Glaise na bFer will be an eternal ancient well,
> the loss of everyone in the tale will live till Judgement's scales.
> Not to walk in the morning on Brega's mead, not to flee from a band of poets
> not to rest for the night at Dún Ráth, not to reward the two warriors.
> Not to lie with the daughter of Bodb of an evening with cries on the battlefield,
> not to walk on Síd Ban Finn by the blaze of a new red fire.
> Finn mac Cumaill of Alma by the Son of Mary of the great oath
> never refused anyone either good or bad, a clear fulfilment.
> The deaths of Cathal and of curly-haired Crimthann, both under the
> green mound, such destruction all at the one time I never saw north or south.
> That Finn of the Fian was killed giving his hero's leap
> broke my heart in three, reduced all my strength to nothing.

Victory and blessing, Caílte, said Conall, you have given us great knowledge to tell to the people of a later time.

They went into the dwelling and were feasting and enjoying themselves until it was time to rest. Caílte arose next morning and said good-bye to Conall Derg mac Néill and all his people.

Now, Caílte said, I must go to another region. He went east to Loch Daim Deirg [Lake of the Red Stag] in Dál nAraide where there were two dignified presbyters, Colmán Éla and Eóganán, followers of Patrick, performing the gentle dominical canon and praising the Creator. Three young ecclesiastics arrived and launched a currach to go fishing while saying their hours and their office. Seeing them, Caílte spoke this poem:

I have seldom listened to chanting on the water
In the past I have listened more often to the murmur of gentle women
Whoever has a pen would have to write a long time
Although I am wretched now, I have known great wonders
Slow my journey from Tráig Lí [Tralee], I waited a long time for it
As for reading from books, a fine work, I seldom listened to them.

Then Colmán Éla and Eóganán saw the tall men with the huge dogs on a leash.

It's true, he said, that's Caílte, one of the Fian, and Saint Patrick's people as well. Bring him to the island so that we may be together.

They were brought in, housed in a secluded part of the house, given the best of every drink, and provided with meals and nourishment.

Colmán asked Caílte, Why was the lough called the Lake of the Red Stag?

The red stag was on the open lands in well-watered Luachair in the south. Three times a year he would escape from the hounds of the Fian. One year the Fian pursued him to this place. Four of us caught up with him: Diarmaid Ó Duibne, Mac Lugach, Glas mac Aencherda Bérra, and myself. I was nearest to him as we approached this lough. We threw our four spears at him at the same time and he fell. I caught one antler, Diarmaid caught the other, and we took him with us to Temair Luachra to show him to Finn. Finn put the bottom of the antler at his feet and the upper tine was at the top of his head and he was the tallest man in the Fian. I put the other antler at the end of this island. If I had light, it is likely it could bring evidence of that casting.

Caílte spoke this poem:

This lake, the Lake of the Red Stag, to which we came step by step,
its name forever from now to the last generation.

If there is enough light for me across the land,
I will bring the antler to you, the complete antler.
We four moved from the west, from Munster land of great hostage,
our vigour and reputation intact until we reached this lake.

Victory and blessing be yours, Caílte, said Colmán, that is great knowledge and true guidance that will live with all of us.

Young ecclesiastic, said Caílte, see if the moon has risen yet in her aerial tent.

She has risen, said the ecclesiastic, sea and land are illuminated by her.

Then Caílte went to the farthest end of the island, put his hand deep into the stream, retrieved the antler and laid it on the floor of the house where the clergy were.

He who was king of Ulster at that time, Eochaid Faeburderg mac Fírglinne, was close to them at the Hill of Weapons, now called Mag Ráth [Moira]. Colmán, Eóganán, and six ecclestiastics rose early and took the antler with them to show it to the king of Ulster and to the Ulstermen, who were with them numbering two hundred armed men. An ecclesiastic brought the antler before the king. All of them could have taken shelter under it from storm or rough weather.

Who got the antler, asked the king, and where was it found?

Caílte found it at the Lake of the Red Stag.

It would please me if he would come to see me for he could tell us the old lore of all our territories, of our hills and of the achievements of each of our families.

Leaving the antler with him, the clergy went back to their own house.

Tell me, Colmán, said Caílte, what is the reason for the eight hours that you attend to both day and night?

There is a serious reason: eight faults adhere to every man's body and soul. The eight hours purge them, said Colmán.

Colmán spoke this poem:

Eight bodily faults bite us to the bone,
eight chosen hours help us to atone:
Prime against the gullet's craving,
Tierce 'gainst anger's wilful raving,
Midday's light 'gainst lustful phases,
Nones 'gainst greed throughout the ages,
Vespers' calm 'gainst sore despair,
Compline's strength 'gainst easeful sloth,
Nocturn's cold 'gainst boasting's stride,

Matins, God's son's, 'gainst stubborn pride.
Jesus, Judge, save me through the eight.

Victory and blessing, Colmán Éla, said Caílte, you have solved that question well. And why should I not practise the Eight Hours since God has kept me here to know about them?

Colmán then asked Caílte, Why is this well at the head of the lough called the Well of the Women?

Niam, daughter of Aengus Tírech, king of the two parts of Munster, eloped with Oisín mac Finn from Dún na mBárc in the province of Munster and came to this well. Oisín was with her here for six weeks, hunting and chasing deer. Each morning the woman and her thirty serving-women came to this blue-tinted water to wash their faces and hands. It weighed heavily on Aengus Tírech that his daughter had run off with Oisín. He gathered the two provinces of Munster about him, five great battalions, three thousand men in each battalion, and came here in pursuit of the Fian. Niam and her women were washing in the well and saw the five battalions on the hill above them.

It is a pity, she said, happy was she who died and was buried before her guardian, her father, her three brothers, and the nobles of the provinces of Munster had seen her like this! She put her face to the ground and she and her thirty women died. Her heart came out of her mouth in a flood of black blood. From that time this hill is known as the Hill of Slaughter. The Well of the Women is the name of the well over there.

Caílte said:

In this hill is the queen that the hosts avenged,
the Hill of Slaughter where all have stayed.

The two provinces of Munster saw the daughter's death, continued Caílte. The king said, Finn and Oisín and the Fian have done a bad thing to us. The king ordered the female runner, Muirenn, daughter of Muiresc, to find Finn and challenge him to battle. She went to the Rath of the Head of the Hound where the Fian were. Finn asked her what news she had and she told him her message. She spoke this poem:

Finn, a clear fight for you, man of the ever-melodious word,
at the Head of the Hound without contradiction, without escape.
The Munsterman contends with Finn and his company,
if they fight one another the clash will be heroic.
I say running in advance, and what I say is true,
if reason does not prevail you will have a fight on your hands, Finn.

Seldom, said Finn, have I been challenged to a fight. Go out, Garb Crónán, and tell the Fian to prepare for battle.

Coming to the camp of the Fian, Garb Crónán gave three fierce war cries in the middle of the encampment. The Fian responded because they realized there was some great reason for his urgency. The Fian assembled, bravely preparing for battle and then asked Finn, What is the cause of this fight?

Fergus Finnbél, the poet of the Fian, said, It is not right, Finn, for you to fight against the king of Munster because of the daughter whose death you have caused.

Then Finn and the nobles of the Fian decided on a plan. Finn said, Where is Smirgat, daughter of Ábartach?

Here, she said.

Go quickly, continued Finn, and tell Aengus Tírech and the nobles of Munster that I will give them the judgement of Cormac of the Hundred Battles and of Eithne Ollamda, daughter of Cathaír Mór, and of Cithruad mac Firchoécat.

The messenger went off with that. The king of Munster answered, If they give guarantees and sureties for that I will accept it.

What guarantees do you want? asked Smirgat.

Oscar mac Oisín, son of the man who did me wrong; Ferdoman, son of the Dagda's son, Bodb Derg; and Diarmaid mac Duinn meic Donnchada.

Finn agreed. The Fian and the king of Munster went to Tara where they were given this judgement: The girl to be raised from the mound in which she lay, placed on a scales, and her weight in gold to be given as a blood-fine and a blood-fine to be given to each king and leader whose daughter had been killed there.

Fian of Ireland, said Finn, how shall we divide these fines?

They replied, A third from Clanna Baíscne and two thirds from us.

And this, cleric, said Caílte, is why these are called the Hill of Slaughter and the Well of the Women.

At this time Eochaid Faeburderg, king of Ulster, sent a message from Ráth Áine to bring Caílte to the Lake of the Red Stag. Caílte said good-bye to Colmán and Eóganán. The clergy promised Heaven to him, to sing his requiem, and to pray for him to the King of heaven and earth.

Caílte went in the king of Ulster's chariot to Ráth Áine in the east where Eochaid Faeburderg was. He was a noble and respected king for he harried no one unlawfully nor deprived anyone of what was lawfully his. The three battalions of the king were assembled in one place. Caílte came to them, descended from the chariot, and was welcomed by the king of Ulster and the hosts.

My word, Caílte, said the king, what would be better than to ask you the history of Ráth Áine?

I know its origins, said Caílte. The men of Scotland and Ireland were always asking Áine, daughter of Modarn, king of Scotland, What's wrong with you, lady, that you have not married a good man from Scotland or Ireland? Except for Finn mac Cumaill, she replied, there is no man in either place that would suit me.

Finn heard that and asked Finn Fer in Champair and Rónán Rígóclach, two Fian-chiefs of Scotland, to go and woo her from her father.

What conditions will we bring? they asked.

Her power over everything in Ireland and Scotland that is mine, Finn answered.

Fian-chief, it is well, they replied but send two trusted men of your original people with us so that the lady may believe us more readily.

Caílte, let you and Mac Lugach go with them, said Finn. Although it is a lot to ask, I will grant it for her.

Then, Caílte continued, we four chief warriors went to Dún Monaid in Scotland where we were given a secluded house. Modarn and his daughter, Áine, came to visit us and asked us the reason for our journey. We told him our message.

You hear that, daughter, said the king, the best man in Ireland and in Scotland.

I will sleep with him, said the young woman.

She married Finn mac Cumaill and everything she asked of him he gave her. We and the woman returned to Ireland to the rath. She brought all kinds of possessions with her. Finn and the three battalions of the Fian came then from Temair Luachra to meet and greet us. They built a fort, a good homestead with a sun-room. Here in the fort, facing us, she attended and served the three battalions of the Fian for a year without lack of food or drink.

At the end of the year Mac Lugach said to Finn, You have enough land and territory, i.e., Áine, daughter of Modarn.

On my word, Mac Lugach, said Finn, whatever I might need in Ireland or in Scotland would be given to the Fian in Áine's house.

She lived with Finn for six years and all the people of Ireland and Scotland were grateful to her. She bore him two sons, Illan Faeburderg and Aed Bec, but died giving birth to Aed Bec.'

Caílte spoke this poem:

> Empty is Ráth Áine today where young men used to laugh,
> crowds and stud horses often on its smooth grassy slope.
> Three hundred women in the mound, many do not know that,
> three hundred favourite men, many fine fosterers.
> She was better than all women, with countless guests,
> all of whom are dead, her place today is empty.

She was buried in the earth, said Caílte. A stone was raised over her, her funeral games were held, and her name written in ogham.

Victory and blessing, Caílte, said the king of Ulster, you have told us a good story. Write that story in the tablets of poets and on the Fian monuments.

Eochaid Faeburderg went to the Rath of the Shields above Rudraige's Strand, now known as Rudraige's Wave. They went into the fort where a secluded house was given to Caílte. He was served well and the entire place from small to large made available to him. They were feasting and enjoying themselves until sunrise next day.

There are, the king said to Caílte, two graves here. How is that?

They are memorials to Art and Eógan, the two sons of Aed mac Fidaig meic Fintain, king of Connaught, who are buried there. They were dear to Finn and to the entire Fian. The reason they were loved was that whatever an artist's excellence or defects he was sure not to go away from the two princes without some reward. Nor were they ever in dispute with Finn or the Fian without making peace within a year. Either of them was an equal match for four hundred warriors. They were seventeen years with Finn, said Caílte, and would have been worthy sons for Cormac mac Airt or for Finn.

One time Finn and the three battalions of the Fian came to Rudraige's Strand on a great hunt through Ireland. Finn ordered that the watch be set. On this night the watch fell to Art and Eógan. They set off, one hundred warriors and four hundred servants and came to the head of this strand. They were not long here when two sons of the king of Lochlann in the north arrived, named Conus and Conmael, whose father had been killed by Finn mac Cumaill in the Battle of Druim Derg over in Scotland. Those two at the head of two hardy and equal battalions came to this strand in order to avenge their father on Finn.

They saw the four hundred with shields and weapons ready for them. Art had a deadly blue-angled spear called Órlasrach that Finn had given to him a year earlier. Finn had also given a spear called Muinderg to Eógan. The men from over the sea asked who was guarding the shore. Art said, Finn's people.

We are lucky indeed to come across so many for not one of them will escape, they replied.

If any group is in danger, Art replied, it is you, not us.

The two big battalions landed and it was very hard for the four hundred warriors to resist them. They engaged in battle and mutual striking from the gathering of the evening shadows until the middle of the night.

At that moment Finn had a dream and this is what he saw, two grey seals sucking his two breasts. The Fian-chief woke from his sleep. Where is Fergus Finnbél? he asked.

Here, said Fergus.

Explain two seals from the sea sucking my two breasts?

Two sons of the king of Connaught whom you sent to guard the Fian tonight are outnumbered by men from overseas, said the poet.

Men, get ready, said Finn, for what the poet says is true.

The Fian assembled quickly and went to Rudraige's Strand where of the entire Fian they found only the two sons of Connaught's king alive. They had their shields about their necks. No man had fought better and not one man of the two battalions from overseas was alive. This was the condition of the two sons: their bodies covered with bloody gashes, their shields and spears holding them up. No two of the Fian had ever equalled a contest like that. The Fian seized and pillaged the ships of the Norsemen and then pulled them up onto the land. Conus and Conmael, the king of Lochlann's two sons, were buried. Art and Eógan died soon afterwards.

The Fian had carried them here above Rudraige's Wave.

My friends, Finn asked, is it possible to cure you?

It is hard that you speak like that, they replied, because you know well how we are. We were surrounded by nine hundred warriors each of whom has fallen. We too are fallen. Prepare our grave. Raise a stone above our resting place. The arms which we have used well and which you gave us as a reward bury with us.

The souls parted from their bodies and the two were placed in the earth. For these reasons their fame and renown have lived after them, said Caílte.

Finn spoke:

> Little tomb of Art and Eógan who are wounded to the quick by it,
> beloved pair of noble birth, boys young and beardless.
> Two sons of Connaught's king who was fosterer of dogs and houndpacks,
> who was fosterer of hirelings, outcasts and parasites.
> I speak of their fame and what I say is true,
> beloved pair, brave and clever, are buried in this tomb.

By virtue of your valour and prowess, Caílte, get those weapons for us out of the grassy mound, said the king of Ulster.

I'm reluctant to do that, said Caílte, for the sake of Finn mac Cumaill and the great company that buried them. But you shall have them.

They went to work, opened the grave and brought the weapons up, the Órlasrach and the Muinderg. The latter they gave to Aengus, the king of Ulster`s son, the other to the king himself. The Battle of Rudraige's Strand is the name of the battle, a landmark in the annals of Fian-lore. They reburied the dead, raised their stone, and wrote their names in ogham.

Victory and blessing, Caílte, said the king of Ulster. You have given us truth and knowledge. They went into the fort, gathered in the feasting-house, and were happy for that night.

Next day Caílte experienced a fit of inertness and old age.

Caílte, my friend, how are you today? asked the king.

If I could hunt and chase on the Mourne Mountains I would be much better.

You will, said Eochaid Faeburderg mac Fírglinne, king of Ulster.

They assembled dogs and packs of hounds and went northwards to the Mournes. Caílte went with them and organized the hunt for that day so that from Ethach to Tonn Tuile, north of the Mournes, each man could pass the leash to another's hand.

Caílte and the king of Ulster were at Tonn Tuile from where they could see out to sea. They saw a young woman out in the waves, swimming on her back, then on her side, then treading water. Sitting on a wave in front of them as though on a hill or a rock, she raised her head and said, Is that not Caílte mac Rónaín?

I am he, certainly, said Caílte.

Many a day we saw you sitting on that rock in the company of the best man in Ireland and Scotland, that is, with Finn mac Cumaill.

Who are you? Caílte asked.

I am Lí Bán, daughter of Eochaid mac Eógain meic Aililla, she replied, who has been a hundred years in the water and has not appeared to anyone since the Fian-chief went away. What made me raise my head today, Caílte, was to see you, son of the best warrior born of woman in Ireland.

Caílte sang:

> Whence comes the tidal wave,
> from the shimmering ocean?
> Whence has come the great beauty?
> What has caused the slumber of the melodies?
>
> Is it the wave of red-haired Rudraige
> that comes from the south or the north
> or is it the drowning wave come hither
> which roars at Tráig Eothaile?
>
> Or is it the cold wave of Benn Étair,
> or the hard wave of Inber Colpa?
> Or the sweet wave of Baile's Strand
> that is directed towards Ireland?
>
> Is it the wave of gifted Clídna
> striking the strong harbour?
> Or is it the wave of Dublin
> or the wave of the son of Dáirine?
>
> Whichever of these waves, one or the other,
> beautiful is its splendid sheen,

sweet its murmur in the rounded bay
cold is the sound that it utters.

After this, the deer, fleeing before the hounds, raced into the sea.

Lend me your spear, Caílte, said Lí Bán, that I may kill a deer and force them back to you on the land.

Caílte put the Coscarach into her hand and she killed the deer. The hunting Caílte did that day was as successful as the greatest hunt Finn ever conducted there. The woman gave the spear back to Caílte and went away.

It is reliably said that a pig, a stag, and a doe fell to every five of the Ulstermen that day and that thirty deer fell to the king of Ulster and to Caílte. They went to Ráth na Scíath now called Ráth Imill. This is the hunting of the Mournes and the colloquy of Lí Bán, daughter of Eochaid mac Eógain, king of Ireland, and Caílte.

They went to the rath where a house for feasting and enjoyment was prepared for them. In the feasting-house Caílte saw something that surprised him: a beautiful yellow-haired girl in the champion's seat giving jewels and treasures for poems and other artistic works.

He asked the king of Ulster, Who is the woman to whom everyone is paying honour and respect?

The daughter of one of my warriors whose only living child she is but she has this problem. She has half of a quatrain but in the whole of Ireland cannot find anyone to complete the other half.

I am not a poet, Caílte said, but, woman, let me hear your half.

The woman spoke her half:

The Dark Man's fort, the fortress
under which our blood lies.

Caílte continued:

All the Fian have gone
Fial lives not after them.

Caílte put the drinking horn out of his hand and wept copious, truly sorrowful tears, wetting his shirt and his chest.

What is the meaning of this verse? asked the king.

I know what it means, said Caílte, but am sad that I have to remember it today. Do you know, king of Ulster, the four who excelled everyone in Ireland and Scotland in generosity in those times: Finn mac Cumaill and his son Oisín, Dub mac Treóin from Ulster and his son Fial mac Duib. Nobody was more generous than the last two. If everything in Ireland and Scotland were given to them they would give it all away to anyone who asked. It seemed a pity to Cormac and to

Finn that they should be so generous and not own the great wealth needed to practice it.

All the men of Ireland came to the Fair of Teltown, that is, Cormac, grandson of Conn, king of Ireland, Finn mac Cumaill, the three battalions of the Fian, and all the tribes as well. Dub mac Treóin and his son Fial mac Duib also arrived and sat before the king of Ireland and his son. Although the king had not met Dub nor his son before this, he had heard of them. Finn mac Cumaill was at Cormac's side, Oisín beside Finn, and Cairbre Lifechair at Cormac's other side.

Tell me, Cormac, said Finn, do you recognize the warrior in front of you?

I do not, said Cormac.

Dub mac Treóin from Ulster and his son Fial mac Duib.

Is he the needy warrior of outstanding generosity we have heard spoken of? asked the king.

He is indeed, said Finn.

Where is your son Fial? the king asked Dub.

Here beside me, said Dub mac Treóin.

How has it come about that you, both father and son, have such generosity even though you are the sons of warriors?

It is a pity, noble Cormac, said Fial, but we know that if we refused anything to anyone we would both die.

Men of Ireland, said Cairbre Lifechair and Oisín, it would be a pity if you did not help Dub mac Treóin and his son.

When the nobles of Ireland heard that, they said, We will give them the assistance you suggest, for whatever is given to them will be given to the men of Ireland.

I, said Cormac, will give them a hundred of each kind of cattle every year.

I, said Finn, will give them the same every year. And the nobles of Ireland also promised them other riches.

Dub mac Treóin returned to his own fort where he spent that wealth for seventeen years, continued Caílte. It would be impossible to count the good he did during that time until death and misfortune came to him one night on the green of his own fort: the enticing fairy cavalry that arrived one night. They asked whose place it was and one of them replied, The fort of Dub mac Treóin, the most generous warrior of all the descendants of Mil or of the Tuatha Dé Danann. Another of them said: It is a pity that we have no one to equal him among the Tuatha Dé Danann. One of them seized a deadly javelin, pierced Dub's dun-coloured nipple and killed him. Fial, his son, succeeded him as king for seventy years.

Tell me, woman, said Caílte, what relationship did you have with those whose story you asked of me?

I am the daughter of Fial mac Duib, that last warrior. Of that great people whom you saw I am the sole survivor which is why the king of Ulster gave his jewels and his treasure into my care so that I may give them away.

What is your name? asked Caílte.

Uaine, daughter of Fial mac Duib, she answered.

Caílte spoke:

> Uaine, daughter of Fial,
> your father was good through the years,
> a friend of poets,
> a truly generous warrior.

And that, said Caílte, is the story you asked me about your father and grandfather. The king of Ulster was right to allow you to give away his wealth and his possessions.

Then Eochaid Faebuderg said to his son, Aengus, marry that girl for you will never find through all the provinces of Ireland a woman with a father and grandfather's history better than hers.

The warrior did that and for the rest of his life had her alone as wife. After that they were feasting and enjoying themselves for three days and three nights.

The king spoke again: Caílte, I would like to go hunting at the Meeting Place of the Fian.

Early next morning Caílte and the three battalions of the Fian made their way there. When they arrived, the nobles and Caílte went into the great mound.

Seeing it, Caílte said, From this place many had their hunger and thirst removed and their craft and art rewarded by Finn mac Cumaill.

The king of Ulster, his nobles, and Caílte sat down. Before long they saw a young man approaching. He wore a beautiful green cloak with a silver clasp, a yellow silk shirt next to his skin, over that a soft satin tunic, and he carried a slender lute across his back.

Where are you from? asked the king of Ulster.

From the fairy mound of Bodb Derg, son of the Dagda, in the south.

What made you come here and who are you?

I am Cas Corach, son of Caincinne, master-poet of the Tuatha Dé Danann, and I myself am a trainee-poet. I have come here to learn wisdom, knowledge and story-telling, and the great exploits of the Fian from Caílte mac Rónaín.

After that he played airs and music for them and put them into a sound sleep.

Tell me, Caílte, he said, what answer do you give me?

Everything you came to find you will get if you have the skill and the intelligence to learn all the Fian's deeds of valour and prowess. There was a warrior here at one time, Finn mac Cumaill. He would have rewarded you well for your music but now the place is empty.

Caílte sang this song:

Empty tonight the Fian's Meeting Place where bladed Finn would come,
empty is noble Alma since the death of the great man without sorrow.

The noble people do not live, princely Finn does not live,
the spear-troops do not live nor the Fian-chief, the overlord.

All of Finn's Fian are dead who roamed from glen to glen,
it is bad to live after Finn, after Diarmaid and Conán.

After Goll mac Morna from the plain, after Ailill of the hundreds,
after Eógan of the bright spear, after Conall of the first attack.

I tell you for sure, and what I say is true,
our losses at Tech Drumann were heavy without Dub Dírma.

Pity I did not die there after the bands and the hundreds,
those who went from end to end, from brimful to empty.

Then Caílte reflected on the absence of friends and companions and the great gatherings he once knew. He shed copious, truly sorrowful tears that wet his shirt and his chest.

They came to the Hill of Three where the king of Ulster, Caílte, and all the others sat down, and the king of Ulster spoke, The ground is beautiful with choice green grass. Why is this hill called the Hill of the Three and why is this river called the River of Two and why is that place called the Tomb of the Dog's Head?

Although the story is not new, I will tell you why it happened for I was not old when they got their names, said Caílte. There was a king in Scotland, Iruath mac Ailpín, who had three daughters named Muiresc, Aífe, and Aillbe, who fell in love with three young men of the Fian of Ireland. These were the sons of Aencherda Bérra, Ger, Glas, and Guba, who fell in love with them and for twenty years there was equal love between them.

But one time the women slipped away and came to this hill where they were overcome by a fit of sleep. Exactly at that time an appalling battle was taking place between Finn mac Cumaill and Fothad Canann, the son of Macma's son, Mac Niad, from the fair province of Leinster. Poets are unable to number those of the Fian who were killed nor of Fothad Canann's people. The three sons of Aencherda Bérra were also killed.

When the three women awoke from their slumber they saw three warriors of the Fian approach. They asked their news and were told of the fight that took place, of the slaughter of the Fian, and of the deaths of Aencherda Bérra's sons.

The women expressed their sorrow on this hill and died here of grief for the three sons whom they loved. The women had two foster-brothers, two sons of king Catt in the north, called Uillenn and Eochair, who made a determined effort after their foster-sisters and had reached this river but it was at the full. Seeing the marvellous rich clothes on the other side, they bravely attempted to cross but were drowned. They lie in these two green graves at the edge of the ford.

Why do they call that grave the Tomb of the Dog's Head? asked the king.

Finn mac Cumaill had a favourite dog called Adnuall, who strayed northwards from the hostel. Three times he roamed throughout Ireland until he came to this ford where he gave three howls and died. That hound was one of the three best that Finn ever had. In the meantime the two Fian chiefs, Goll Gulban and Cas Cuailnge, were hunting on this plain when they saw three yellow-haired women dead upon this hill with the rarest clothes of every colour on them. They grieved over them for a long time, then buried them. Down at the ford they saw the two men who had drowned. These, too, they placed in the earth.

Caílte said farewell then to the king of Ulster and came by hill and rock to the top of the green grassy Fews to the Rowan of the Meadow of Two Stags, to the Space of Chariots where the Ulstermen left their chariots as they went to the battles of Gairech and Ilgairech. As Caílte reached that place, it happened that Saint Patrick also arrived with one hundred and fifty bishops, one hundred and fifty priests, one hundred and fifty deacons, and one hundred and fifty psalmists. They sat down and Patrick said the Hours, praising the Redeemer in front of the Space of Chariots.

Caílte arrived then with the nine members of the Fian and Cas Corach mac Caincinne, the minstrel. Welcoming him, the clerics asked for news and he told them what he had been doing during the year.

Where is Broccán the scribe? said Patrick, and he answered. Write and record everything that Caílte has related from the time that he left us at the stone on the top of Uisnech to this time.

Tell me, Caílte, said Patrick, who is the dark-faced, handsome young man with a musical instrument?

Cas Corach mac Caincinne, son of the minstrel of the Tuatha Dé Danann, who has come to learn knowledge and wisdom from me.

He has chosen well, Caílte, said Patrick. You have survived for great goodness to a time of faith, saints, and truth, when you can belong to the people of the King of heaven and earth. And you, Cas Corach, play some of your poetry and craft for us.

I will indeed, Cas Corach replied, and, holy cleric, I have never done so for anyone whom I would more gladly please than you.

He took his lute, tuned it, and played music of such beauty that, apart from the canonical praising and adoration of the King of heaven and earth, no one had ever heard any as sweet. From hearing that enticing fairy music a fit of sleep fell on the clergy.

When he finished playing, Cas Corach said, Holy cleric, give me a reward for my music.

What reward do you want?

Heaven for myself, since that is the best payment, and good luck for my craft forever and for the artists who come after me.

Heaven for you, Patrick replied, and may this be one of the three arts which will be rewarded to the end of time in Ireland and, however great the inhospitality to the artist, let him perform the music or tell stories despite begrudgery. Because of your art you will be the bedfellows of kings and rewards will come provided they do not perform carelessly.

Cas Corach returned his lute to its case.

That was skilful art, said Broccán.

It was good, said Patrick. Were it not for the fairy spell that infuses it there would be nothing to equal it except the music of the King of heaven and earth.

If there is music in Heaven, asked Broccán, why can it not be on earth also? It is not right to forbid playing.

I do not say that, said Patrick, but I must not advocate it.

Before long they saw a mature silver-grey warrior coming towards them wearing a purple cloak with a gold pin, a golden sword across his back, and a staff of white hazel in his hand. He placed his head on Patrick's chest and bowed before him.

What is your name? asked Patrick.

My name is Eógan, the arch-hospitaller, from the family of Diarmaid mac Cerbaill, the king of Ireland.

Have we not heard that you are a man of much wealth? asked Patrick.

Yes, I am.

Tonight, said Bishop Soichell, Patrick's chief steward, we would like to avail of your resources.

What night is it? Eógan asked.

It is Hallowe'en, said Patrick.

I will welcome you, he said, from Hallowe'en to May Day, all of you, your guests and your people.

They saw fifty big men approaching with iron pins in their cloaks.

Who are these? asked Patrick.

My hospitallers and my victuallers, Eógan answered.

They came together and genuflected before Patrick.

Your offerings in life and your offerings after death to Armagh forever, said Patrick.

Heavy snow and distressful cold afflicted the whole province. The snow reached to men's sides, to the shoulders of soldiers and to the axle-trees of chariots and made twisted wicker-work of the tops of the red branches so that nobody could get through.

It is a good time now, said Caílte, for the wild stags and the does to go to the tops of the hill rocks and for salmon to go into the hollows in the banks.

Caílte spoke this poem:

Winter is cold, the wind has arisen,
the wild, red, unquelled stag rises.
Tonight the whole mountain is cold,
although the hardy stag is belling.

The stag of Sliab Cairn of the gatherings
does not put his side to the ground.
The stag on Echtge's cold height
also hears the song of the wolves.

I, Caílte, with noble Diarmaid
and Oscar, light of foot,
used hear the cry of the wolves
in the sharp cold night.

The brown stag sleeps
with his hide to the bulging rock
as though under the land's cloak
at the end of the bitter night.

Today I am an old man,
I know but few men.
I shook a sharp spear fiercely
on a freezing cold morning.

I thank the King of Heaven,
and Virgin Mary's Son,
I put great quiet on many
who are truly cold tonight.

It is time for us to go to our forts and good homesteads, said Eógan.

They went away and saw the fort in front of them. It was given over to their needs. Caílte and his people were assigned to a sun-room at the back where they spent three days and three nights feasting and enjoying themselves except when the clergy were saying mass, making the hours, or praising the Creator.

Then Eógan, the arch-hospitaller, went to speak with Patrick and told him that there was no water nearby, that the people were tired carrying water to the dwelling. It was surprising that day that the place was a hole hidden in the earth with a mountain above and about it and only one door and that the one for going out. No matter how much any man might want to despoil or destroy it he would not have been able.

Did you find evidence of hosts or bands there before you? Patrick asked.

Eógan replied, We found a spear, a sword, and an iron vessel.

We'll ask Caílte, said Patrick.

They sent for Caílte and brought him to Patrick.

Tell me, Caílte, said Patrick, who lived here before Eógan?

I can answer that easily, said Caílte, for I was one of the eight men who gave this place to the man to whom Finn mac Cumaill assigned it, Conán mac Léith Luachra in the west, the only man who compelled Finn to make friendship with him. It was he who happened to do great harm to Finn, killing a dog, a servant, and a warrior of the Fian between one Hallowe'en and the next and in addition killing one of the three best men of the Clanna Rónáin, Aed Rind mac Rónáin, together with his three sons: Aed, Eógan, and Eóbrán. The Fian-chief had come south to Carn Luigdech in the province of Munster and, while sitting there after hunting, Conán came at him from the rear and caught the Fian-chief about his body and his weapon before he knew it. Finn, however, r**ecognized** the man who had seized him.

What do you want, Conán, he asked.

My guarantee of friendship and trust with you for I have been plundering and pillaging you for seven years and I am not able to endure your anger.

Even if I were to accept you, said Finn, you have done so much evil and wrong to the Fian of Ireland that I do not believe they would accept the peace.

Just accept me and leave the rest between the Fian and me, said Conán.

I will, said Finn, although the agreement is forced upon me.

So Finn accepted him and made a pledge and friendship with him. The Fian arrived and drew near in their bands and groups. Each group was amazed as they approached to see in one place the two who had been the greatest enemies in Ireland and Scotland.

Conán, said the Fian, what recompense will you give us for the great wrongs you have done to us?

Conán answered forcibly: Every battle, every risk, every wrong that will be done to you I will face it but on two conditions: you can heap your resentment on me if I fall, otherwise the fame and glory will be all yours.

On my word, said Oisín, we have never been given better terms.

So they made peace with Conán, said Caílte.

How many are your people, Conán? asked Finn.

Five hundred warriors, five hundred servants, and five hundred dogs.

Since there is that number, said Finn, search through Ireland and whatever cantred you yourself will choose I will give you.

Eight of us, said Caílte, went with him until we came to this place. Although the Fian had made peace with him, Conán did not feel secure until he came here and saw how secluded and impregnable it was. He came here with his entire hosts and people and had it for thirty years and every battle and every fight that came to the Fian he first confronted each challenge.

How did Conán die? asked Patrick.

He was one of the four Fian, said Caílte, who died in his bed. A poisonous worm entered his head and he died instantly.

Where did he get water? asked Patrick.

There is a spring well here, said Caílte.

It is in a secluded place, said Eógan, for we cannot find it.

Only a few of the Fian knew of it, said Caílte, until one warrior hit upon it. I discovered it after him. Then the man of the place found it.

Who was that first warrior? asked Patrick.

Aed mac Finn, said Caílte. There was no place in Ireland from which people could draw the full of a goblet of water from a cliff, a river, an estuary or an inaccessible place, but he could find it even at midnight. The well is in the side of a hard rock and protected by an equally strong, hermetically sealed rock over it. Long ago Smirgat and Dér Dub from Dubshliab found it.'

Caílte spoke:

A well on the southern side will give you good health,
will bring you clear blue water from the centre.
Water the fort will never have,' said Eógan without malice,
unless heaven's King, son of gentle Mary, helps.

My battle prowess was good against the sea-strangers,
three times fifty fell by me, a gallant show.
Smirgat, daughter of generous Fothach and Dér Dub of Dubshliab,
a valued pair, would go far for the Fian to spy on enemies.

I, the well-formed Caílte, forced many to say 'ugh'
by the quality of my running I gathered every kind of deer.

Finn's people were good people, a pity to be after them in Ireland!
Great vigour in the swift troop, wide the lands they knew.

Go now, said Patrick, and find the well.

I am afraid to find it, said Caílte, for nine men would raise its cover from it and the same number put it back again. I am afraid that water from the well will drown the place.

God will manage its distribution in a suitable manner, said Patrick.

Caílte went and they went with him. There was a massive stone on the edge of the dwelling. Caílte put his two hands about it and pulled it to him. A great spout of beautiful clear bright blue water burst from the rock and began to flood the area. Then Patrick raised his gentle hand of faith that could relieve every difficulty and every distress that it met and the water was swallowed back into the mountain and into the same rock. All that remained was the full of Patrick's palm from which the water trickled gently out.

The well's name from now on, said Benignus, will be Patrick's palm.

I agree to that, said Patrick, unless the people of the country engage in racial strife at a later time.

Patrick and Caílte came out on the green together with those who were in the fort. Before long they saw a warrior approaching dressed in a silken yellow shirt with a beautiful green cloak over it fastened across his chest with a golden pin.

Who are you? asked Caílte.

Aed mac Aeda from Cnoc Ardmulla out to sea, now called Rathlin, a youth of the Tuatha Dé Danann and I want to ask you something.

What do you want to ask me, Aed?

I would ask you more than anything why this mound is called Carn Manannáin?

A warrior of the Tuatha Dé Danann, said Caílte, Aillén mac Eogabál, fell in love with the wife of Manannán mac Lir. Aillén's sister, Áine, whom Manannán loved more than than anyone in the world, loved Manannán.

Áine then asked her brother, What has taken away your supreme kingly appearance?

On my word, sister, said Aillén, you are the one person to whom I would reveal that. And he told her: I am in love with Uchtdelb, daughter of Aengus Finn, wife of Manannán.

I have the remedy for that, Áine replied. Manannán loves me, and if he were to give his wife to you, I will live with him and bring you relief.

Aillén and Áine came to this hill and Manannán and his wife also arrived. Áine sat on Manannán's right side and gave him three hard loving kisses. Then they asked each other for news. When Manannán's wife saw Aillén, she fell in love with him.

Then Patrick said, This is a complicated story: Aillén mac Eogabál's sister loves Manannán and Manannán's wife loves Aillén.

As the proverb has it, said Caílte, storytelling is a complicated matter.

Manannán gave his wife to Aillén and took Áine for himself. Áine, daughter of Eogabál, charmed Manannán.

Caílte made this poem:

> Mac Lir, come with me to Daire Dairbre better than any place,
> cocks will call over the stepping stones of the hound.
>
> Many songs will be sung for you, both known and unknown,
> the cuckoo's voice will leap above the dark wood at the sound of the belling stag.
>
> You will hear the breeze whistling as it fitfully tosses the trees,
> the sound of the harsh wind, the grouse on the cold night.
>
> Hearing the warbling sound, the varied music,
> beautiful women in our house will be got for you, Mac Lir.

Aillén took Manannán's wife to the mound of Eogabál and Manannán took Áine with him to the Land of Promise. And these, Aed, said Caílte, are the answers to the two questions you asked me.

They remained in that place for a week, then said farewell to Eógan, the arch-hospitaller, and Patrick gave heaven to him for all that he had done for him.

They went eastwards after that to the Valley of the Hero, now called Muinter Diugra, where Patrick had been a slave to Miliuc moccu Buain, king of Dál nAraide. They saw a church in which thirty ecclesiastics were fervently praising the Redeemer. When they looked to the other side they saw another church on the field beside it.

We give thanks to the King of heaven and earth, said Caílte, what was an abode of hosts and gatherings is now a place for saints and believers.

Which of the Fian were here? asked Patrick.

Raigne Roisclethan mac Finn was in one place and Caince Corcarderg mac Finn in the other but the Clanna Morna killed Raigne. The Plain of Raigne is named after him. They killed the other son also and from him comes the name Sliab Caince, answered Caílte.

Before long they saw a gentle girl of marriageable age with yellow hair coming towards them. She sat beside them on the turfbuilt gravemound. Who are you? Patrick asked.

I am Étaín Fairhaired, daughter of Baetán, king of Dál nAraide.

Why have you come?

To give the service of our living and our dead to you, holy Patrick, for my brother and I are the only survivors of our seed.

She put her hand inside her shirt and took out fifty ingots of gold and fifty ingots of silver. They were a gospel penny for Patrick. Then she genuflected to him.

What is your brother's name?

Loingsech mac Baetáin.

I give him the rule of Ireland, said Patrick, 'and three of his seed to rule after him.

Everything we own we give to you, she replied.

She said good-bye to them then and they remained on the hill after she had gone.

Corc mac Dáirine, son of the king of Corca Duibne, was one of Patrick's company. He was closely associated with Muiredach mac Finnachta, king of Connaught.

Caílte, he said, there is a question I want to ask you. Why is one wave called Tonn Clídna and another Tonn Teíte?

I remember that well, said Caílte. Finn had a favourite warrior, Ciabán mac Echach Imdeirg, king of Ulster. As the moon in her fifteenth day outshines the high stars in the heavens so in form and appearance he surpassed the sons of kings and leaders in the world. But the Fian of Ireland became weary of Ciabán because there was no woman whether married or single who was not in love with him. Finn therefore renounced Ciabán although he was reluctant to do so but he feared the great jealousy of the Fian of Ireland.

Ciabán went to Tráig an Chairn, now called the Strand of the Strong Man, in the province of Ulster between Dunseverick and the sea. There he saw a high-prowed sword-straight boat of bronze with two young men in it robed about the shoulders. Ciabán greeted them and asked, What are your names?

I am Lodán, son of the king of India, one said, and the other man is Eolus, son of the king of Greece. The sea has driven us and the wind has propelled us and we do not know in what country or among what race in the world we are.

Would you allow someone into your boat who wants to sail with you? asked Ciabán.

If you are on your own, we will, they said.

Ciabán, his people asked, do you want to leave Ireland?

I do, he said, for I do not have protection or security here.

Ciabán went into the boat and left his people downhearted and dispirited, their parting like the separation of body and soul. Ciabán became friendly with the men in the boat. Bright bellowing waves rose about them each equal in height to Sliab Mis, Sliab Étair, or Sliab Elga, each wave huge and towering like a wall and all the speckled salmon that seek the sea's depths were along the sides of the boat. As a result the men were seized by fear and terror.

On my word, said Ciabán, if we were on land we could put up a good fight.

Ciabán sang:

> The three of us on the sea had a precarious time,
> in great danger in that state of attaining sharp death.
>
> Myself and the two on the sea full of valour and courage,
> if we were in a pitched bloody fight we would quell a hundred.
>
> Since the wave to the south greatly withholds a good result,
> great is the grief, the grief of the chiefs for we are only two or three.

They were in that strait, said Caílte, until they saw a single warrior approach on a dark grey horse with a golden bridle. For nine waves he was undersea and on the ninth he rose without his shirt or his chest being wet. The warrior asked them, What fee would you pay him who would rescue you?

We do not know if the price asked is within our hands?

It is that you will be in agreement and friendship with him who would rescue you.

They agreed and shook hands with the warrior. The warrior brought the three of them out of the boat onto his horse. The boat sailed along beside the horse until they reached harbour and haven in The Land of Promise. They dismounted and went to the Lake of Brightness and to Manannán's dwelling. A feasting-house had been prepared and they attended and ministered to the four warriors, serving them from brown yew vats so that they raised horns, goblets, and cups. Beautiful, warlike, dark-browed servants circulated with smooth polished buffalo horns. They played sweet stringed lutes for them and fresh, melodious, nine-stringed harps so that the house was filled with music.

Then long-snouted, long-heeled, lean-buttocked, foxy, bald fellows appeared and performed games and tricks. This was one of the tricks they did: they held nine osier rods in one hand and, standing on one foot with one hand free, threw them up to the rooftree of the hostel and caught them again. They did this to shame any noble well-bred family that came there from powerful foreign parts. This night one performed the feat as before and, approaching Ciabán, put the nine rods into his hand for he was the best in form, bearing, and reputation among the Tuatha Dé Danann and the sons of Mil that were in Manannán's house.

Ciabán got up and performed the feat in the presence of Manannán and the nobles of the Land of Promise as though it had been his one and only skill. He gave the rods to Eolus, son of the king of Greece, and he performed in the same manner. He gave the rods to Lodán, son of the king of India, and he performed it likewise.

In the Land of Promise, continued Caílte, Manannán had a chief judge, Libra, a leading physician, who had three daughters – Clídna, Aífe, and yellow-haired Étaín – who were the Tuatha Dé Danann's vessels of chastity and celibacy whom it was feared only the deadly pang of chastity might kill. Yet all at once they fell in love with the three and arranged to run away with them on the next fine day. They went to a harbour to meet the three warriors. Lodán and Eolus went in one boat, Ciabán and Clídna were in another. They raised the silken-threaded sail to the top of the mast and travelled from there to Tráig Téite in the south of Ireland. This is how it was called Téite's Strand: Téite Brec, daughter of Ragamnach, went there with one hundred and fifty women to play the wave-game and were drowned there so it is called Téite's Strand after her.

Ciabán mac Echach Imdeirg found harbour and haven on this strand. He went hunting through the territory near it but a wave from afar came over Clídna and drowned her. Since then it is called the Wave of Clídna. Mannanán's household came after her, Ildathach and his two sons who also loved the girl and were drowned on the same strand.

Caílte sang:

Clídna fair-haired, a lasting tragedy, her death came on the strand,
cause of her mother's death was what led to the old name.
When the people of the Land of Promise held the fair,
Ciabán mac Echach Imdeirg took the woman off by stealth.
The queen of that distant gathering, beautiful Clídna,
curly-haired Ciabán took over the wide ship-filled sea.
He left her on the sea and went on light adventure,
went hunting, happily, into the forest's tangled hair.
The wave came when he'd gone, not a good thing for Ciabán,
a disaster that grieved me, the drowning of fair-haired Clídna.

It was called the wave of Téite's fort of the chiefs
until the wave drowned the woman known as Clídna.
Téite's grave is north of this strand, she was slain among a great host,
Clídna's grave on the south near the mound of Dorn Buide.
The hair of yellow Dorn is drenched by waves in the heavy tide,
although there were many there it is Clídna they drown.
Fifty ships went over the salt sea, the household of Mannanán,
a gathering not without glory, drowned by the Wave of Clídna.

Ildathach and two sons all three drowned on their wooing,
a pity they trusted a ship not spared by the Wave of Clídna.

Then Ciabán Casmongach came to us at Druim Assail mac Úmair. That night Eochaid Imderg, king of Ulster, died and Finn invested Ciabán Casmongach with the kingship of Ulster in succession to his father. This, Corc mac Dáire, is the story you asked me for, said Caílte.

After that the entire host, including Patrick, went to the Ráth of Medb.

Who was Medb? asked Patrick.

Medb, daughter of Echach Feidlech, answered Caílte.

Was she from here?

She was not, said Caílte, but she would come here for the festival days of Hallowe'en to talk with her druids and her poets to find out what would be good or bad for her in the year ahead. She was accustomed to travel by nine chariots: nine chariots in front, nine behind, and nine on either side of her.

Why did she do that? asked Patrick.

So that neither miry spattering along the way nor spit from the muzzle-heads of the horses would touch her or soil her clean fresh clothes.

That's laughable, said Patrick. What is the name of this field?

The Field of Staying, said Caílte.

What was that staying?

One of Finn's warriors was about to leave because his wage was a long time coming to him. He was brave Druimderg mac Dubdechelt from Connaught. The three battalions of the Fian came to restrain him but he would not remain. Then Finn came to stop him because he was good at detaining young warriors. One of Finn's gifts was that if he made three couplets on him he would become content.

Finn said:

You, brave Druimderg, glorying in the fight,
although you go from me with honour, it is foolish to leave.
At Ráth Chró, I gave you thrice fifty ounces in one day,
at Carn Ruide, the full of my goblet of silver and yellow gold.
At Ráth nAí, remember, we got two women,
and when we had the nuts, I was there and you were there.

The whole company went to the Grove of the Horses, now called Elphin. It is called the Grove of the Horses because when the provincial kings feasted at Cruachan they tied their horses there in a fenced paddock.

Victory and blessing be yours, Caílte, said Patrick, you have great knowledge and lore.

They were not long there when they saw a woman approaching. She wore a green cloak, a shirt of smooth silk next to her skin, and on her head a glittering plate of yellow gold.

Where have you come from? asked Caílte. From the cave at Cruachain, said the woman.

And who are you?

I am Scothniam, daughter of Bodb Derg, the Dagda's son.

Why have you come here? asked Caílte.

To get my bride-price from you because you promised it to me at one time, she said.

Why did you not come to seek it at Carn Caireda to the south in the province of Leinster? asked Caílte.

You speak untruthfully, said the girl, in view of the separation that took place between us.

We are amazed when I look at you, said Patrick, a girl in all her beauty and you, Caílte, an old man, stooped and grey.

I can explain that, said Caílte. We are not contemporaries. She belongs to the Tuatha Dé Danann, who never die. I belong to the race of Mil, who do.

Caílte, said Patrick, give the woman her answer. I will, said Caílte.

Caílte went to Carn Subaltaigh on the north-west of Cruachain, put his elbow to the cairn, pushed it partly to one side, put in his hand, and took out the Lughbordad, a hamper that had been given to Finn mac Cumaill as rent and tribute and which Finn gave in payment to Conán Mael mac Morna, who hid it in this cairn. The hamper was full of gold and Caílte gave it as a bride-gift to the young woman.

You got that, Caílte, said Patrick, a short distance from the path and track of the chariots.

Caílte sang:

People of wealth and skill have been here in the past
yet few have found treasure though it is not far from the roads.
Hidden in the Fews is what would make Ireland wealthy:
three hundred ounces of red gold, Red Leaf as well.

There are four vats of gold on the summit of Sliab Smóil,
the smallest of them wide enough for two or even three.
I tell you how it is, holy son of Calpurn,
The treasures survive, the people do not.

When Patrick had finished his hours, his orders, and the Mass, he asked Caílte, Why is the glen below called the Hag's Glen?

One day Finn and the Fian were here. We saw a crooked-shinned jet-black hag coming to us. She challenged us to a race on the usual stake: his head to be cut off from whoever was left behind. Three of us ran against her: Oisín, Diarmaid Ó Duibne, and myself.

We ran to Áth Mór, called Áth Moga today, and I was first crossing the ford west. I turned to face the hag and gave her a belt of my sword that took her head from her body. Since then this glen has been called after her.

The clerics went into the house which they blessed. After that blessing there was a legion of angels over it. They remained there for six weeks.

PART III

One day Patrick was reciting his hours and when he had finished he and Caílte heard the sound of hunting in Berrobol, a hill beside them.

The cry of the hounds is weak, said Caílte, and it is in the absence of Finn, the chief, that this hunt is being carried out and in the absence of brave Mac Lugach; of Diarmaid Ó Duibne; of Little Aed, son of Finn who was slain in England at the battle of Confaite, of Dub Dá Conn; in the absence of Dub Dithruib, the son of the king of Leinster; of Dithrubach, son of Scál, killed by Caílte Coscair Ríg, son of the king of France; after the burial of Conán Mael, son of Morna, and of Ferdoman, son of Bodb, because of Findine, Bodb's daughter.

Then Patrick said to Caílte, Your cry of regret to be left without the Fian is pitiful. You should not believe like that from now on but in the true illustrious God who created heaven and earth.

Believe me, holy cleric, said Caílte, had you known the Fian you would have loved them just as you love me who have lost my agility and prowess.

The entire host heard that and were sad for what had happened: the brave warrior left without his Fian.

Caílte, my soul, said Patrick, why do you not go to see the hunt?

I'd like to go but for the shooting pain of a cast that Seiscenn, son of Ferdub, gave me at the battle of Cenn Mara [Kenmare]. It was his last shot for he himself fell there. I thank the King of heaven and earth that I am able to listen to the crow of the cock in this place.

Where did the spear hit you? asked Patrick.

Here on my right side where the shield did not protect me.

Then Patrick put his right hand into the wound and the head of the spear came out. The knee of the biggest man in the host would have gone into that spear's socket. Mael Tréna mac Dínertaig was closest to Caílte in the church.

Hold my hand, boy, said Caílte, for the Adzehead has gone to see the hunt.

Then Caílte came out and Mael Tréna, Patrick's chief pupil, held his hand and took him to the bed-house after the spear had been removed and there he remained for the night, lamenting sadly. They remained there for three days and three nights.

Then they all came to the Valley of the Fian on the far side of Cruachain and sat down above it on Árd Senaig.

Why was this height called Árd Senaig? asked Patrick.

Finn had a fine minstrel called Senach of the Daigri, who died here after being sick for an hour. They raised this mound over him, it is called Árd Senaig after him.

Caílte spoke this poem:

> What Senach got from Finn for his music, I remember,
> thirty ounces each quarter, no small amount.
> A golden penny from each man, to handsome red-haired Senach
> for his singing, a great feat, that put them to sleep.

Caílte, said Patrick, that was a big amount.

It was, said Caílte. The treasure Finn gave to women and minstrels alone was a great amount.

And did he oblige many women in that way?

He did indeed.

Caílte said:

> Finn gave three hundred women, by the King above,
> a bride-price for every woman, the amount truly very large.

The warrior's generosity was great, said Patrick.

It was, Caílte said, for he left no woman without her bride-price, nor servant without his rightful wage, nor man without his pay. He never promised at night what he did not fulfil next day and he never promised by day what he did not fulfil that night.

They were not long there when they saw a warrior approaching. In form and appearance he made a good impression. He sat on the grassy mound in front of them.

Young man, said Patrick, who are you?

Aed, son of Eochaid Leithderg, son of the king of Leinster. We were playing hurley at the fairy mound of Liaman. My father and mother, Bé Binn, daughter of Cúán mac Fintain, king of Connaught, whose only child I am, were present. I scored seven goals against all the boys but at the end of the game two women dressed in green cloaks came up to me. Their names were Slat and Mumain, daughters of Bodb Derg, son of the Dagda. Each of the women took me by the hand and brought me with them to the glittering hostel of Bruig. For three years my people have been grieving for me and the fairy people looking after me. But last night I got a chance to escape. One hundred and fifty of us young men came out of the fairy mound onto the green. There I reflected carefully on the seriousness of the situation in which the fairy people had me and I came running from the Bruig to find you, Saint Patrick.

You will have protection, said Patrick, so that neither their strength nor their magic power will prevail.

Then Caílte said, We must go south to Leinster to bring his son back to the king, to sow the faith there, and to obtain endowment for the church.

Where, Patrick asked, is Cas Corach mac Caincinne?

Here, said the minstrel.

The son of the king of Leinster will share bed and sustenance with you until we get to Leinster.

Leinster

They went to Leinster and arrived at the grave of Roíriu, daughter of Rónán Ruad, in the middle of the hero-plain of Leinster. Caílte told them how that grave got its name. My only sister, he said, whose name was Roíriu was Goll mac Morna's wife. She died on this hill giving birth to a son who died with her.
Caílte sang:

> Roíriu, daughter of Rónán Ruad, your grave's in this green field,
> your spirit's here beneath this hill without a shadow of doubt.

I'd like to make a request, said Caílte.

What is it? asked Patrick.

I'd like my sister to be delivered from torment now that I have become one of your followers and favoured ones.

May she, your father and mother and your lord Finn mac Cumaill be delivered from torment for your sake if it be God's will, said Patrick.

Caílte thanked the Táilchenn. It was the best gift he ever got.

They went to the Cairn of Heroes known at this time as Garbhthanach [Rough Washing] of Hy-Murray.

Tell us, Caílte, said Patrick, why is this place called Rough Washing?

A High-King, Tuathal Techtmar, conquered Ireland. This Tuathal cut the heads off the provincial kings and as a result was called Tuathal the Taker because of his conquering and because he forced the provinces to serve him at Tara. He had two daughters, Fithir and Dáirine. The king of Leinster, Eochaid son of Eochaid Ainchinn, came to seek one of them. Tuathal asked, King of Leinster, which of the two girls do you want? Fithir, said the king. But, said the king of Ireland, I will not give the younger before the elder.

So they gave Dáirine. As a bride-price Eochaid gave one hundred of every kind of stock and she was with him for a year. But the king of Leinster did not love her. One night in bed he resolved by guile and cunning to take the king of Ireland's daughter into the middle of the dark forest, to fell trees about her, to make a secret hidden house for her and the nine foster-sisters that she had with her and then to say she was dead. His horses were harnessed and his chariot prepared. He went to Tara to speak with the king of Ireland.

The king asked him for news.

Bad news, he replied, the good daughter you gave me died last night.

And why have you come to me? asked Tuathal, for I've never heard a sadder story.

I have come to seek your other daughter for I do not want to be separated from your friendship.

On my word, said the king of Ireland, giving you my daughter doesn't bring me ease or happiness.

I did not have control of her life, said the king of Leinster.

Caílte sang:

He did not stop his bare asking and hard pleading
until he took Fithir to his house away from her people.

The other daughter was given to him and he took her with him to the place where we are now but when she got here, her sister was here before her.

Caílte sang:

Fithir put her mouth to the ground, this was not a good alliance,
her heart broke in three, her strength went to nothing.

When the other sister saw her sister dead before her eyes, she too died of grief.

Fithir and Dáirine, Tuathal's two happy daughters
Fithir dead for shame, Dáirine dead from grief.

The king of Leinster had them washed here. This, he said, is a rough washing.

The name Garbthanach has been on the place ever since. They were laid together in this green grassy grave and that, holy Patrick, is the story you asked me for.

Victory and blessing be yours, Caílte, my friend, said Patrick, you have told us a good story.

They saw a hostel beside them in a fenced grassy field. There was a genial serene-looking young man in it and he had a hundred and fifty horses gathered before him. Patrick approached and the young man came to meet him.

May you have the support of kings, said Patrick, and a good man in your place. What is your name?

Muiredach mac Tuathail meic Finnachta, son of the king of this country.

What is that fort we see over there?

The fort of a hospitaller to the king of Leinster's people, said Muiredach, Coscrach Cét [Coscrach of the Hundreds].

Why is he called that? asked Patrick.

Because it is not possible to count his stock or his herds except in hundreds.

Will we get lodging there for the night? asked Patrick.

You will, for I have power and command in this place since the warrior himself is not at home.

They went into the dwelling then and the young man put Patrick and his people in a large kingly house belonging to Coscrach and they were attended with due reverence.

Caílte went to the Stone of Arms south of the fort where every year the Fian used to sharpen their weapons on a king-sized stone. He wept copious, sorrowful tears remembering the great company who had often stood on top of it with him in former times. Before long he saw a young warrior coming towards him in a purple cloak fastened with a brooch of gold. He looked like a good man with his princely carriage and soft curly hair. He sat on one end of the stone with Caílte.

What is your name? asked Caílte.

Coscrach Cét. And are you who I think you are?

Who do you think I am?

I think you're Caílte mac Rónaín.

That's right, said Caílte.

I'm pleased that I've met you.

Why is that?

I have twenty-nine ploughlands and when it is time to harvest the crop a wild very fierce deer comes, damages, and destroys it all so that we have no profit from it. Since you are a man of valour and prowess, give help and relief to me from the deprivation, said Coscrach.

When I had my agility and strength, said Caílte, I would have removed him for you.

Then Caílte asked him if he could send messengers to Cluain Caín in the province of Munster to Daire na Fingaile [Oakgrove of Fratricide]. My seven hunting nets are there.

The messengers went, brought the nets back to him and Caílte arranged the hunt. Putting most of the men and almost all the dogs in the direction from which he thought the stag would come, he stretched his nets on the cliffs, waterfalls and inlets of the country.

The great deer approached as he did every year. Seeing the wild deer coming to the Stag's Ford on the Sláine [Slaney], Caílte seized his spear, the Slayer, and when the deer became entangled in the net threw it at him so that a part of the spear equal to a warrior`s hand showed through.

It seems to me, said Coscrach, the deer has been bloodied and what better name to give this ford than the Ford of the Bloodied Stag?

And that was its name from that day to this. They brought his chine to Broad Ridge, now known as the Red Ridge of the Deer.

Caílte, said Coscrach, it was a good thing you came here.

Coscrach spoke this poem:

> Where have you come from, old man, where have you left your people?
> The decrepitude of age has come over you, your generation does not survive.
>
> They are of the same period to me, they who walk the earth,
> Finn and his distinguished people, great and mighty hunters.
>
> I would take compassion on you since you are naked,
> if you would kill for me perilously the old, withered, familiar deer.
>
> How would I kill him, man who gave good appearance to us,
> to kill him, a hard task, without hounds, without nets?
>
> My nets are at Cluain Caín, bring them to me if you would,
> his killing will be famous, the old deer will go into the snare.
>
> Bring all my nets to the Red Ridge of the deer,
> let the hard-horned one be killed, on the hillside to the north of us.
>
> Caílte went after the deer, without camp, without a dog,
> after the pack of hounds which loved me, a tale pitiful to sing.

Then Coscrach and Caílte came to where Saint Patrick was. Coscrach placed his head on the saint's chest, as did his seven sons and his seven daughters, and all of them bowed before him for on this night two good things happened to Coscrach: Patrick saved his soul and Caílte saved his crops by killing the deer that had been destroying them.

They were feasting and enjoying themselves that night and next day the entire company and Saint Patrick emerged onto the green.

Coscrach then asked Caílte, Why was this sturdy pillar-stone called the Stone of the Arms?

On this stone every year at Hallowe'en, Caílte replied, the Fian used to grind their weapons. It had the best guarantee of a secure peace in Ireland and Scotland during the reigns of Conn, Art, Cormac, and Cairbre Lifechair: a bracelet of red gold, twenty-eight ounces of gold that was exposed there. There was a hole in the stone and even though the bracelet was fitted through it the rule of those kings was so firm no one dared steal it. In addition to the authority of the kings the divination of the druids was so excellent that no one dared move it. Those kings departed until the time of Cairbre Lifechair, who fell at the Battle of Gabair. Then those of us of the Fian who were left, said Caílte, came back to this place. I turned the stone, putting the half that was up down as you see it now.

If we could see the hole and the guarantee, said the host, we would believe.

Give me a few minutes, said Caílte, till I take the half that is at the bottom and put it on top, for the Irish are impetuous.

All of them together tried to shift it but could not.

Then Caílte tried. Putting his two arms around it he raised it out of the earth and there it was: a bracelet of gold in a hole at the lower part and they all saw it. Caílte took the bracelet and divided it in two, giving one half to Patrick and the other to the people in that place.

From that time until now it is known as Cluain Falach, the Meadow of the Bracelet, and the stone is called the Stone of the Weapons.

Caílte spoke:

> Coscrach, do you recognize the stone that kings used to frequent?
> To it the king would come, Finn mac Cumaill of Alma.
> Known as the Stone of Arms, for many it was the stone of death,
> and it remains ever since in the same place.
> Many a spear that caused much hurt and swords of handsome heroes,
> were, Coscrach, ground on the stone before every battle.

Victory and blessing, Caílte, said Patrick, you have given us a good story and good lore.

They caught Coscrach's horses, prepared his chariot and he went east to the Broad Ridge of Laegaire mac Úgaine to talk with Eochaid Leithderg, king of Leinster. He told him about Caílte.

I am much displeased, said the king, that you did not tell us Caílte was with you.

The king of Leinster assembled three great battalions and went to Ráth Mór [Great Fort] of Maig Fea, at present known as Rathmore in the plain of Fea, to see Patrick and Caílte.

Saint Patrick was sitting at the door of the rath with his people, a place now known as Patrick's Seat. The king of Leinster and all his people also sat down. He placed his head on Patrick's chest and entrusted his powers to him, both great and small.

Although I have come to see you, holy cleric, said the king of Leinster, we are in great trouble elsewhere. Ailill mac Scannláin meic Dungaile, king of the Déise, has challenged us to battle at the Wood of Conflict, now called Raigne's Plain. I have allowed him to burn the country while I come to consult with you and to do what you want.

You shall have instead the burial place for the kings of Ireland, said Patrick, if you walk around this stone on which I am sitting.

Caílte sang:

> There is a stone that lies at Laegaire's Broad Ridge,
> victory to Leinster's king, if the noble man goes round it
> righthandwise.

May the ground at Raigne's Plain swallow him, said Patrick.

And so it was done. The king of the Déise was swallowed there because of Patrick's words. No one ever prevailed against the king of Leinster.

The king of Leinster said, Caílte, you would be very welcome even if you came on your own. You have a right to be here since your mother was Tadg's daughter. But tell me, why is the well at the entrance to this rath called Scáthderc's Well?

Scáthderc, daughter of Cumall, was drowned in it while she was looking at the water-monster of Loch Lurgan. It was out of the well that the coiling cold waters of Loch Lurgan rose and spread from the crooked apple-tree on the top of Sliab Smóil mac Etlecair, then called Sliab Bladma, all the way here and it threatened to spread throughout the entire province. Then Finn performed the greatest deed that anyone has ever performed before or since: he got the sucker from the land of India, the magicians from the land of Almáin [Germany], the warrior women from the lands of England and France so that they drained that coiling cold lake, answered Caílte.

The first Fian of Finn mac Cumaill were noble, said the king of Leinster.

Although they did not survive until your time, continued Caílte, each man of them was no worse than those who have survived. The shepherds and cowboys enjoyed assembling arms and clothing here for the three battalions of the Fian, Finn mac Cumaill's and those of Ferdoman mac Imomain from distant Lathrach in the province of the Leinstermen.

By virtue of your valour and prowess, Caílte, tell us the companies and the divisions of all those who were drowned by the water-monster of Loch Lurgan.

Faelán of Finnloch from the province of Connaught; Aengus and Dobarchú from Leinster; Druimderg from Derry and Dub Dá Dét from Cenél Conaill in the north; Ibar, Aicher, Aed, and Art, the four sons of the king of Coill in Chosnama, now known as Ossory; Cairell, Caicher, Cormac, and Caem, the four sons of the king of Dál nAraide in the north; Maine, Art, and Aralt, the three sons of the king of Scotland; Eobrán, Aed, and Eógan, the three sons of the king of Britain; Blaí, king of Islay, and his two sons, Cern and Cernabrog, the two kings of the Hebrides in the north; Diure, Barrae, and Idae, the three sons of the king of Lochlann; Luath, Indell, and Eógan, the three kings of Mairtin in Munster; Glas, Delga, and Duibne, three sons of the king of the people of Brega and of Mide; Illann, Aed, and Eóganán, three sons of the king of Cenél Eógain in the north; Samaisc, Artúr, and Inber, three sons of the king of Gall-Gaedil.

These were the names of the princes, chiefs, and men of the territory of Finn mac Cumaill's original Fian who were drowned by the water-monster of Loch Lurgan, said Caílte and added, although my vigour and casting have decreased, I knew this plain when it was a full cold lough of clear blue water.

Caílte then said:

> Water in a bright stream, sharp whine, whirr of the shaft of yew,
> garb of the warrior band entice the boy who herds the cattle.
> Ten men, ten twenties, ten hundred, that many, no lie,
> fierce warriors, dear strength, everyone dead.
> I would make it my main concern, in every battle I ever fought,
> to kill there only the sons of kings or great men.
> My shape and form collapsed, I am slow, cowardly, unhappy,
> sense and body gone, only lamenting remains.

Then Caílte became acutely aware that he was now without his Fian, his great people, without his agility and casting and began to grieve greatly.

My soul, Caílte, said Patrick, you should not feel sad. Your condition and your hope are better than all the others since I have come to you and because the rewards of the true God, faith, holiness, and prayer with the arms crossed have come to you and not to any others of the Fian.

As the end of the day drew near, Coscrach of the Hundreds said to the king of Leinster, I have a marvellous banquet ready for you: a hundred and twenty vats of delicious, tasty ale.

I have never before been offered a banquet that pleased me better than that, replied the king.

All those who were in the host, including Saint Patrick and his clergy, went to that feast. There was a cup-bearer to pour, a porter to open the door, and a food distributor to serve. They removed the spigots from the vats of sweet red yew. Young boys arrived with cups of bright gold, and food and drink were served to everyone.

The king of Leinster said to Patrick, Did we not see a minstrel with you this morning?

You did indeed, Cas Corach mac Caincinne, who is acquiring knowledge and learning from Caílte, said Patrick.

Where is he? asked the king.

Here I am, Cas Corach answered.

Go out and bring back Aed, son of Eochaid Leithderg, son of the king of Leinster, who minds Cas Corach's lute but has a dark blue hood over him.

He was brought like that to Patrick and the king. Cas Corach played his lute and gave it such a fairy cadence it was said that wounded men would have slept having that bewitching music played for them. They gave jewels and valuables to the minstrel who put them into the hands of his attendant and the attendant gave them to everyone.

Which is the most generous, people asked, those who give the jewels, the minstrel, or the attendant?

The attendant is the most generous, said the king of Leinster, for he gives what he gets to everyone.

Everything I get, said the minstrel, he gives away, for I have not come to the Táilchenn and Caílte to seek wealth but to acquire knowledge and learning from Caílte and Heaven for my soul from Patrick.

Minstrel, where did you get your attendant, asked the king of Leinster, who is more generous even than yourself?

In Ulster.

What is his name? asked the king.

He is a lad we found without knowing his name, or his mother or father.

The king got up with a great bugle-horn in his hand and said, Patrick, one time when we were at the fairy mound of Liaman Lennchaem, the daughter of Dobrán Dubthaire in the south, two beautiful yellow-haired women came to us and carried off my son from the middle of the assembly. I do not know whether they took him up to Heaven or down into the earth. I am like a solitary tree in the wind after my only son and miss him from that time until this, not knowing his fate in the world. I would like to know whether he is alive or dead.

If it be God's will that knowledge will be given to you, replied Patrick.

They remained there until it was time to get up next morning and the sun had risen from his fiery zone.

The king of Leinster said, I would like to go hunting stag and deer on Tulach an Máil in the plain of Leinster. You should come with me for it will please you more than remaining here since the hosts and gatherings of Leinster will be there.

Two great companies went with them: the band for faith and prayer with Patrick, the other band concerned with deeds of valour and weapons among the Fian of Ireland with Caílte and the king of Leinster. They all arrived at Tulach an Máil.

There Eochaid Leithderg asked Caílte, Why is this hill called Tulach an Máil and why is that hill called Cnoc Aífe?

There was a High-King Aeil mac Domnall Dubloingsig, who ruled the kingdom of Scotland and had one son, Mál mac Aeil, who had a wife, Aífe, the daughter of Scoa's son, Alb, king of Lochlann. Mál had a fort, a good homestead, at Rinn Ruis in Scotland. When storytellers, ollaves, and poets of the men of Ireland went there they would bear witness to Finn and the Fian in the presence of Mál and Aífe. Finn mac Cumaill had a warrior, Mac Lugach, and when they made poems in praise of the Fian, both of Ireland and Scotland, they praised him in particular. When Aífe, the daughter of the king of Scotland, heard the great testimony that poets and ollaves made about Mac Lugach she loved him for what was said about him.

Mál mac Aeil went hunting to Sliab Mór Monaid in Scotland with three hundred warriors. The woman formed a plan in her own sun-room to take nine foster-sisters to Ireland with her. The nine of them came across the sea's tresses to Benn Étair where the Fian were hunting. The hunt extended from the little field of Meille mac Lurgan Luime's house at the base of Sliab Smóil, now known as Sliab Bladma, to Benn. Finn was there in his hunting-seat with his gentle affectionate fosterling, Dubrind, son of the king of Cenél Conaill in the north.

Caílte sang:

Brown Dubrind who could fight,
I often called to the ale-feast,
my pleasant fosterling, full of deeds,
lively Dubrind close to my heart.

When he looked far and wide about him the young man saw a ship making for the narrow strand in front of him. There was a wide-eyed queen with nine women in the stern. They came to Finn with their arms and all their valuables. The woman Aífe sat on his left hand. The chief of the Fian looked at her and asked her story. The queen told him from beginning to end: she had come across the sea's mane to find Mac Lugach because she had fallen in love with him. Finn welcomed her for he was closely related to the man she sought.

When the hunting ended, the nobles of the Fian returned in their bands and their companies and each band as it arrived asked him, Finn, who is the wide-eyed queen? Finn told them her name and her lineage and why she had come. We welcome her, they said, for except for the chief of the Fian there is not a better man in Ireland or Scotland than the man for whom she has come.

On that day the hunting of the western side of Sliab Bladma fell to Mac Lugach with the result that he was the last one to return. Finn's tent had been erected and the woman and the nobles of the Fian brought into it. Mac Lugach arrived and sat down on one side of Finn. She took the other. And like all the others, Mac Lugach asked about the woman. Finn told her story from beginning to end and said, It is for you she has come. She passes from my hand to yours, together with her conflicts and her battles but these will not be a greater burden for you than for the entire Fian.

That night, continued Caílte, Finn came to Alma with the three battalions, the queen, and her women. That night also she and Mac Lugach were bedded and she was with him for a year and a month unsought for coming after him. But one day on this hill we saw three large, powerful, well-matched battalions approaching. We asked them who they were. They replied that they came from Mál mac Aeil meic Domnaill Dubloingsig, king of Scotland, to avenge his wife on the Fian. Finn answered, He comes at a good time when we are all in the one place.

The battalions advanced on one another. Mál mac Aeil advanced, seized his arms, and charged twelve times through the three great battalions of the Fian. He killed a hundred brave warriors in each attack, twelve hundred in all. He and Mac Lugach met in the middle of the battle. Each took four steps towards the other beyond the smooth hard necks of the shields and each struck the other on the head with the sword. Mac Lugach killed Mál mac Aeil, who is buried in this hill.

Caílte sang:

> This is Mál's hill, a hill which was the place of great slaughter,
> there were warriors there in their blood, strength in swift wounding.
> Mál came with seven score ships over the glittering sea,
> none escaped alive but the crew of one ship.
> For shield and battle sword and many-coloured clothes,
> brave Mál crossed the sea, his hand swift to slaughter.
> Many a cliff, many a bright inlet, many a river, many a stream,
> many vicissitudes, much misfortune, many sighs, until he reached this hill.

So this hill is called Mál's Hill, the battle is called the Battle of Mál's Hill and Aífe's Hill is the name of the hill below us for the queen was there during the battle, said Caílte, and from then on she lived with Mac Lugach and was the mother of his children.

Patrick and the entire host arose at the same time from the hill and went west to the Mound of the Deer. Caílte saw two forts there, the Fort of Spelán and the Fort of Mál.

Those are two big forts, said the king of Leinster. Who lived in them?

Two hospitallers of Cormac, king of Ireland, said Caílte. The hostages of the men of Ireland lived in them every year from the end of the month of Trogan, now called Lugnasad, to the day of Samain and were maintained by those two hospitallers, Becán Bóaire and Spelán mac Dubáin.

They saw another hill near them.

Caílte, why is this hill called the Slender Rib, asked the king of Leinster.

I remember why, he replied. Milid mac Trechossaig, son of the king of the big world to the east, came with three hundred warriors to seize the kingship of Ireland. He sought pledges from Finn mac Cumaill. Finn said he would not give hostages or guarantees nor any amount of gifts in the entire world. Milid challenged Finn to single combat but I got up since at that time I could fight a good man and I killed him when he tired of the fight. The men of Ireland were so elated by his fall that they put a piece of him on every significant hill. Two of his slender ribs were left on this hill and from them it gets its name. And that, king of Leinster, said Caílte, is the lore of this mound and this hill.

They went to Ráth Mór of Maig Fea to the king of Leinster's fort and that night the feasting-house was prepared by Eochaid Leithderg.

Give his lute to Cas Corach, said the king, so that he may make music for us.

Let the boy we found, his own attendant, bring it to him, said Patrick.

The attendant brought the instrument and placed it in the minstrel's hands. At that moment the roof-tree of the house caught fire and they were all looking at it. The minstrel went to put the lute back into its case but his attendant said, Do not interrupt your art or your minstrelsy, allow me to save the house.

He took a stone out of the fold of his tunic and made such a cast that it drove both the roof-tree and the fire beyond the dwelling's long high palisades with the result that the place has been called the Height of the Roof-tree from that day until this.

Caílte sang:

He saved the house from fire,
fair-handed Aed, son of Leinster's king,

Height of the Roof-tree on the green
its name ever since.

Success to your casting, your sharing, and your attack, said Patrick.

All those in the house that night declared, We have never seen a minstrel's attendant that was better for agility, casting or generosity than this attendant.

They stayed in that house until the sun rose next day. Saint Patrick and the entire gathering went to the Hill of Kings, now called Maistiu.

The king of Leinster began hunting at the place called the Hill of the Young Men, now known as the Hill of the Schools, as far as the fairy mound of Morrígu. Except for the minstrel and his attendant none of the clergy was with him. None of the king's company was able to draw first blood of a pig or a deer except the minstrel and the attendant and since the time of the Fian no hunt had been as successful as this.

Patrick stood up and preached a sermon. The province of Leinster dedicated a third of its children and a third of their wealth to Saint Patrick so that Tithe Hill is the name of that hill from that time until this. The Plain of the Third Part is the name of the plain and the Hill of the Preaching is the name of the hill.

After giving the sermon Patrick felt a great thirst. They saw a place before them called the House of Wood where a great feast was taking place. They asked Maelán mac Dubáin, the man of the house, for a drink for Patrick but he refused. Angered by such niggardliness, Patrick said, Neither a son nor a daughter will be born to you, Dubán, nor relatives nor a single kinsman.

Neither was there.

Patrick sang:

A greedy house in his native place,
a man without son or wife,
my curse and the curse of Heaven's king
on all those in that house.

The host came to Árd Cuillinn in the Plain of Leinster where they looked about at the cliffs, the river before them, and at Árd Cuanaide. The king of Leinster asked Caílte, Why is that height called Árd Cuanaide and why is this place called Árd Cuillinn?

Caílte wept such copious, truly sorrowful tears that his shirt and chest were wet.

I had a fosterling here, he said, Cuanaide mac Lind meic Faebair, the son of the king of Leinster here, whose mother, Cuillenn, daughter of Dubthach, was not a lady. We were on the trail of Clanna Morna. One hundred and fifty shield-bearers from the armourclad young men of the Fian of Ireland came here. No shoulder was without a shield, no head without a helmet. I asked brave Cael, grandson of Nemnan of the hundred wounds, to follow the trail. He stayed on the track until he came to where there was a she-miller. Cael saw a dark-browed servant talking with her. The man wore a shirt of regal satin next to his skin and had a fringed purple-red cloak fastened.

My dear son, said Cuillenn, you should not be here talking with me. You should leave for Clanna Morna, the original enemies of the Fian, have crossed the ford and the river.

Brave Cael came to us, continued Caílte, and told us that news. We rose up as one and overtook the attacker but we did not recognize him, Cuanaide mac Lind meic Faebair, my fosterling. He turned his face to us, charged through us three times, and on the third charge made a spear-cast at me that went through my knees so that when I go up every hill and every rock the consequences of that spear affect me. I sent a cast that struck him in front and broke his back in two so that he died on that height, known ever since as Cuanaide's Height.

The warrior died like that, said Caílte, and I do not remember anyone before that whose death was a greater sorrow to me.

The host together with Patrick went into Ráth Mór of Maig Fea and were feasting and enjoying themselves there for a while.

Have your lute brought to you, Cas Corach, said the king of Leinster and his attendant brought the lute to him.

I wonder, said Bé Binn, daughter of Cobán, king of Connaught, why that large dark hood about the minstrel's attendant is not removed day or night.

How do we know that his head, said the king, is not disfigured although every feature we see has no lack of shape?

Then he said to Caílte, My good friend, I have a spear-shaft and I'd like you to give it a magical finish for I've heard there was nobody in Ireland or in Scotland better than you at making a shaft.

I tell you, said Caílte, the spear-shaft that no man in Ireland could make I could make.

They gave that shaft to Caílte, who bound it so well that there was no better-made shaft in Ireland or Scotland. Now, said the king, make the spear's fitting.

Caílte put his foot against the solid post of the house and drove the head of the spear into the post. He took the spear-shaft, hurled it at the head and aimed it with such force that it entered its socket as though it had been its fitting for some time. Here is your spear, he said.

The king took the spear and it was good. Caílte, he said, I give you two horses and my chariot in payment for that fitting.

Those were the two horses and the chariot that carried Caílte at the end in Ireland. Those horses were part of the story told about him, that is, the departure of Caílte. The names were Err and Indell.

When the king looked at the spear in his hand, he was sorry he had no son to inherit it and he shed watery tears over his cheeks so that Patrick asked Why are you so sorrowful?

I have cause.

What cause? asked Patrick.

Because of the son I told you about, said the king, and being without a close loving son to inherit the spear Caílte made for me.

My good friend, said Patrick, give it to the minstrel's attendant until we see if his grip will be filled with its shaft and socket.

They handed the spear to the attendant who wielded and bore it bravely.

Take off that big dark hood, said Patrick to Cas Corach's attendant, and handle your father's spear well. He took off his hood and there was no one there who did not recognize him.

On my word, said the assembly, this is the gift of a good cleric.

Cleric, said the king, do not let the Tuatha Dé Danann have power over my son in the future since it is they have aided and fostered him before today.

He will have the death ensured by the King of heaven and earth, said Patrick.

Then the assembled host rose up and professed fealty and friendship with the young man with the result that before the time of rising next day he had six thousand followers.

Once again the entire gathering moved forward with Patrick in their midst and Caílte riding in the chariot the king of Leinster had given him. They came to the Height of the Fian's Steadying across the Sláine. Caílte got out of his chariot and arranged a hunt.

Caílte, my friend, said the king, why is this height called the Height of the Fian's Steadying?

I remember why. One day Finn mac Cumaill and the three battalions of the Fian came to this ford and while sitting here we saw a single woman on the rock over there at the head of the ford. She was wearing satin and a green single-coloured cloak fastened with a golden brooch and a golden diadem, sign of a queen, on her head. Fian of Ireland, said the queen, let one of your young men come to talk with me. Scíathbrec mac Dathcháin responded and went to talk with her. Whom do you want? he asked. Finn mac Cumaill, she answered. Finn crossed the ford to speak with her, continued Caílte.

Who are you? Finn asked, and what do you want?

I am Dairenn, daughter of Bodb Derg, son of the Dagda, and I have come here to sleep with you after we've arranged bride-price and gifts.

What bride-price and gift? Finn asked.

That I will be your only wife for one year and have half of your sexual intercourse thereafter.

I do not give that, said Finn, to any woman in the world and I will not give it to you.

The woman put her hand into an obscure recess in her clothes and from her waist produced a silver goblet full of sweet mead and handed it to him.

What is this? asked Finn.

Sweet mead, delectably intoxicating, she replied.

It was a taboo for Finn to refuse drink. He took the goblet, drank from it, and became drunk. As a result he turned his face against the Fian and every evil, every fault, and every mishap of battle that he knew against every man he threw in his face. The nobles of the Fian got up and and left him. Every one of them went to his own region and place so that only Finn and myself were left on that mound. I got up then, went after the Fian, and said, Men, do not abandon your chief and your lord because of confusion caused by an enticing fairy woman.

Twelve times I mustered and mastered them on this hill. At the end of the day the venom went from Finn's tongue. As I restrained them for the last time, sense and memory returned to him. He would have preferred to fall on his weapons and die rather than continue living. That was one of the two worst days I ever had, that day restraining the Fian and the day I released Finn from Cormac and gave the odd drove to him. This is why it is called the Height of Steadying and the Ford of Steadying.

Caílte sang:

> Flann and Finn Finnabrach lie at Sengabar na Sreth,
> Aed and Congal Clídna in the one grave.
> A great loss to Finn's Fian our going to them at Iubarglenn,
> great the loss of heads also at the awful battle of Finntrága.
> Our loss at the battle of Monad, the cruel destruction of Deicell,
> the death of Alb mac Main and fleet Merge.
> Our loss in the battle of Clídna where death came to Idna,
> the killing of three hundred men, of very fierce warriors.
> Four times nine and a thousand wounds I gave
> there were many who died, all of them good men.

I tell you, and what I say is true,
although my heart is sad, I did not yield.

Many evil battles and contests happened at that time, Caílte, said Eochaid Leithderg.

Today, said Caílte, nothing remains for us but age and decrepitude.

The entire gathering together with Patrick proceeded by the Black Wood, now called the Dark Wood, to Sliab Bladma, now called the Mountain of Aige, son of Iugaine. They went to the top of the mountain where they remained for a while.

The king of Leinster asked, What is this mountain and this place where we are?

This mountain and the fairy mound on it, said Caílte, were never found by anyone but Finn and six young men. We roused a beautiful skittish wild fawn at Torach in the north and followed her to this mountain where she disappeared head-first into the ground and we could not discover where she had gone. A heavy snowstorm fell and made a twisted wicker-work of the tops of the trees. The severity of the storm and the foul weather took away our agility and our resolve. Finn said, Caílte, can you find shelter for us this night from this foul weather?

I supplied myself and went south round the shoulder of the mountain. There, looking about, I saw a fairy mound all lit up and with many horns, cups, and yellow and golden goblets. For a while I was in the doorway gazing into it, I was thinking whether I should go in and find out about it, or whether I should return to Finn. I decided to go into the mound and sat down on a crystal chair on the hero-floor. I looked about and saw twenty-eight young men on one side.

Each had an attractive beautiful woman by his side. On the other side were six beautiful women with yellow hair with woolly cloaks hanging about their shoulders. An attractive yellow-haired woman sat in a chair in the middle of the house with a harp in her hand on which she played and performed. Sweet as pipe-tunes was the melodious sound of the girl's voice and her Irish. Every time she had sung, a goblet was handed to her that she might drink from it and then she would hand it back to the man who had given it to her. They all sat about her and all were enjoying themselves.

Caílte, said the woman, will you be served?

I will not, I replied, for I have a company with me nobler than me, namely, Finn mac Cumaill, who would like to find lodging and provision in your mound for tonight.

Then the young man said to me, Caílte, my friend, bring Finn mac Cumaill for he never refused his house to anyone and he will not be refused by us.

I went to get Finn. You were a long time away, said Finn, for since the day I took up arms I have never spent a night that afflicted me more than this night.

Finn said:

> Help us, Caílte, for you are our princely equal,
> if you find fire and a house on the sides of this splendid mountain.
>
> I think I have found a house, prince of the true-striking Fian,
> no one alive has seen any other house more beautiful.
>
> A lone woman in that great house, in which all are at the feast,
> melodious as harp strings is her refined, beautiful speech.
>
> Our raiment was removed in the mound, we found there mead and wine,
> and we were there afterwards until the year was complete.
>
> Anywhere I sought south and north in the wonderful world,
> a day comparable to this, I did not find, till this day, Caílte.

After that, said Caílte, the six of us with shield and weapon, that is, Finn mac Cumaill and myself, Diarmaid Ó Duibne, Oisín, Oscar, and Mac Lugach came back to the spacious brightly-lit fairy mound. We sat there at the back of a column and a gentle pleasant-looking, yellow-haired girl came to serve us. She placed us on a luminous crystal chair and they brought us the oldest of wine and the freshest of food.

When we had relieved the keenness of our hunger and satisfied our thirst, the chief of the Fian said, Which of you will I ask for information?

Ask anyone you yourself prefer, said the tallest of the young men.

Who are you? asked Finn. For I did not know there are so many young men in Ireland whom I do not recognize.

Donn mac Midir, he answered. Those twenty-eight young men that you see over there have the same mother and father. They are the sons of Midir of the yellow-hair, son of the Dagda and of Finnchaem from the fairy mound of Monad in the east. It will be thirty years tomorrow since the Tuatha Dé Danann assembled to confer the kingship on Bodb Derg, son of the Dagda, in the spacious brightly-lit, hospitable mound in the north. He has begun to demand hostages from us according to our number, but we replied that until the Tuatha Dé Danann would give hostages we would not. Bodb Derg said to our father, Midir, If you do not give up your children we will destroy your fairy mound. We came out, the twenty-eight of us, to find a mound for ourselves. We searched Ireland until we found this secret hidden place and we have been here ever since. We are twenty-eight brothers and each of us had a thousand warriors but all the clan has been destroyed except for the twenty-eight brothers.

How were you destroyed? asked Finn.

The Tuatha Dé Danann came for three years in succession and attacked us on that grassy green outside.

Whose is the long fresh grave that we saw on it? asked Finn.

The grave of the druid Diangalach, the best druid the Tuatha Dé Danann had and one of the three great losses suffered by them.

How did he die?

I killed him, answered Donn.

What was the other loss?

I'll tell you. All that the Tuatha Dé Danann possessed in jewels, wealth, treasures, cups, vessels, and of yellow and gold goblets we took away with us all at the same time.

What was the third loss? asked Finn.

Fethnaid, daughter of Fidach, the Tuatha Dé Danann's minstrel, their music, and the alleviation of all their spirits, said Donn. They are determined to fight us tomorrow but our total number of fighting men is the twenty-eight brothers before you. Realizing we would be in danger against them, we sent Mál to Torach in the shape of a timorous fawn to bring you and you followed her. She is the woman you see with a green cloak about her. The empty half of the mound that you see is the place for those the Tuatha Dé Danann have killed.

They were feasting and enjoying themselves for that night, continued Caílte, and, when they arose next day, Donn mac Midir said to Finn, Come out with me onto the green so that you may see the place where we do battle with the Tuatha Dé Danann every year.

They came out and looked at the graves and the stones. The Tuatha Dé Danann are destined to come to us, said Donn.

Which of them, asked Finn, are determined to attack you?

Bodb Derg and his seven sons; Aengus Óg, son of the Dagda with his seven sons; Finnbar of Knockma with his seventeen sons; Lir from the fairy mound of Finnachad with his twenty-seven sons and their families as well; Tadg, son of Nuada, from the beautiful fairy mound of Alma; Donn Ailéin and Donn Dumaige and the two Glases from the fairy mound of Glas in the country of Ossory; Dobrán of the Dubthaire from the fairy mound of Liaman Lennchaem in the province of Leinster; Aed Aillén from Rathlin in the north; Fer Aí, Ailéan, Lí Bán, and Fainnle, sons of Eogabál from Munster, from the fairy mound of Eogabál; Cian, Coban, and Conn, three sons of the king of the fairy mound of Monad in Scotland; Aed Minbrec from Assaroe with his seven sons; the children of the Morrígu, daughter of Ernmas with her twenty-six women-warriors and twenty-six male warriors; the two Luaths from the plain of Liffey in Moyliffey; Brattán, Ballgel, and Ubalrosc from the fairy mound of Cleitech in the plain of Brega; Cathal, Caithre, and Catharnach from the fairy mound of Druim Derg in the territory of Tirconnell in the north; Derg and Drecán from the fairy mound of Benn Étair; Bodb Derg, himself, with his great household: ten men, ten score, and ten hundred in all. These are the chiefs and territorial rulers of the Tuatha Dé Danann that come to destroy our fairy mound year after year.

After that, Caílte continued, they went back into the mound where Finn spoke to his followers: Comrades, he said, the people here are experiencing great violence, oppression and distress. If you do not perform well in their defence there is the danger that you will not see any of the Fian or their followers again.

Finn, said Diarmaid Ó Duibne, when did you ever find us slack in fighting that you are warning us?

I give you my word, Finn replied, were I to search the whole world I would have no fear if I had this number of the Fian of Ireland with me.

They remained there until it was time to get up next day. Then the people of the fairy mound went out with Finn and his six warriors.

Tell me, Donn, said Finn, is it by day or by night that the Tuatha Dé Danann attack you?

At the fall of night that they may do the greater amount of damage, answered Donn.

They remained there until night came and Finn said, One of you go out on the green and keep watch so that the Tuatha Dé Danann may not attack us without knowledge and hearing.

The sentry had not gone far when he saw five hardy battalions of equal size approaching. I think, he said, many warriors and fighters surround the druid's grave and this time are a match for heroes.

Finn said:

A band of warriors at the mound with many red sharp-pointed spears,
let us mention the mass of spears in the forefront of the band.
Let Diarmaid go out and Oisín, who gives protection,
Mac Lugach of the clear, clean deed and Oscar, to defend us.
The hosts gather in the white rath. Caílte and I will go to meet them
and we will go out, both of us and the people of the house.
The three times three fifties of the most courageous warriors in the world
will ward off every second man of that brave host
I tell you, and what I tell you is the truth,
I will enter that hard fight, the enemy will flee before me.

Where is Oscar? asked Finn.

Here.

Fight well in the battle against the Tuatha Dé Danann, said Finn. Diarmaid, Mac Lugach, Caílte, Oisín, and I are senior to you. Leave the rear of the battle to us. Bring the sons of Midir, the few that they are, safely back to us. Should harm come to them, now that we have joined them, would be for us a betrayal of generosity and loyalty.

We fought the battle, said Caílte, from the coming of darkness over the territories until early morning. The Tuatha Dé Danann lost ten men, ten score, and ten hundred.

Then Bodb Derg, Midir, and Finnbar said, What will we do with the dead? Let Lir from the fairy mound of Finnachad advise us since he is the oldest of the Tuatha Dé Danann.

My advice, said Lir, is that each of you should carry friends, comrades, fosterlings, sons, and brothers to their own mounds. Have a wall of fire made on one side of us and a wall of water on the other.

The Tuatha Dé Danann raised their dead nor did they leave on the green as much as a raven might stand on of those slaughtered by the people of the fairy mound. Finn and the people of the fairy mound went back into the mound. They were wasting in pools of blood and three of us were in a bad way, Mac Lugach, Oscar, and Diarmaid. Three times that year the Tuatha Dé Danann attacked the same mound and three times we fought against them, continued Caílte. We lost Conn Cruthach mac Midir in the last battle and were sorely distressed. Oscar and Diarmaid felt the venom and the fierceness of the fight with the result that, as they lay bloodied on their litter-beds their clothes were raised about them with bent hazel rods. We four who had survived – Finn, Mac Lugach, Oisín, and myself – walked out onto the green. Oisín spoke, It was a bad journey we made to the fairy mound of Midir's sons. I've lost my son and my foster-brother, Oscar and Diarmaid.

It would be a pity to face the Fian, said Mac Lugach, after leaving Diarmaid and Oscar for no two served the Fian better in arms.

Whoever faces them, said Finn, it will not be me.

Bring Donn mac Midir to us, I said.

Tell me, Donn, said Finn, do you know of anything that would cure these men?

I do not but there is a physician with the Tuatha Dé Danann who could bring remedy and relief to them within nine days unless the spine has been severed from the back. They would become unscarred and sound of body.

How can we get him, asked Finn, since those with whom he is are no friends of ours.

I'll tell you how. Early each day he comes out of the fairy mound to collect healing herbs while they bear the moisture-bead of the morning.

Find me the one, Donn, I said, who will identify that physician and he will come with me, dead or alive.

Aed mac Midir and Flann Fuilech mac Midir approached: Come with us, Caílte, they said. We made our way to the mound's dew sparkling green and when we arrived there saw a sturdy young man wearing a woollen cloak from the wethers of the flock-abounding Land of Promise. He filled the bottom of his cloak with healing medicinal herbs for putting into the wounds and bones of those among the Tuatha Dé Danann, who were hurt in battle.

Tell me, Aed, I said, who is that?

He is the man we have come to get. Attend him well so that he may not escape back into the mound.

We ran about him all at the one time, said Caílte. I caught him by the shoulders and we took him to Slaney Ford in the great plain of Leinster where the Fian were. A magic mist rose about us so that we were invisible. When we had reached the hill where the ford is we saw four in fringed crimson cloaks with four golden swords in their hands and four hunting dogs with them. We were not visible to them because of the magic mist but we could see them. We saw them in conversation: Colla mac Caílte, Faelán mac Caílte, Raigne Rosclethan mac Finn, and Caince mac Finn. They were speaking of the loss for a whole year of Finn mac Cumaill, their leader and lord. When I heard the conversation of my two sons and of Finn's two sons, I was sad.

What will the Fian of Ireland do? asked Raigne Rosclethan, without leader and lord?

They can do nothing, said Colla, except go to Tara, disband, and choose a Fian-chief for themselves.

After that the sons wept sorely for the loss of their fathers and their leader. We came away, continued Caílte, until we reached the fairy mound of the two birds, now known as the Mountain of Aige mac Iugaine, and there we went into the mound. Finn and Donn mac Midir welcomed Libra, the physician, and showed him Oscar and Diarmaid.

These, said Donn, are my two brothers. See if you can cure them.

The healer examined them and said, They can be cured and can convalesce if my fee is healthy.

It will be good for sure, I said. How long will it take to cure them?

Nine days.

I will give you a good fee, I said. Your life will be spared but if the young men do not recover I will cut your head off with my own hand.

The young man healed and cured them within nine days, making them unscarred and sound.

After this a messenger came from Cormac, king of Ireland, to bring the Fian to Tara in the absence of Finn mac Cumaill, their leader and chief, in order to hold the Festival of Tara with Conn of the Hundred Battles. All the Fian of Ireland – men, women, attendants, and the minstrel – went to the Grave of the Druid on the green at Tara. Goll mac Morna sat on one side of the king of Ireland and the representatives of the provinces of Ireland were also seated

The absence of Finn mac Cumaill, your leader and chief, Fian of Ireland, said Cormac, is a great loss for you.

It is great, said Goll. With the three comparable losses that took place in Ireland before this of Lugh, Conn, and Conaire, this is the fourth greatest.

Tell me, Cormac, said Goll mac Morna, what organization will you give to the Fian of Ireland now?

Goll, said Cormac, I will give you the hunting and deer-killing until we find out if Finn has really disappeared and to Clanna Baíscne, Finn's family, their choice of hunting for the year from you.

The Fian of Ireland agreed to this.

Until Finn has been missing for three years and no one in Ireland expects to see him, said Goll, I will make no claim against him concerning the kingship of the Fian of Ireland.

The freckled-faced Ailbe said to Cormac, What will happen to Finn's fair women, the seventeen queens?

A secure and secluded sun-room will be built for each of them, with her company of women, for a month, a season, and a year, until we find out if Finn is alive or dead. During that time they will be given all that they need of food and drink.

Then the minstrels of the Fian came to Cormac, that is, Daigre mac Morna, Dér mac Daigre, Senach mac Senaig, and Súanach mac Seinchinn, the teller of old tales, it was he who played the sweetest lute in Ireland and Scotland, and Cnú Dereóil, the dwarf, and Bláthnait his wife.

Cormac spoke to them: Remain in Tara. I will give you half your wages and a payment equal to what Finn would have given you.

Fergus Finnbél, poet of the Fian, approached. They numbered a thousand, poets and artists.

I give you the chief honour of Ireland, said Cormac, from the Wave of Clídna to Rudraige's Wave.

Then Finn's servants approached with Garbchrónán, chief of the senior attendants. Provide for us, they said.

For your sustenance I will give you, said Cormac, from the wide Ford of Loch, now called Athlone, in the west to Benn Étair in the east.

They went to Tara. Cormac entered the great Banquet Hall where he arranged for each with due regard for the heredity of their father and grandfather. He gave Goll mac Morna the place of the Fian-chief; he gave Eithne Ollamda, Cathair's daughter, wife of the king of Ireland, the queen's place, with Alb Gruadbrec at her side and Maiginis, daughter of Garad Glúndub, beside Ailbe; and he arranged the great Banquet Hall in that manner, served drink, and provided food for them.

Rising up with a polished drinking-horn in his hand, Cormac said, Men of Ireland, it would be a good thing if any of you could find news of Finn for us in waterfall, or estuary, cliff or river, fastness or inaccessible place, mound or fairy mound.

Berngal Bóchétach, chief hospitaller to the king of Ireland from the borders of the Fews, answered: On the day that the Fian-chief came from the north with six warriors in pursuit of a fairy-deer, he gave me a deadly spear with a blue-angled head and a dog's collar. He told me to keep them until we would come together again in the one place.

Berngal Bóchétach then gave the spear and the collar to Cormac. Cormac gave them to Goll. They all looked at them and Cormac said, The man who owned this spear and this collar is a great loss to the men of Ireland.

Cormac questioned the young man as to whether or not Finn and his people had hounds with them.

They had, the hospitaller replied.

What hounds were they, Goll?

Bran and Sceolaing in Finn's hand, said Goll, Adnuall and Fer Úaine in Oisín's; Iarratach and Fostud with Oscar; Baeth and Buide with Diarmaid; Brec, Luath, and Lánbind in Caílte's hand; Conuall and Conrith in the hand of Mac Lugach.

Where is Fergus Finnbél, asked Cormac.

Here he said.

Do you know how long the Fian-chief has been missing?

For a month, a quarter and a year, Fergus Finnbél said.

Fergus Finnbél spoke:

> I count Finn so long away, a week, a month and a year,
> it is time today for the Fians of Ireland to separate all at once.
> A quarter, a month, and a year since the man went hunting,
> since the king went to destruction, Finn mac Cumaill of Alma.
> Great loss for Mac Lugach, the cheerful warrior chief,
> to be without swift-spirited Oscar and Oisín, the beautiful friend.
> Great is the loss of noble Diarmaid the best pupil of the Fian,
> Finn, Caílte, best of men, the great loss I count.

Then the king of Ireland said, It is a great loss for we do not think, Cithruad, that those six, the best in Ireland and Scotland, will be found. The Fian-chief gave you great jewels and wealth. Tell us, is Finn alive or dead?

Cithruad answered, The Fian-chief is alive but I will not reveal his story for Finn would not want it.

All were rejoicing at that for they knew that everything that Cithruad had foretold had come true.

Put a date on it, said Cormac.

On the last day of the Festival of Tara, the Fian-chief will be seen at the drinking, I said.

It was a question in *Acallam na Senórach* [The Dialogue of the Ancients].

> How long was Finn at Sliab Én?
> Caílte, answer a difficult question.

Who was wounded in the mound,
Because our anxiety is great?

After this, said Caílte, we were in the mound for six weeks while the Festival of Tara was being held and until we had taken hostages from the Tuatha Dé Danann for Donn mac Midir. From then on the Fian of Ireland had no more intercourse with the households of the Tuatha Dé Danann.

While Caílte was telling this story to the king of Leinster and to Patrick, they saw a warrior approaching with a shirt of royal silk next to his skin and over it a tunic of soft silk. He wore a fringed crimson cloak fastened over his chest with a golden pin, had a sword with a gold hilt in his hand, and a helmet of gold about his head. He was Donn mac Midir, who placed his head on Patrick's chest and gave him power over the Tuatha Dé Danann.

All bowed before Patrick.

Donn mac Midir gave hospitality to Patrick and his people that night and after that the entire host together with Patrick came to Ráth Mór of Maig Fea. That night messengers came to Patrick from the king of Munster asking him to preach the gospel. Patrick said farewell to the king of Leinster and the nobles of the whole kingdom and went to the Mound of Warriors, now called Cashel of the Kings.

MUNSTER

Eógan Leithderg mac Aengusa, king of the two provinces of Munster, arrived along with six great battalions before Saint Patrick. All the nobles of Munster genuflected and dedicated their kingdom, patrimony and wealth to Patrick.

A gospel penny for Saint Patrick, king of Munster, said Benignus mac Aeda.

What penny is that? asked the king.

Country and land for the clerics.

This place where he is, said the king of Munster, will serve him and his people after him forever.

How will it be given to us? asked Benignus.

Like this, said the king. The cleric himself will go on to the Stone of the Hundreds and as much as he can see of Munster's plain on every side will be his.

Patrick mounted the Stone of Hundreds and the sun rose to give light to him on all sides. As soon as Patrick put his foot on the stone, eleven thousand demons rose from the edges of the rock and went into the air to escape from the saintly man. He blessed the stone and bestowed on it the gift of giving counsel and blessing: that an angel would pass over it every evening; that should the king of Munster and his nine sons fast on it he would get whatever request he desired; and that it would be one of the three fires to be alive and flourishing in Ireland until the end.

Eógan Leithderg and all the Munster nobles then welcomed Caílte.

Caílte, my friend, said the king of Munster, why is this stone called the Stone of the Hundreds?

I remember how it came about, said Caílte. We had no knowledge of heaven until Finn sat on that stone and put his thumb under his tooth of wisdom for the first time. Heaven and earth were revealed to him, the great glory of faith in the true God and, Táilchenn, your coming to Ireland, when saints, good men, belief in the Cross and faith would flourish.

Who was it first erected a fort and a good homestead here? asked the king.

Fiacha Muillethan mac Eógain, who ruled the two provinces of Munster for thirty years, and it was he who built a strong dyke about the dwelling and had his house there, answered Caílte.

Patrick said:

This stone is called Stone of the Hundreds, crowds once about it,
It will be a place of piety and crosses after every abode that I found.
Cashel, head of all Ireland, rock where the fire will come,
will dispense knowledge of heaven without tribute to a heedless king.

My church in the north was good, in great-hosted Connaught,
if I might get a clean burial in my pure clear cloak.
My place in the territory of Ulster is dear to my heart,
its lie is good, the beautiful three in the one place.
Ten men, ten twenties, ten hundred, it is true and no lie,
they took my far-off refuge, place of abbots and the faithful.
They will have psalms, faith, paternosters and gospel,
they will have psalms early among cairn and stone.

Victory and blessing be yours, Patrick, said the king of Munster, you too have given us great knowledge and wisdom.

The entire gathering remained there until the sun rose from his fiery circle and filled the world with light. The crowd then went westwards to the Little Rath of Wonders in Mag Femin. The king of Munster and his nobles sat at one end of the rath and Saint Patrick and Caílte at the other.

Then Eógan Leithderg mac Aengusa asked, Why is this small rath called the Little Rath of Wonders?

Caílte gave this answer:

Finn found a wonderful windfall
waiting for him on this hill,

three men of fair fame
with one hound between them.

On that day, said Caílte, when the three battalions of the Fian came to this mound we saw three warriors before us with one hound. There was no colour in the whole world that was not in that dog and compared to other dogs he was extremely big. They sat in front of Finn, who asked, Young men, where have you come from? From great Iruaith [Norway] in the east, they replied. And why have you come? To make a contract with and offer companionship to you, they said.

What will we gain from your being with us? asked Finn.

We three have each a particular use.

What uses are they?

The safe-guarding of the Fian of Ireland and of Scotland, said the first of the warriors.

Every duty of battle and of single combat that shall come to the Fian I will undergo and let everyone else keep quiet, said the second.

Tell me, said Finn to the third, what qualfication do you have?

I tell you, he replied, every difficulty that will come to my lord I will meet it and every demand that will be made of him I will respond to. As for the dog, as long as there are deer in Ireland he will provide for the Fian every second night and I will provide on the other nights.

What will you ask of me, said Finn, for helping us in that manner?

Three conditions, they replied.

What are they? asked Finn.

That no one shall come to our camp either from a distance or close to it once night falls; that nothing either small or large be provided for us; and that the Fian of Ireland will assign to us the poorest hunting.

Why do you request that no one see you once night falls? asked Finn.

We have reason and cause, they replied, and whether it be for a long or short time do not inquire about anything else from us. Of the three warriors that you see, one will be dead every third night, that is why we do not want anyone to see us, and the other two will watch over him.

For Finn it was taboo to see a dead man unless killed by weapons but this time he had the solution to hand: not to come near this little rath, said Caílte.

Caílte sang:

It was taboo for Finn to see someone dead
unless killed by weapons,
if he did not approach, fair his fame,
about this rath.

Seven poets, continued Caílte, from the people of Cithruad mac Airm meic Fhir Choecat approached Finn to request the fee for a poem: one hundred and fifty ounces of gold and of silver to bring to Tara for Cithruad.

We will find help with that, said Scandal, grandson of Líathán, a favourite warrior of Finn.

Now, poets, said the three warriors, would you prefer to get the fee for your poem tonight or to tomorrow?

Tomorrow will suit us.

Those three warriors and their dog went to the dog's bed in the Little Rath of Wonders. The dog vomited one hundred and fifty ounces of gold and one hundred and fifty ounces of silver which they gave to the poets who then departed.

What, Finn asked, will the three battalions of the Fian do tonight without water?

One of the three warriors asked, How many drinking horns has Finn?

Three hundred and twelve, I replied:

> Three hundred and twelve horns,
> golden drinking horns, had Finn,
> at the time we came to the feast
> they had the full amount of wine.

Put the horns in my hand, said the warrior, and although it comes from the fairy mound drink whatever you find in them.

Three times the warrior filled them for the Fian of Ireland and at the third filling they were cheerfully drunk and jolly.

I am surprised, said Finn, by the conduct of this feast.

The Mound of the Banquet is the name given to it by Finn and the Dog's Bed is the name of the lair. For this reason also this rath was called The Little Rath of Wonders, that rath the Rath of the Banquet, and that the Rath of the Dog's Head. The Fian remained there for a year, said Caílte.

Then Eógan Leithderg, accompanied by Patrick and Caílte, went to the Rath of the Dog's Head, to the south of Mag Femin, and to the Mound of the Women. The whole company sat upon the rath. Caílte sat before Eógan Leithderg.

Tell me, Caílte, said Eógan, why is this rath called the Rath of the Dog's Head and this mound the Mound of Women?

There was a princely hospitaller here, said Caílte, Cellach mac Duibdét his name, whose possessions and wealth when counted covered the great plain of Femen. No one in the world had a greater share of meanness and niggardliness than him. Thirty of us bearing shields and armour came to the Fian-chief of Ireland and Scotland after hunting on Sliab Cua. We sat down by the bed-posts but before they had finished serving us the man of the house had disgraced and insulted every one of us except Finn.

A fierce member of the Fian, Cuinnscleó mac Ainscleó, king of Britain, replied, This boorish fellow is a big chunk of dog's head snarling at the Fian.

You have found the right word for him, said Finn. Let him be known as Dog's Head.

And why, the king asked Caílte, was this rath called the Rath of the Women?

The Fian-chief gathered fifty seamstresses, the best in Ireland, at this rath to make clothes and garments for the Fian of Ireland. He put the king of Britain's daughter whose name was Dergoda, wife of Oisín's son, Oscar, in charge of them and they were here for many years, hence the names the Rath of the Women and the Rath of the Dog's Head.

And what, asked the king, is that great stone pillar in the middle of the rath?

That was the women's candelabra, answered Caílte, for they would only have a fire three times a year so that neither dirt, dust, nor smoke of the fire would harm them or their clothes. They were here for many years doing embroidery and making clothes for the Fian. These women – Finnchas, Finnruine, and Finningen – three daughters of the king of Uí Chennselaigh, had a pleasant way of passing the time. They had a small lute with a silver neck and pegs of yellow gold and even women in the childbed would have found sleep because of the enticing music they played.

Caílte, asked the king, what are the two great graves that we see?

The three warriors and their dog who entered into friendship with Finn at the Little Rath of Wonders killed the two warriors whose graves these are, Donn and Dubán, the king of Ulster's sons in the north.

How were they killed?

The three of them and their dog were away from the Fian and, when night fell, a wall of fire would surround them so that no one might look at them, said Caílte. Donn and Dubán kept watch for the Fian that night. Three times they made a circuit of the Fian and on the third saw the fiery wall.

Donn said, It is strange how these three warriors and their dog have been for a year with their warning that nobody must see them after the fall of night.

They drew nearer and went through the wall of fire. Drawing their weapons, they looked at the warriors and their dog. The great dog they had with them each day hunting and chasing was not bigger than a lord's pet marten. One of the warriors kept watch over the dog with a naked sword in his hand. Another was at the dog's mouth with a silver goblet and the choicest of drink that any man might desire issued from the dog's mouth into the goblet.

Then one of the warriors said to the dog, It is a good thing, noble fellow, take note that the chief of the Fian is spying on you.

The hound wagged his tail, creating such a factitious magic wind that their shields fell from their shoulders, their spears from their hands, their swords from their sides and were cast before their eyes into the fiery wall. The warriors killed them. The dog turned towards the dead men, blew his breath over their bodies, and turned them into ashes and dust so that neither blood, flesh, nor bone remained. Theirs are the two graves you asked about. If you opened them, you would find nothing but clay and sand.

No one has ever told us, said Eógan Leithderg, a more wonderful and more mysterious story but what is the high post at the side of that stone in the rath?

The women's annual wage from Finn was hidden by Oscar under the bottom of that stone: six hundred ounces of gold, said Caílte. The gathering went over, dug down, and took up the gold. They gave a third to the king of Munster, a third to Saint Patrick and to me, and a third to the clerics. The gold survives but neither the Fian-chief nor Oscar who hid it, survives.

Caílte sang:

> The Rath of the Dog's Head exists today without beauty, without strife,
> and the king, Finn mac Cumaill of Alma, does not live.
> The stones of the rath exist which we frequented at all times
> durable red gold lives and Oscar does not live.
> The death of Donn and of sweet Dubán, died in slaughter
> we searched for them for a week, a month and a year,
> Finnchas and Finnruine, it is true, and Finningen, pitiful the deed,
> in the famous estuaries, three daughters of Cheinnselaig.
> Dear was the small beautiful harp, ear never heard so soft,
> the host of the world would sleep at the one time, a great gift.
> The little harp the women had with its white silver rim,
> with its golden yellow pegs, with its white bronze strings.
> Fifty beds inside there, fifty drinking horns, fifty chessboards,
> fifty ounces of red gold, their wage every year.
> I tell you before, and it is true what I declare,
> the best of every good time we enjoyed in that rath.

As for the three warriors, asked the king, did they stay with you or did they go away?

They stayed, said Caílte, until the three battalions of the Fian were divided into small bands of nine at the Rath of Nines in Leinster's great plain. Nine warriors and nine servants from the east went to every part of Ireland to find the two sons of the king of Ulster killed by the sons of the king of Iruaith. After the dispersal Finn mac Cumaill went to Temair Luachra with only camp followers and inexperienced servants. The bands of nine came together at Temair Luachra on the same night to meet Finn; they did not know whether the two men were alive or dead.

Patrick and the king of Munster went south to the White Hill of Running between Sliab Cláire and Sliab Crot. Patrick, Caílte, and the entire crowd sat down and the king asked, Why is this peak called the White Hill of Running?

Once upon a time, Caílte answered, when Finn mac Cumaill was on this hill, he saw a woman waiting on it. She wore a crimson-fringed cloak fastened with a golden brooch and had a frontlet of yellow gold on her forehead. Finn asked her for news of whence she came and she replied: From Benn Étair.

What is your name? asked Finn.

Étaín Fairhaired, daughter of Aed Whitebreast, from the fairy mound of Benn Étair.

Why have you come here?

To ask one of the Fian to race against me, she said.

How do you run? asked Diarmaid Ó Duibne.

I run well, said the woman, whether the ground under my feet is long or short it is the same to me to be running.

Caílte said:

When we arrived at White Hill a woman came to us,
challenged our Fian to a race however hard.
I ran to the height above Badamair,
we climbed fast, a difficult task for me.
We ran then to the hill above Badamair,
past caves and eight glens to Dublin.
I got there first, I do not deny it,
and ran past them all, both dogs and people.

We went after that to the side of Benn Étair,
that pleased all the host in the mound.
We came to the mound, got mead and wine,
and stayed there twenty nights after that.
My heart breaks, my soul is unprepared,
as I see each famous hill, the living heights.

This was our number when we got there, said Caílte, two thousand of the Fian of Ireland including Finn mac Cumaill. We sat at the posts of the royal house in the fairy mound, our feet were washed, our hunger satisfied and our thirst quenched. While we were there, Finn, the chief, saw a mild yellow-haired woman in front of the vats with a goblet of white silver in her hand serving everyone.

Then Finn said, It seems to us that she is the woman who challenged the Fian to run and race from the Fort of Sliab Crot in the west to Benn Étair.

It was not she in any case, said Aed Whitebreast, king of the fairy mound, for she is the slowest woman that we have.

Then who was it? asked Finn.

Bé Mannair, daughter of Aincél, replied Aed, the messenger of the Tuatha Dé Danann. She changes into the shape of a water-spider or a big animal and transforms herself into the appearance of a fly or a true lover, both male and female, so that all leave their secret with her. It was she who outran you in the east not that woman who was drinking and enjoying herself at the vats here in the fairy mound.

What is that woman's name? asked Finn.

Étaín Fairhaired, said Aed, my daughter, much-loved by all the Tuatha Dé Danann. She has a lover among the Fian of Ireland.

Dear friend, said Finn, which of us is that lover?

Oscar, son of Oisín, and it was she who sent the messenger for you to the Fort of Sliab Crot in the south. Cairbre Lifechair, son of Cormac, king of Ireland, has offered to give the Tuatha Dé Danann as her bride-price and wooing-gift the cantred nearest to Brega and Mide and to put himself and an equal weight of gold and silver into a scales and to give it all to her.

Why did you not agree on this for her with the king of Ireland's son?

We did not accept him, said Aed, for since she had not the slightest wish or desire for him we made neither agreement nor match concerning her.

Well, Finn asked, what condition do you require from us? Tell me, woman, what condition do you seek from Oscar, grandson of the Fian chief?

She replied, Never to leave me unless my own evil actions come against me.

You will certainly get that condition, said Oscar.

Give sureties and guarantors for it, she said.

What guarantors do you want? asked Oscar.

Goll mac Morna of the family of Morna and Finn mac Cumaill of the Fian of Ireland.

Those guarantors were given to her and she and Oscar were married. We remained there for twenty nights afterwards.

Then Oscar asked Finn, Where will I take my wife?

To broad green Alma in Leinster, Finn replied, until the end of seven years. After that you will provide a place for her.

The banded battle of Benn Étair took place after that, said Caílte, and in it Oscar was seriously wounded. The Fian were distressed. Finn, too, was distressed. One night Étaín Fairhaired came to watch over Oscar's bed. She saw that his great royal form had departed. Greenness and darkness overcame her, she raised up her pitiful cries and her high grieving wail. She went to her own bed where the heart within her breast broke like a nut and she died of grief for her husband and her first-love. She was taken to her own fairy mound, the fairy mound of Benn Étair, and was buried in the earth. Étaín's Grave is its name. Oscar left three noble sons named Luath, Indell, and Oscar. That is the story you asked me for and therefore this place is called the White Peak of the Race.'

They remained there that night until the bright light of the next day arrived. Saint Patrick and the entire gathering arose and went on to Cuillenn and to Callann in Uí-Chuanach. There Patrick sat down so that Patrick's Seat is the name of that place from that time until now. The king of Munster sat at Patrick's shoulder and Caílte in front of him.

Then Eógan Leithderg mac Aengusa asked Caílte, Why is this place called Callann and Cuillenn? And why is that hill called the Warrior's Grave and this dyke surrounding the land called the Dyke of the Fian?

One day, answered Caílte, Finn mac Cumaill was at Ráth Cuire between Dundalk and the sea at the end of Baile's Strand. The Bed of the Vessel was on one side of Finn and the Rath of the Horses, the place of the Dub Sainglenn and the Grey of Macha, on the other with Dundalk behind us. We were not long there when we saw thirty charioteers coming towards us across the strand to the north. They alighted, unyoked their horses, and the great wide-eyed warrior, the eldest and the noblest of them, sat by Finn's shoulder.

Finn asked him for news: Where have you come from and who are you?

I am Callann, son of Fergus Find, son of the king of Ulster, and my own brother, Aed Donn, has banished me. He does not allow me to be with Cormac, grandson of Conn, and denies me my own inheritance. I have come to speak with you, king of the Fian, since we are of the one family. Mess Muingel, daughter of Aengus, king of Ulster, your grandmother, is my father's sister and mother of Cumall.

If that is so, said Oisín, it is from Ulster we have derived our fury and fierceness.

From them for certain, said Finn. Is it in Ulster you want to get land?

No, Callann replied, since we do not want to commit parricide.

In that case, said Finn, I will go tomorrow to Eógan Faeburderg mac Finn, king of the two provinces of Munster, and ask him for land for you for a time and a season. Unless I get land willingly from him I will do battle with the king of Ulster at the end of Baile's Strand for your own land.

Then the three battalions of the Fian with Callann, son of the king of Ulster, in front of them marched south to the Fort of Sliab Crot where the king of Munster was living.

The king came out to meet Finn and the Fian of Ireland and said, I welcome your coming, Finn, and greet you loyally.

It is indeed loyal, said the chief.

Then they went into the fort and all were served. The feasting-house was prepared for them. Goll mac Morna was placed at one side of Finn and the son of the king of Ulster on the other.

Then said the king of Munster, Have you seen among the men of Ireland or the men of the entire world any three whose shape surpasses that of the warrior at Finn mac Cumaill's shoulder? Finn, who is the warrior with you?

Finn told him Callann's name and family and that Callann had come to ask him for land and heritage.

By my word, said the king, if someone as good as him came by himself to seek land and territory it were advisable to give them to him but when you, king of the Fian, seek it, it is proper to give it. I will give him two cantreds.

And a third for my sake and the sake of the Fian, said Finn.

That, too, was given to Callann so that he had three cantreds.

Where is the land that you are giving him? asked Finn.

Brecthír, now called Uí Chuanach, and Tulach na Dála, now called Cuillenn, said the king.

My people, said Callann mac Fergusa, are rough like Ulstermen and how will they react?

My advice to you, said the king of Munster, is to let the Fian build a rampart as a fortification around your land.

The three battalions of the Fian rose up and built it in seven days and a host door of contention was made in it. When it was built, Finn and the three battalions of the Fian and Callann, son of Fergus, son of the king of Ulster, went with them again to the Fort of Sliab Crot.

Then Finn said, Well, king of Munster, do you know for what other reason we came to you? I do not.

To ask your daughter, Cuillenn, for Callann, said Finn.

What is her bride-price and her gift? her father asked.

A bride-price in hundreds, said Finn, that is, a hundred of every kind of cattle and of each kind of animal and by my word she will have it.

So that was secured for her and that night the king of Munster's daughter was married to the son of the king of Ulster.

Callann went north for his people and they came with him to the land which the king of Munster had given him and there he built a great fort. The woman bore him a famous and beautiful son called Fer Óc and there was no one in the whole of Ireland whose shape, agility, and casting surpassed his.

We, the three battalions of the Fian, went there with three thousand in each battalion. As we were standing there, we saw a boy playing on the green with a heavy lump of stone on his palm. He would throw it so that it would fly over ten furrows and run beneath it and catch it with his hand in the air. We watched him for a long time.

Never, said Finn, have we seen better casting than that and who, men, is the boy doing the casting?

The son of the owner of this place, everyone answered, Fer Óc, son of Callann, son of the king of Ulster.

Never has there come from the Ulstermen since their great and gallant men died better makings of a warrior than that youth, said Finn.

Never indeed, they all replied. And he does another casting that is harder than that.

What is it? asked Finn.

He puts the shafts of his two spears against the ground with his back to the house and jumps over the host door with the spearshafts and lands on the stone on the other side with the spears in his hand. Then he leaps back with them over the house and lands on this green, they replied.

Fer Óc, said Finn, by virtue of your conscience do this feat in our presence.

I will do it, said the boy. But I am ashamed to do it before the Fian of Ireland unless I do it well.

He performed the feat in the presence of Finn and the Fian as well as he had ever done it. Callann and Cuillenn, the father and mother of the boy, then came to them and welcomed Finn and the rest of the Fian with true gentliness.

Well, beloved son, they said, make your contract and friendship with Finn.

I will, he replied.

He rose up and made peace and fellowship with Finn and shook hands with him. After that we went into the fort and there we remained feasting and enjoying ourselves.

Then the Fian-chief said, Where is Berrach, daughter of Cas Cuailnge?

Here I am, said the woman.

Take the measure for hundreds and place in it three times its fill of gold and three times its fill of silver and give it to Fer Óc as his wage, said Finn.

The boy divided it into three, a third to his father, a third to his mother, and another third to the poets and judges and to the treasurers of the Fian of Ireland.

The wage has been divided wisely, said Finn.

They remained there until the following day came with its full brightness, said Caílte, then the three battalions of the Fian held a hunt and a breaking-up of deer. However, that day because of Fer Óc, none of the Fian got first blood of pig or deer.

When they returned to the house after the hunt, a severe sickness seized Fer Óc caused by the malignant eyes of the people and the envy of the great gathering, and killed him, outright, at the end of nine days. He was buried on that green grassy hill and the shining stone that he held when he was playing and performing is the one rising above his head. Therefore the Hill of the Boy is the name of that hill.

His mother remained in his place after her son for a year. Every day she would go to her son's grave. All that year she lamented him. Then one day she died of grief and she, too, was interred in this hill. From her comes the name Cuillenn. And this, said Caílte, is one of four places where the Fians of Ireland used to put on their fine comely-mantled clothes, namely, Tara of Brega, Tara of Luachair, the great broad Alma of Leinster, and here in Cuillenn. Here, too, every year chief Finn used to assemble the three battalions of the Fian. Champions were brought and chosen for valour in place of all the Fian who were killed. Here the fierce wild stags and the heavy-sided boar were brought to us to the floor of the house of feasting and pleasure. That day Cuillenn was a place of deer and game.

Caílte sang:

Cuillenn a place of hunting, a fort of a king with authority,
beautiful in the hour of battle for its clothes of many colours.
What youth did Finn give the gold to, the great upright king,
and how many nights thereafter before his soul left his body?
No greater deed of valour was done than that by Conán Cerr
and Conán Mael on the plain at the battle of Berramain.
Not less were the deeds of valour performed by myself,
Diarmaid and Oisín at the heroic battle of Lámrach.
Nor better deed under the sun than that performed by Finn himself,
its profit accrued to us, the day of the battle of Ollarba.
Pitiful what was done by the noble king when the host went early to meet him,
there live with us here today only myself and Oisín.
I tell you before, and it is the truth I tell you,
they came proudly to the height the host that Cuillenn loved.

Victory and blessing be yours, said Eógan Leithderg mac Aengusa, and, Caílte, it is a sad story you have told us, the story of Fer Óc.

They were not long there when they saw a large brave group of men coming towards them in two divisions: eight score armed with shields in each group with bulwarks of red brown shields around them, a wood of tall spears at their shoulders; a boy, brown, assured, beautiful in front of the group with a diadem of gold on his head as a sign of royalty; a crimson cloak around another warrior who was their chief with a helmet of gold on his head. They knelt before Patrick and placed their heads on his chest.

Warriors, who are you? asked Patrick.

Two kings of west Munster. I am Derg mac Dínertaig meic Maeldúin and the other is Flann mac Flainn meic Failbe. We have a great beautiful banquet for you, king of Munster, and we would like you to bring Saint Patrick with you to enjoy our feast. We want to have our lands and our territories blessed by him and to give him our life-service and our death-service for we have never had a clerical friend except him.

Go before us, said the king of Munster, and we will follow after you.

They remained there that night until the bright light of the next day came.

The entire host, Patrick and his people, came south to Cathair of the Hundreds on one of the two summits of Sliab Mis. The two kings of west Munster came to meet them and welcomed Patrick and the king of Munster. They gave Saint Patrick a gospel penny, sixty ounces of gold, and sixty ounces of silver from each of them.

Then Eógan Leithderg asked Caílte, Why is this place called the Oakwood of the Conspiracy and why is this ridge called the Ridge of the Dead Woman and why is this small rath called the Little Rath of the Incantation?

I know why, Caílte replied, although its origin is not new. One time Finn mac Cumaill and the three battalions of the Fian came here for hunting and dispersal of deer. We were not long here when we saw someone approaching. She sat down with us on this hill, this woman with a shirt of royal satin next her skin. She had a soft crimson cloak with a golden brooch, a soft folded breastplate of gold, and a diadem of gold on her head. What we compared her to was not insignificant, the mast of a tall ship over a high summit. There were few of us who were not seized with horror, dread, and awe at the woman's outstanding shape and size. For we were not people of the same period as she for she was bigger, much bigger.

Goll mac Morna was at Finn's right hand at that time and I gave a great testimony for him in the presence of Munster's two provinces. He was the upper hand in fighting, a wave of death over fierce bands, brave as a lion, one of the five best warriors of his period and time in Ireland and Scotland behind shield, sword and spear. On my word these were the five whose bravery was best at one time in Ireland: Finn mac Cumaill; Lugaid Lága; Oscar, son of Oisín; Goll mac Morna; and I, without bragging words, am the fifth.

Then Finn said to Goll across the woman: Have you ever seen a woman bigger than that?

On my word, Goll replied, I never saw a bigger woman nor has any one else.

The woman took her long deft hand out of her breast. She was wearing three rings of gold on that hand, two on the other, each one as thick as a three-ox yoke.

We ought to question her, said Goll.

How can we do that? asked Finn, unless we stand up and even then there is the risk that she might not hear us.

The entire crowd stood up all together to talk and converse with her but at the same time she also rose up.

Sit down, woman, Finn said, lean your elbow against the hill if you want to hear anything we say or us to hear anything you say.

She lay down on the side of the hill and the Fian-chief asked for her story.

Good woman, he asked, what country are you from and who are you?

I come from the Land of Women in the west where the sun sets. I am the daughter of the king of that country.

What is your name?

My name is Bé Binn, daughter of Tréon.

Why is that country called the Land of Women? asked Finn.

There are no men there, she explained, except my father and his three sons but he has one hundred and forty-nine daughters. Therefore the land is called the Land of Women.

What country is closest to you?

The Land of Men, she replied.

Who is king over it? asked Finn.

Cétach Crobderg, who has twenty-eight sons and only one daughter. I was given to one of his sons, the beautiful Aed mac Cétaig Crobdeirg. I was given to him three times and three times I escaped from him and this is the third.

Who told you about this country? asked Finn.

Three fishermen driven from here by the wind and over to us. They told us about this country and said there was a fine warrior in the land, Finn mac Cumaill. If you are that warrior I have come to find you and to secure your protection.

She removed the glove from her hand and placed her hand in Finn's but he said, Place your hand in the hand of Goll mac Morna. No warrior in Ireland is more suited to have a bond of friendship and guarantee with you than him.

She placed her hand in Goll's and made those bonds with him. Just then they saw a very fierce stag approaching in full flight pursued by some of the hounds of the Fian.

Leave the deer alone, said Finn, for, Fian of Ireland, we will not spend this night hunting but with one of the young warriors of the Fian. Where is Finn mac Cúáin?

Here I am, he answered.

Go before us into your house and provide service and attendance for us.

It is an honour for us to do something for you, said Finn mac Cúáin, for I have one hundred and sixty herds in the pastures of Luachair and I got all of them from you.

One of Finn mac Cumaill's virtues was that no matter how much he had given to anyone, he never mentioned it to him by night or by day. Finn mac Cúáin proceeded to serve Finn and the Fian in his own fort. The woman removed her smooth burnished helmet, releasing her beautiful fair hair about her in eight score tresses so that all wondered at its abundance when it was let down.

Then Finn exclaimed: Great gods whom we adore, the sight of Bé Binn, daughter of Tréon, will be a great wonder for Cormac, grandson of Conn, the king of Ireland, and for Eithne Ollamda, poet daughter of Cathaír Mór, and for the women of the Fian!

Then the Fian-chief said to her, Tell me, good woman, would you think it too little if we gave you the division of a thousand?

The woman looked at the dwarf, Cnú Dereóil, who was playing the harp and said, Whatever share you give to that little man who plays the harp, be it small or large, the same amount will not be small for me.

The woman then asked Finn for a drink.

He asked, Where is Saltrán Sálfhota?

Here I am, Fian-chief, said the servant.

Bring me the full of the goblet of Smir Tuill of water from that ford.

There was a draught for twenty-seven of the Fian in that goblet. The servant brought the full of the goblet and gave it to the woman. She poured the water into her right palm, drank three sips of it, then raised her hand and sprinkled the rest over the entire gathering which made them and her burst out laughing.

Finn said, On your conscience, woman, why did you not drink from the goblet?

I have never drunk anything from a vessel that did not have a rim either of gold or of silver, she replied.

I happened to look about me at this time, said Caílte, and I saw a single tall warrior approaching and, if the woman was big, he was bigger still. He had a woollen cape about his shoulders with no beard and it seemed to us that if the men of the world were all in one place not one of them would be more beautiful than him. He was wearing a green cloak with a brooch of gold in it and a shirt of royal satin next to his skin. He had a branchy shield red as the rowanberry on his back, a gold-hilted sword in one hand, and a deadly blue-angled spear in the other.

The entire host looked at him and there were few of us except the true warriors who were not seized with horror and fear of him but Finn had a strong spirit for he was never afraid of anyone by day or by night. Then the Fian-chief said, Let not servant or warrior among you speak, nor anyone move. Do any of you know that man?

I know him, said the woman, he is the man I've come to escape.

After she had said that she came and sat between Finn and Goll mac Morna. The young man approached and, as he did, none of us knew what was in his mind. For when he came up to Finn and Goll he raised his hand and made a very wicked thrust of his spear at the woman so that the shaft of the weapon appeared through her back to the length of a warrior's hand. He withdrew his spear and went on out through the host.

You saw that, said Finn, and let him who will not avenge this terrible deed upon the doer not think any more of being in the Fian.

The three battalions of the Fian got up at the one time so that there were only three left on the hill, Finn, Goll mac Morna, and the woman, fatally wounded. We all went in pursuit of the warrior to the Rath of the Youths, now called the Rath of the Sheep in Mag Lí to the south; from there to the marsh of Ulster's plain in the west where the Ulstermen camped when besieging the Fort of the Sloping Rath at the time they killed Cú Roí mac Daire; north to the Place of the Ships where Clanna Deagaidh kept their boats; to the harbour of Labarthonn which means either Labar Wave, because Labar, daughter of Míl of Spain, was drowned there, or Speaking Wave, because there the surf spoke to the land; to the Well of the Lazy Warrior west of Tráig Lí; and west to Tribute Point where the men from overseas used to pay rent and tribute to Cú Roí mac Dáire every year.

There he faced out to the broad harbour. We four warriors – Diarmaid Ó Duibne, Glas mac Aencherda Bérra, Oscar mac Oisín, and myself – were well up with him. We also faced out to the waves but as I ran after him bounding at full speed I made a cast at him. The spear penetrated the sling of his shield and his left shoulder and the buckler fell off into the sea. I met his shield with my left hand. When he used his right hand to remove that spear, I caught the one that was in his other hand and pulled it away. But when I would have made a cast with his own spear, the bulk of the waves and the sea's depth intervened. Then as we were watching him we saw a great ship approaching from the west rowed by two people. He went on board but we never knew which direction they went.

The three battalions came back to this hill. Finn asked us for news and I told him our story from the time we left to the time of our return and we placed the weapons in front of him.

They are good weapons, said the woman, the spear is called Performer of the Hundred-feat and the shield Red-arabesqued. The woman added, It is well. Prepare well my grave and my burial for it was for your protection I came to Ireland and I died while in your care.

She gave her bracelets to Cnú Dereóil, Bláthnait, and Daigre, the harper. Her soul left her body and she was buried here in the ground. From her the Ridge of the Dead Woman got its name, said Caílte, and, king of Munster, that is the story you asked of me.

And, Caílte, why was this grove called the Oak-grove of the Whisper? asked the king.

The four you have heard about from me were at the Little Rath of Wonders, that is, the three warriors and the dog. It was here that the Fian conspired to kill them, replied Caílte.

What reason had they to conspire against them since they were on their side?

The Fian did not understand the procedure that they chose to follow: to have a camp apart with a wall of fire around them and no one to see them until sunrise next day.

Finn said, By no means do I want them killed for those three are the best in the world at casting and agility. They have three arts but it would not be right to kill them because they have those arts. If any man were sick or diseased, he would be made smooth and without scars if one of them applied herbs to his ailment. Whatever is asked of the second man, he gives. As for the third, let the needs of the world be told him and they will be fully satisfied by him. In addition and beyond any of these he has a pipe that would put men to sleep however great their sickness. As for the dog, if none of us were to kill a deer or other animal we would not be short, thanks to it.

Then the Fian-chief said, Do you know why you have been brought to talk with me?

We do not, replied the warriors.

The Fians of Ireland think you are disloyal because of the arts that you practise. They want to order you away and to give you your wage.

What evil have we done that we are ordered to depart? they asked.

We do not know of any evil, said the Fian, except that you have customs we have never seen nor heard of being practised by men before you: a wall of fire about you every night. You do not like anyone to see you so you place that wall of fire about you after dark.

And what harm does that do you, Finn? asked the warriors, for we will not be a burden to you, every good thing we do belongs to you.

The Fian-chief spoke: That is the speech of noble people. Neither I nor any of the Fian of Ireland will ever show you spite or reproach you day or night. There is something I would like to ask you.

If we know it, they replied, we will tell you.

What are your names?

I am called Dub, said the warrior who had performed the cures.

I am Ág, said the middle warrior.

I am Ilar, said the other warrior.

Caílte sang, describing them and their dog:

Dub, Ág, and Ilar, a dear trio in that gentle place,
and Fermac, good the hound, who used to be with them.
A camp apart for them from the blood-stained camp the Fian had,
so that nobody would observe them, the four bright distinguished ones.
The four came from afar and were not known to Finn himself,
nor were they known to any of the host, that beautiful frightening four.
A place to themselves apart from the camp of the Irish
so that no one visited their house, unless someone going astray.
A wall of fire around them, my grief, alternating with a ditch of water
so that no one went out until rising time the next day.

> No man of the people of Finn, the Fian-chief, was ever wounded
> with any seizure or sorrow that Dub did not cure.

Finn, said Caílte, told them: Go to your homes and as long as anyone will follow me you will be free and the fellowship you have not found you will have from now on. That is why this grove that you asked me about is called the Oak-grove of the Whisper.

Victory and blessing on you, said Eógan Leithderg to Caílte, well have you answered those two questions. But you were asked a third that is still unanswered: Why was this rath called the Little Rath of the Incantation?

One day when Finn was sitting here with the three battalions of the Fian we saw three bald young men approaching with three red dogs in their hands and three spears and venom on their weapons, their clothes, their hands, their feet, on everything they touched.

Men, where have you come from? asked Finn, and who are you?

We are the three sons of Uar mac Innaist, they replied, of the Tuatha Dé Danann. One of your people killed our father in the battle on Sliab Én, now called the Mountain of Aige mac Iugaine. We have come to request the bloodfine for our father.

You've been a long time coming for it, said Finn.

Until you came to Feis Temrach [Festival of Tara], they said, we assumed that it was Midir's sons who fought that battle. The men of Ireland knew that it was you who took hostages from the Tuatha Dé Danann for the sons of Midir in that battle.

What warrior of my people asked Finn, do you accuse of killing your father?

Caílte mac Rónaín, they replied.

By my word, said Finn, he was one of the six warriors who were with me there. What are your names?

Aincél, Digbáil, and Espaid are our names. What answer do you give us, Finn?

No one before me has given a bloodfine for a man killed in battle and I will not give one, said Finn.

We will inflict pillage and plunder on you, they said.

What plunder is that?

We are three brothers, they replied, and each of us will inflict plunder.

This is what I will do, said Aincél, whether three or two or four of the Fian happen to meet me I will take their feet and hands completely from them.

This is what I will do, said Digbáil, I will not go away for a day without depriving the Fians of Ireland of a hound, servant, or warrior.

And I, said the third, will not leave them without depriving them of a band or company, foot, hand, or an eye.

If we do not get help against them, I said, none of us will be alive at the end of the year.

Then said the Fian-chief, Fians of Ireland, make a fort and fortress here where those men met me for I will not retreat throughout Ireland before them with them following until I find out which of us is the stronger.

The Fian rose then and each leader built a little rath and fort about him and his territory from the summit of Sliab Mis as far as here.

It seems to us, said the king of Munster, that for some reason these little raths were called the Little Rath of the Healings.

That's right, said Caílte, for the three remained here for a month, a quarter, and a year inflicting every distress and destruction on the Fian. It was here that the healing of the Fian from those afflictions was performed.

At that time the three sons of the king of Iruaith who were in Finn's company came to talk with him and, taking him aside on a sod of scrutiny and prudence, said, Finn, we want to give you a circuit of our hound, that is, to let him go around you three times every day. Then although many might wish to do you harm or to plunder you they will achieve nothing from one day to the next provided there is neither fire nor weapon nor another dog in the same house with him. For it is a taboo of his to have one of these in the same house.

None of them, said Finn, will be in the same house as your dog and he will return safely to you.

So the dog was sent to Finn every day with a chain about his neck of ridged red gold in which there were fifty plates of refined gold. The dog would go round Finn three times and put his tongue on him three times. The smell that came from him when he entered Finn's house seemed to those who were closest to him like the smell from a vat of mead that had been strained and to others like the perfume of a fragrant apple-orchard. Those three committed great plundering on the Fian during that year but for every sickness and every evil that Aincél caused, Dub would apply his herbs and his medicine so that all were healthy next day. And those whom Espaid and Digbáil harmed Ág and Ilar would help and comfort.

Then, said Caílte, Cormac, grandson of Conn, was told of those enemies who were doing harm to Finn.

It is from them the wonderful proverbs are derived, namely, to those to whom harm or want comes: Aincél has visited you. To one to whom damage or want comes: Digbáil and Espaid have visited you.

It was then that a gathering was made by Cormac, grandson of Conn, king of Ireland. Twenty-eight battalions with three thousand in each came to this hill to work with Finn and the Fians of Ireland. Finn welcomed Cormac and the other nobles of the men of Ireland and told them of the great affliction which he and the Fian had suffered throughout the year except that the three sons of the king of Iruaith were helping us against them.

Why, Cormac asked, should people who have such arts not find some spell, charm, or craft that would drive the sons of Uar out of Ireland?

He told me to go for the three sons of the king of Iruaith, continued Caílte. I went and brought them. Cormac looked at them and said, The men are beautiful, their shape and appearance are good. Well, my sons, could you find a spell or charm that would remove those three enemies who are destroying the Fians?

If we had them near us, said the warriors, we would cause them to depart, driving them away from the men of Ireland.

Where, asked Finn, is Ág, son of the king of Iruaith?

Here, replied one of the warriors.

Where are those three enemies who are destroying Ireland?

They are on Dáire's Cairn, here at the end of the camp, answered Ag.

Where are Garbhcrónán and Saltrán Sálfhota? asked Finn.

We are here, Fian-chief, replied the servants.

Go to those men, said Finn. Tell them I will give what the king of Ireland awards in relation to their father.

The servants went for them to this place and gave them the message. Then they came with the messengers to Cormac and Finn. The three sat down on the dyke of this rath. Cormac was there with twenty-eight battalions and we were the three battalions of the Fian.

Cormac spoke: Arise, Dub, son of the king of Iruaith, and command them by charm or spell to leave Ireland.

Dub rose up and said, By the power of this spell and charm, leave, you three enemies, one-eyed, lame-thighed, foul-thighed, half-blind, left-handed of the race of extraordinary evil from the gravelly plains of Hell below and of the race of Buadnat, Herod's daughter, daughter of him who gave up and betrayed God and the Lord of all humans, go forth on the bitter-deep ocean and let each of you give a sword-blow on the head of each of his brothers. You have been plundering and pillaging the fair-minded royal champion, Finn mac Cumaill, long enough. Go to the original people of your father, mother, and grandfather to the gravelly hills of Hell below and may fire consume you there.

Then the dog raised his tail and sent a blast under them from his arse and off they went on the fruitful green-sided sea, and each struck a sword blow on the head of the others. So the three brothers died and went to Hell.

Caílte sang:

They went away from us
on the rough heaving sea,
each one killed another,
great their torment.

Aincél, Digbáil, and Espaid
got a sudden death,
drowned at sea, wounded,
that rough unlucky three.

Because of that spell, added Caílte, this little rath is called the Little Rath of the Incantation.

Then said Flann mac Flainn and Derg mac Dínertaig, We would like to have that spell, Caílte.

What for? asked the king of Munster.

Each of our men, said Flann mac Flainn, including us, owns eight cantreds which add up to the whole kingdom of West Munster and at the very time when we are reaping our harvest, three flocks of birds come to us from the western sea. They have beaks of bone and breaths of fire and the wind that comes from their wings is as cold as the wind of spring. When everyone wants to work in the fields they come to us. Once a year a bird attacks every ear in our cornfield and they carry it off. The second time they take away our fruit and leave neither apple on appletree nor nut on hazel nor berry on rowan. When they come the third time they leave neither fledging nor fawn on the ground nor innocent little child nor is there anything they can lift that they do not remove.

Where do they come from? asked Caílte. Or what are they or to what end do they come?

Some of us say, replied Derg, that they come from the fairy mounds, from the Tuatha Dé Danann. Others say they are a birdflock sent from Hell to do injury and harm to the men of Ireland.

Wherever they come from, said the warriors, we have to leave them our territory and land because we are no longer able to put up with them.

Then Caílte said to Patrick, Where is the lord of knowledge and calculation, that is, Saint Patrick?

Whatever you wish to ask I will answer, if I know the answer, said Patrick, for I have often put questions to you.

In what year, Caílte asked, is there a month without a moon, and a moon without a month, and a month that contains three moons?

The year of the Quartile, said Patrick, which is between two millennia, that is, a thousand years before it and a thousand after it. The first month of that year has no moon. In the following month there is a moon, but it is not a month in this case because of the month following it. The third month has three moons, the first moon of the first month which we reckoned during the question before us; and the first moon of the quarter before us of the same month that passed, and the third moon is the moon of the kalends of that month's actual time.

Victory and blessing be yours, Saint Patrick, said Caílte, a blessing came to the generation of men of Ireland the day you came amongst them. For there was a demon at the bottom of every single blade of grass before your arrival but today there is an angel at the bottom of every blade of grass. Blessing to the men of Ireland who will see you and to those who will not see you because your marvels and miracles will serve them.

But tell me, Patrick, Caílte continued, when is that Quartile year that you mentioned?'

Last night was its first night, said Patrick.

And the month that has the three moons? asked Caílte. When does that come?

It begins tomorrow night and the following day.

And when, asked Caílte, are your cornfields ripe, Derg mac Dínertaig?

We will reap tomorrow unless that ill-omened flock of birds arrives, said the warrior.

When do you expect them?

Tomorrow for sure, replied Flann mac Flainn. Tomorrow is the anniversary of the day on which Dub, son of the king of Iruaith, put a charm and spell on the three sons of Uar mac Innaist, when weapons killed them and the wave of the sea drowned the three brothers.

Why then, said Caílte, should I not give a charm and spell to Flann and Derg, the two kings of West Munster, in the name of the Trinity, unchanged and unchangeable, against the birds that come to ruin them every year?

Early next day Caílte set out with the nobles of the provinces of Munster and Patrick with them to the summit of Sliab Mis. Then the birds came to the cornfields as they used to come every year and everyone saw them and they lit on the cornfields.

And Caílte said:

> Depart, children of Rúadmael, daughter of Rugatal, of the seed of the Miller of Hell who destroys the cattle, food, gold, and silver of the world and all its many other treasures. Everything that is gathered and hoarded he casts into the mouth of his mill and makes ashes and dust of it.
>
> And go, children of Bolcán mac Nemid, the worst that is and that will be. Go, by power of this charm and spell, out to the choice blue-fronted sea so that each of you may kill the others and make dust and ashes of one another and that you may not know the just and true-judging apostle of the Gaels, Patrick, son of Calpurn, chief of the devotion and faith of the Gaels. Take yourselves to the Mountain of Witness and leave Ireland to him for it is not right that you should be there opposing him.

Then the birdflock rose in response to that charm and went out to sea and each killed the others with their beaks of bone and their breaths of fire. Wherefore Crag of the Birdflock is the name of the crag at the edge of Sliab Mis by the sea and the Spell of the Birds of the Cornfields is the name of that spell from then on.

Caílte said:

> Good my journey, vehement Derg, to reach you from afar,
> since I sent the birds away from you on the fierce stormy sea.

Then Patrick consecrated the land and the district so that neither horror nor witch nor destruction came into it from then on. The host went into the fortress and Patrick with them and were there until the end of the week, merry and relaxed, enjoying the feast. Aed mac Muiredach meic Fhinnachta was king of Connaught when that birdflock was cast out of Ireland.

Part IV

Connaught

The king of Connaught was then at the foot of Dún Leoda Loingsig, partaking of a great feast that he held. One night at the fall of evening he came out on the green grassy lawn. He was there with the nobles of his house about him when he saw to one side a gentle yellow-haired girl who looked not at the host but at the king alone. Her fashion was strange.

Where have you come from, the king asked.

From the glittering hostel in the east.

Why have you come?

You are my love, said the girl.

Whose daughter are you? said the king, and what is your name?

I am Aillenn Fhialchorcra, daughter of Bodb Derg, the Dagda's son.

Did you know, dear, that a severe lung-disease struck me as though my father and mother had given me draughts of sudden death but that the Adzehead, Saint Patrick, brought me back to life and bound me to have only one wife, Aífe Ilchrothach daughter of Eógan Leithderg, king of Leinster? Yet, on my word, said the king, never have I seen a woman I would rather have as a wife than you, were I not subject to the cleric's discipline and to fear of the King of heaven and earth. Tell me, would you like to be seen by the nobles of the province?

I would, the girl said, for I am not a fairy woman although one of the Tuatha Dé Danann. I have my own body.

The girl showed herself to the host and they never saw, before or after, a lovelier woman.

What judgement do you give me, king of Connaught? asked the girl.

Truly, said the king, I will give whatever judgement Saint Patrick will give.

The king ordered seven of his household to go to Cathair na Claenrátha in the south to the summit of Sliab Mis to get Patrick. They went there and found him. Saying farewell to the two provinces of Munster and leaving a blessing with them, Patrick and Caílte came with the two messengers to Benn Bailb, now called Benbulben in Moinmoy.

Aed, king of Connaught, came to meet him, he placed his head on Patrick's chest, knelt before him, and gave him power over the province from small to great. The king told Patrick the story of the girl.

Are you, asked Patrick, the girl who loves the king of Connaught?

I am, she replied.

It is well, said Patrick, and your appearance and shape are pleasing. What is it keeps you at the height of your form and shape?

All of us, said the girl, who drank of Goibniu's feast do not suffer pain or illness but, holy cleric, what is your judgement on the king of Connaught and me?

It has been established by God and by me, said Patrick, that a man should be bound to one wife only and we cannot go against this decision.

What am I to do? asked the girl.

You should go back to your home and fairy mound, Patrick said, and if the daughter of the king of Leinster dies before you that man you love may take you as his only wife from then on. But if, whether by day or by night, you do harm either to the king or his present wife, I will harm you so that neither your mother nor your father nor your guardian would wish to see you.

Patrick sang:

> Aillenn of the purple veil, daughter of Bodb,
> I will not heed you, proceed to your feast.
>
> Neither your knowledge of fairy friendship coming to silent Benn Bailb,
> nor your especial gifts bring you success.
>
> The gospel of powerful Christ keeping us from pain
> will be a fair sign of our protection, woman from afar.
>
> I bless this province from my reason and my sense
> that foreigners may not destroy it; that they be entirely destroyed.
>
> Do not make offerings to us, gentle good woman,
> rise, blessing on you, proceed in peace.

So it is your fixed opinion, said the girl, that I must not be given to the king while he has his wife?

That is so, answered Patrick.

In that case, said the girl, I ask you on your solemn word that I will be given to him, if the king's wife should die before me.

I promise you faithfully, said Patrick, that if she dies you will be given to him.

Then the girl wept copious tears.

I am dear to you, said the king.

Dear indeed, she replied.

There is no one in all mankind who is more loved by me than you, said the king, but I cannot bypass the conditions and rules of the Táilchenn and God.

The girl went away to her fairy mound until such time as the story again touches on her.

Patrick, Caílte, and the host remained at Benbulben for three days and three nights. Then they went to Fiadmór's Grave on the Hero's Plain, now called the Plain of Aí, where the entire host sat down. Patrick also sat so that the place is known as Patrick's Seat.

Then the king of Connaught greeted Caílte and asked, Well, Caílte, why was this place called Fiadmór's Grave and this height Circall's Hill and the hill beside it Conga's Hill?

Caílte answered these questions because he knew what they referred to.

Finn mac Cumaill had a good very loveable daughter whose name was Aí Árdúallach and Fiadmór mac Airist, king of Scotland, sought her of her father. Finn said that if she wished to marry Fiadmór he would not refuse him. So they asked the daughter who said that she would never sleep with a man outside of Ireland. Then Finn said to her, I will give you to the man you have refused, the king of Scotland.

The girl had a lover among the Fians of Ireland, Ailbe Armderg from Athlis, from the borders of Fid Gaible.

Aí said to him, Ailbe, my love, what will you do for me, with Finn giving me to the king of Scotland?

Ailbe answered, Go under the safeguard of Goll mac Morna and the Fian of Ireland so that a compulsory marriage will not be forced upon you.

The girl then bound her safeguard on the three equal families of the Fian: Clanna Morna, Clanna Baíscne, and Clanna Nemnan. She bound her safeguard also on the entire Fian and the Fian accepted.

This was the very time when Fiadmór mac Airist, king of Scotland, came to Tráig Eothaille [Ballysodare] with three great battalions. His two brothers, Circall and Conga, were with him. A message about the wife came from them to Finn, to this cairn. But the girl refused. So Fiadmór said that unless she was given to him he would declare war on the Fian. He would not leave Ireland, he said, until either his wife was given to him, dead or alive, or the head of Finn.

Then Finn said, Three of you go to the Cataract of the Birds, called Ballysodare today, and keep watch against the foreigners who are on beautiful Tráig Eothaile.

Three of the Fian obeyed that order, Diarmaid Ó Duibne, Oscar mac Oisín, and myself. When we reached the end of the strand we saw three large men approaching. The six of us met in the middle of the strand. We asked news of them and they said that the king of Scotland was there, three warriors in all, himself and his two brothers, Circall and Conga, to seek a chance of slaughter on the Fian.

By my word, I said, if you wish the Fian to suffer shame or loss you should face us, otherwise we would be as nothing in Finn's opinion.

And if, said the king of Scotland, in his opinion you are lacking, what is that to us? What do we care?

Then we fought a duel, continued Caílte, bloody, aggressive, truly venomous. Hands were quickly moved, deadly blows were struck, hearts were hardened and feet were stayed. We were engaged in conflict from the fall of evening to the next morning. Our bodies were running blood but by next morning we were the stronger in the fight and cut off the three heads.

We decided to bring the heads back with us but had to give up this plan and go against the ships on the strand. We killed three hundred warriors in the first onslaught. Then the three battalions came at us and we fought with them for the whole of that fine day until night. When they saw that their champions had fallen they fled to their ships and swift galleys and we came away badly wounded and bleeding. At that time the Fian-chief became afraid for us and said, Rise up, Fian, go after the three warriors who went away.

But just as they arose in their three joined ranks, said Caílte, we came up to them at this hill, placed the heads in front of Finn, and spoke this poem:

We three went north to join in a red-sworded fight,
we each killed a hundred on the smooth shining strand.
I, alone, noble Diarmaid, and keen lightfooted Oscar
killed three hundred of the foreign hosts in that battle.
We took the three heads with us nor was that a sad journey,
for they gave the names to the three chosen hills.
I tell you something, and what I say is true,
I got the head of Fiadmór, it is true, on the afternoon we fought.
Great our strength and our fame, great our presence and our prowess,
there was no kind of shield that we did not handle, we three.

It was I, said Caílte, who killed Fiadmór, Diarmaid who killed Circall, and Oscar who killed Conga. The three heads were placed on those hills and so they have their names while the Battle of Tráig Eothaile is the name of the battle in the history of the Fian.

Victory and blessing, Caílte, said the king of Connaught, if you wish for jewels and fine things we would give them to you.

You are all the better for making that offer, Caílte replied, but I do not want them.

Then the host came to Breicshliab that is Sliab Formaile in Connaught, now called Slieveformoyle and to Finn's Seat on the top of the mountain. While they were sitting there, Caílte wept copious tears that wet his beard, looking at the place where Finn mac Cumaill used to sit.

What makes you weep? asked the king of Connaught, is it because you look at the place where Finn used to sit, Formoyle of the Fian?

It is indeed, said Caílte, for this mountain was the favourite hunting-place of the Fian, the Lake of the Does, now called Formoyle Lake, and the Meadow of Stags, now called Cell Tulach, which was Conán Mael mac Mórna's place; and the Wood of the Horse-Team, now called the Place, where some of the Fian horses were kept; to the Fort of Saltrán Sálfhota, now known as Cell Chaimín on the river Suck; then to the Moor of Staying, now known as the Moor of the Causeway of Conned; and finally to the Rock of the Pirate, now called Dunmore.

The king of Connaught asked Caílte, Where was Finn mac Cumaill from?

From Leinster.

From what people?

The Uí Tairsig, answered Caílte.

From what place?

Glas Bolcáin. He was Finn mac Cumaill mac Trénmóir meic Cairbre Garbshrón meic Fiacha Fobreach of the Uí Fhailge.

Where did his mother come from? asked the king.

She was Muirne Muinchaem, daughter of Tadg mac Nuadat, of the Tuatha Dé Danann. He had the most generous hand for jewels, treasures, and wealth in the northwest of the world. He was one of the five best warriors that ever carried shield and sword, the best in the world at giving jewels and wages, one of the three best men that ever came from the island of Ireland. He never refused anyone who had a head to eat and legs to carry him nor did he ever turn and look behind him so that no one could say in the end that he was moved by fear. And this, said Caílte, was the favourite hunting place of the Fian.

What were the usual names in the Fian? asked the king of Connaught.

Finn mac Cumaill was the leading man, Caílte answered. Finn mac Casurla, the Fian-chief of the Fian of Brega and Mide; Oisín with his four sons: Oscar, Oisín, Échtach, and Ulach; Raigne Rosclethan; Caince Corcairderg mac Finn; Uillenn Faebuderg mac Finn; Faelán Feramail mac Finn and Aed Bec mac Finn; Finn Mór mac Cúáin meic Murchada, chief leader of the Munster Fian; Finn mac Temenain, chief of the Fian in the Munster Décies; Finn mac Urgna, chief of the Tirconnell Fian; Finn mac Fogaeth and Finn mac Abratruad, the two chiefs of the Fian of Dál nAraide in the north; Finn Bán, grandson of Bresal, chief of the Fian in Uí Chennselaigh; Finn Fer in Champair, Fian-chief of Scotland; Goll Guban and Cas Cuailnge, the two Fian-chiefs of Ulster; Degóc's three sons, Fead, Faeth, and Foscad; Aencherda Bérra's three sons, Glas, Ger, and Guba; Caílte mac Rónaín and his two sons, Faelán and Colla; Goth Gaíthe mac Rónaín, who when he wanted to show his running ability was a javelin cast before all the Fian; Lergan Luath from Luachair in the west who would bring in the wild deer as another would bring home his own cattle; Diarmaid Ó Duibne of the men of Munster who never had weariness of foot nor shortness of breath nor weariness of plain or house; Mac Lugach, very strong, foremost young man of the Fian of Ireland and Scotland, the exemplary fighting-man in all the Fian story; Bran Bec, grandson of Buadachán, chief steward of the Fian of Ireland and Scotland; Scannal, descendant of Liathán, chief of the servants of Ireland and Scotland; Scíathbrec mac Dathcháin, outstanding at games; Goll Mór mac Morna with his thirty brothers and fifteen hundred sons; three musicians from the borders of the flowery-soiled Fews in the north with their three instruments which they played facing one another and those who heard the music were never again afflicted by distress or difficulty.

What were the names of those men? asked the king of Connaught.

Luath, Léitmech, and Lánláitir, Caílte replied, members of the regular Fian. Those were the names of the chiefs, leaders, and men of territory whom Finn had. They attended and supplied him in his own fort three times every year and sounded the chant of the Fian.

These then, king of Connaught, are the questions you asked.

Caílte fell onto the hill in a swoon and a weakness and for three days and three nights was unable to travel or to leave, as he grieved for his comrades and companions. Therefore the king of Connaught made camp and bathed Caílte.

The host then came to the Meadow of Stags, now called the Meadow of Shame, where they camped. Patrick blessed the place and the king of Connaught asked Caílte, Why is this place called the Meadow of Stags and why is this plain called the Meadow of Shame?

Caílte replied, Finn and the three battalions of the Fian used to receive the fruits of the hunt there, a deer to every two of the Fian and three deer to Finn and that is why the place was called the Meadow of Stags. But the Meadow of Shame was given to it for this reason. Clanna Morna were plundering Finn but one time they were so taken up with their meal and the helpings in front of them they did not notice until we, the three battalions of the Fian, came and surrounded them on this ridge.

Then Goll mac Morna said, These men have caused us great shame. May it be called the Meadow of Shame from now on.

From then on it was called the Meadow of Shame.

But we must not make a secret of the worth of the Clanna Morna for they broke out strongly in close formation through the battalions of the Fian. We did not draw blood on them or make even a light reddening. Here we sat down by their fires. A basin of pale gold was brought to Finn with water in it. He washed his face and his hands and put his thumb underneath the tooth of wisdom. The truth was revealed to him and he prophesied that saints and good men would come here.

Finn said:

> A peaceful church will rise on the lake's ridge,
> though a place of king-people before this.
> Honour will come to the Meadow of Shame,
> before the end of the world.

The host came west to the Meadow of the Chariot in Breicthír, now called Firchuing. Patrick's chariot broke down. The saint sat down on the mound of sods when the axle had broken. They were not long there when they saw a chariot approaching with a servant in it. Each of his cheeks was as red as valerian, each of his eyes blue as a hyacinth, every limb of his body was white, and the shaggy cloak about him was black as coal. He came towards them.

Charioteer, said Benignus, would you be able to help Saint Patrick?

Who is he? asked the youth.

Patrick mac Calpuirn, head of faith and devotion among the men of Ireland.

The young man got out of the chariot, placed his head on Patrick's chest, and said, This chariot is not given to breaking down. It is all for Patrick.

Undivided grace on you, your son, and your grandson. What is your name? asked Patrick.

I am Dub mac Muirgissa meic Tomaltaig.

It is true, said Benignus, for he is very black.

On my word, said Patrick, because of your helpful service the name of your race and seed forever will be Rodub's descendants.

The service of our family, both living and dead, to you, said the youth.

More than that, said Patrick. At the end of a hundred years from today your living and dead will belong to me and to God forever.

Patrick said:

> Rodub of Roduib, your people will have much grace from now on,
> one of the three gifted families of great-hosted Connaught.
> Clanna Rodub of great wealth will be here after the slaughter,
> they will receive a fair burial at Fore and at Cruachán.
> I leave them this place, a gift of abbots and of poets,
> well known for housekeeping, well known for mind and advice.
> I tell you about it now, and what I say is true,
> All of this favours men descended from Rodub.

It is my wish, said Patrick, that the outcome of every decree and every covenant concerning one of your race is to be made in his favour provided it is just. For you have given the chariot to me with affection.

Before long they saw another chariot approaching, drawn by two well-matched horses. In it was a blood-red woman with a red cloak fastened by a golden brooch and a frontlet of yellow gold on her forehead. She descended from the chariot, placed her head on Patrick's chest, and knelt before him.

Who are you? Patrick asked.

I am Aífe Derg, daughter of Conall Costadach, king of Connaught, she replied. I have much wealth and treasure and I have come to talk with you as to what man I should marry since you are the best man in Ireland.

There he is, said Patrick, to one side of you.

Who is he?

Dub mac Roduib.

What bride-price and gift does he have for me? she asked.

What bride-price do you require?

That I should be the only wife to him who marries me, she replied, for I do not think it right that he should leave me.

Young man, asked Patrick, do you accept that?

I accept, he replied, whatever you tell me to do.

In that case, said Patrick, marry the woman and let your children and your family be from her and grant her that condition.

So he married her on Patrick's advice.

But, said the woman, we have no land at present and that is a pity.

Where is the king of Connaught? asked Patrick.

I am here, holy cleric, he answered.

For my sake, said Patrick, give land to this pair who came to me for advice.

The cantred of land, said the king, which belongs to him will belong to both of them equally.

So they parted from him.

That night the host came to the Gap of the Dogs. The king of that country was Tigernach mac Cuinn Chumachtaig. When he heard the host approaching, he was seized by meanness and niggardliness and, leaving his land and his territory, fled from Patrick and the king of Connaught.

Hearing of this, Patrick said, I pray to God that the rule of another sept be over them forever.

Then the host sat down on the two raths that were there, one half of the host on each rath. The king of Connaught asked Caílte, What are these two raths on which we are?

Two of Finn mac Cumaill's favourite warriors lived in them, Conall Coscarach and Cobthach Cass, two sons of the king of Tirconnell in the north, two heroes and fighters and two defenders of a gap of hundreds. They had fixed enemies, Clanna Morna. The cause of their enmity was as follows: Finn and the Fian of Ireland held a hunt on Sliab Gam and Conán Mael mac Morna and his men happened to be hunting on the same day. He was the troublemaker in his household, the quarrelsome one of the council, and the contentious one of the assembly. He never sought justice from any one and he cursed the man who gave him justice and because of Conán Mael's curse the entire Clanna Morna died and disappeared. When they raised a fierce savage stag there, Conán cast his spear. The two sons of the king of Tirconnell also cast spears at the stag so that they went right through him.

Conán said, Let the deer go.

We will not, they said.

You have not killed him more than me, said Conán, and I wounded him first.

On our word, said the men, even though you wounded him he will not be given up to you. Instead we will do what Finn decides.

But Conán replied, cursing: Curse him who will give me justice. I do not give it to anyone.

Then Conall raised his hand and struck Conán a blow with the shaft of his spear, leaving a lump and a mark on him as thick as the shaft of the spear. Then the bulk of the Fian came between them and intervened. Conán, however, neither showed grudge nor made reproach until the Clanna Morna began to plunder and pillage Finn. They were killing his foster sons and his beloved ones and they came to Forba na Fer, now called Lenna in Baili.

Then Conán said to Goll, Do you know, Goll, Fian-chief, that the son of the king of Tirconnell gave me the blow of a spearshaft during the hunt of Sliab Gam? Tonight I want to go and take vengeance on them for that.

On our word, said Goll, we would not want a friend of ours to fight them for they have the grunting of a single's sow's litter.

I will attack them with four hundred warriors, said Conán.

He and two sons of his brothers, Taman and Trén, got up and came to this place in the middle of the day with the four hundred warriors. But four hundred then attacked them and Taman and Trén fell at once by the two sons of the king of Tirconnell. No one escaped to tell the tale or earn the wage, except Conán alone with the sling of his shield around his neck. He went back to where his brothers were.

Conán, this is a bad journey, said the brothers. We have fallen because of you, as have the two sons of our brothers, and the four hundred who marched with you.

So, Caílte continued, those eight hundred warriors were buried here and their gravestones raised above their graves with their names inscribed on them in ogham.

Caílte sang:

> Raths of Conall and Cobthach Cass under the green grassy hill,
> there they are from that to this in the hill dwelling.
> The graves of Ailbe and Étaín facing Atha Immeal,
> they died in great grief, at the same time from a bad illness.
> Great war, great battle, great strength, a great host that did us damage,
> it breaks the heart in my breast, looking at these raths.

You have told us great knowledge and true wisdom, Caílte, said the king of Connaught.

Then the entire host and Patrick continued westward to the Witches' Thicket, now called Patrick's Well. The king of the country, Conn Cumachtach, came to see Patrick.

Tell us, said Caílte, why this is called the Witches' Thicket?

Nine women were practising witchcraft, said the king. They did not allow either woman or man to go away without killing them. For twenty years they have been destroying the heritage and the land.

Conn then said to Patrick, Holy cleric, drive these witches away from us and the distress that is ruining the country and the earth.

Then Patrick said, Where is the acolyte?

I am here, he replied.

See if there is water near us.

I see none here.

Then Patrick raised his hand and stuck his staff into the ground from which a clear bright well broke out. Patrick blessed the water:

> 'The water we have here', said sinless Patrick,
> 'will be famous for all, this well of shining water.'

I grant, said Patrick, protection for three days and three nights and help and assistance in every distress for anyone who drinks from it.

They were not long there before they saw the nine dark repulsive witches approaching them. If the dead were accustomed to rise from the ground they would have uttered such shrieks as these made on all sides. Patrick took the holy water and sprinkled it on the witches and they fled from him until they reached the Island of Tears, now called the Isle of the Shrine, in Loch Carra. There they heard their wailing at the end.

The host sat down afterwards on the mound of sods and then the king of Connaught said, You have given the demons a good cleric's hunting.

Caílte said to Patrick, Do you know about the bad luck I suffered in the troop-battle of Benn Étair?

What bad luck was that?

Maine, son of the king of Lochlann, had a deadly spear. No one struck by it escaped death or injury. There were a hundred brave warriors fighting against me and I was in the vanguard of the fight when, unnoticed by me, Maine aimed a cast at me in the middle of the battle. I did not know where the cast had come from but hearing the rushing sound of the spear as it came towards me, I lifted my shield to protect head and body. But this did not save me. The spear struck below the calf and sinew of my leg and left its poison so that I have to go for help and assistance.

Where do you want to go? asked Patrick.

Northward to Aed Mindbrec of Assaroe, said Caílte, for he has a wife, Bé Binn, daughter of Elcmar of the Bruig, and she has the healing and curative drink of the Tuatha Dé Danann. She has all that remains of Goibniu's ale and she distributes it. My knowledge and my road would be short, if Finn mac Cumaill, Oisín, Diarmaid, and Oscar were alive.

Caílte spoke this lay:

> A sure way be mine on this road north to the Falls of Modarn of the great host,
> to have my leg healed so that my term may be the longer.
> I am Caílte in distress, only son of bright gentle Eithne,
> I put the great host under stress, they learned my prowess.
> Alas without Oisín, without Finn, and without Diarmaid whom I remember,
> without greatly distinguised Oscar may my way still be sure.

Where is Cas Corach mac Caincinne? asked Caílte.

I am here.

Rise up and bring your lute so that we may make our way.

They arose and a paternoster was said for them.

Patrick spoke to Caílte, At the end of the year there will be an assembly of the men of Ireland at Tara. Come to meet us there so that you can tell some of your great brave deeds and the deeds of Finn and the Fians of Ireland.

Caílte agreed to this and said, I will do everything I promised.

It is right you should say that for you are dear and loveable to me, answered Patrick.

Then Caílte said farewell to Patrick, the king of Connaught, and the whole host and they went on to the fairy mound of Druim Nemed, now called the fairy mound of Síd Duma, in Leyny in Connaught.

When they reached the green of the fairy mound they saw a young man in a green cloak with a pin of gold in it and on his head a golden diadem. He was singing a sweet song. Cas Corach mac Caincinne came and the young man kissed him three times.

What is the reason for your affection, Caílte asked, for we have not known of it before this?

Good reason, replied the young man, we have the same mother.

What is your name? asked Caílte.

My name is Fer Maise mac Eogabáil, he answered.

It is not an inappropriate name for your beauty justifies it.

Come into the house, he said.

I will not go, said Caílte, until you get permission from the people of the fairy mound lest they blame you for my intrusion.

The young man went into the fairy mound and reported this to Fergus Foltfhind, the son of the Dagda.

Go out, they replied, and bring them in for we have never heard of a warrior's son in his time who was better than Caílte.

They were brought into the mound, were well entertained with all the best they had and stayed there for the night.

Well, my friend, said Fergus, the Dagda's son, I have the hilt of a sword that I want you to fix for the Tuatha Dé Danann have refused to do so.

Give it to me, said Caílte.

The sword was given to him and for the whole of that fine day until night he was working at it. He finished by night and gave it complete into Fergus's hand.

Caílte, Fergus asked, do you know our real reason for repairing that sword?

I do not, replied Caílte.

There is a warrior who has been an enemy of the Tuatha Dé Danann for a long time, namely, Garb mac Tairb, king of Lochlann. He and Eolus, his brother, come to us every third year with a great fleet. They have with them a woman warrior called Bé Drecain, daughter of Iruath. Nothing can be concealed from her from fairy mound to fairy mound of the Tuatha Dé Danann. She was fostered by a woman of dark magic with the result that there were no jewels or wealth or valuables in the mounds that she did not succeed in carrying away as a result of her knowledge. She brings a host to the middle of every fairy mound of the Tuatha Dé Danann to sack and plunder them. See that spear in your hand, he said, fit it against that woman-warrior.

He put the spear into Caílte's hand and he fitted it.

See, Fergus said, the barbed javelin in your hand? Fit it against another of that three.

Caílte took the shaft and it broke in its socket. Seven shafts were brought to him and they also broke in the socket. But the eighth shaft they gave him he fitted strongly and skilfully.

Happy he would be, said Fergus, who could get a friend to ensure that the three against whom these weapons were made would fall by them.

What are the names of these weapons? asked Caílte.

Gore-maker is the name of the sword, War Woman is the name of the spear, and Death Drink the name of the javelin.

It used to be my fate, said Caílte, to do some deed for which the men of Ireland and Scotland and the Tuatha Dé Danann would be grateful. I have not done so since I was young. Who knows but I am fated to do it today?

Who will fall by the sword? asked Cas Corach.

The woman-warrior, answered Fergus.

Who will fall by the javelin? asked Fer Maise.

One of the two kings of the world, a king of Lochlann or of Ireland, said Fergus, son of the Dagda.

Who will fall by the spear? asked Caílte.

Garb mac Tairb, king of Lochlann. The Tuatha Dé Danann have a prophecy that he will fall by it, answered Fergus.

Let me have the spear in my hand, said Caílte.

They remained there for three days and three nights.

Then they said goodbye to the people of the fairy mound and brought those weapons with them. Fer Maise went with them and they proceeded to the Falls of the Birds, now called Ballysodare; on to the Bridge of the Nine, now called the Bridge of Slaughter; northward to Druim Derg of the Fian, now called Druim Cliab [Drumcliff]; over the Ford of the Grey Stag to Cailli in Chosnuma, now called Buadnatan's Church; to the Grave of the Hero where the magic pig killed Diarmaid Ó Duibne; northward to the Plain of Céitine mac Allguba where the Fomorians used to collect their tribute from the men of Ireland; and up to Coiscéim of Assaroe; and to the Height of the Boys where the boys of the Tuatha Dé Danann used to play hurley.

Aed of Assaroe and Ilbrec of Assaroe were in front of the fairy mound. They welcomed Caílte without guile or deceit.

We are pleased with this welcome, said Caílte.

Then Bé Binn, daughter of Elcmar of the Bruig, came out with one hundred and fifty fair women. She sat on the grassy mound and in a loving and fervent manner kissed each of the two, Cas Corach mac Caincinne and Fer Maise mac Eogabáil. The people of the fairy mound welcomed Caílte and the others.

Your friendship would be bad, they said, if you heard that we were in great necessity and did not come to help us.

I was not asked here, said Cas Corach, because of my prowess but when you think it appropriate and desirable for me to demonstrate my skill I will do so.

We have not come here at all, said Fer Maise, for our military skills but we will help you when you need it.

Then Caílte told the people of the fairy mound of his errand and his journey.

We will cure you well, they said.

All entered the mound and remained there for three days and three nights feasting and enjoying themselves.

A man came to the door and said that the harbour was full of ships and boats and that a large army had landed on the strand.

That, said Caílte, cannot be counted:

> In all a thousand ships have arrived
> Scythe-heads and longships at the end of the strand.

Caílte, royal Fian, they asked, what should we do now?

You should ask them for a truce, said Caílte, until the Tuatha Dé Danann can assemble and muster.

They did that. The Tuatha Dé Danann assembled with the result that next day there were twelve battalions on the green of the fairy mound. Envoys came from the ships.

Let the Tuatha Dé Danann give us hostages, they said.

How can we do that, Caílte? asked the people of the fairy mound and the chiefs of the Tuatha Dé Danann.

Let us send our twelve battalions to the end of the strand to observe them, Caílte replied.

The twelve battalions moved out.

Have any of you got a crystal chariot?

I have, said Midir, yellow-haired son of the Dagda.

It was brought to Caílte. The strangers arranged a fence of shields about them. Placing his left knee against the chariot, putting his brave finger into the thong of the spear, Caílte made a cast at the king of Lochlann so that the spear went straight through and miserably broke his back in two.

Caílte said:

> Garb was killed at first in the van of his host;
> Caílte killed him fiercely by a cruel fatal shot.

Then his people carried Garb into his ship and the army said, The man has done a great deed, killing the best in the world with a single cast.

So the name of the strand after that was Garb's Strand.

Then the warrior-woman said to the host, Board your ships and I myself will face the Tuatha Dé Danann. Then Cas Corach asked the Tuatha Dé Danann, Have you a hard strong shield for me?

I have one, said Donn mac Midir.

Give it to me, said Cas Corach.

The shield was given to him. He took the sword in his hand and immediately came straight to where the woman-warrior watched and warded the strangers.

What are you? she asked.

I'm here to fight with you.

Never until this day, she said, have I been matched only with one man, or even two. Furthermore I have often filled a brave host with fear. As for you, young man, seeing that you have come to fight me, it is certain that you have not been able to find room anywhere else in the world.

They fought a bloody, aggressive, skilful fight, inflicting on each other thirty great wounds that needed the doctor's attention. But the young man got round her with speed and determination, struck her with deadly blows and with a stroke that got past the rim of her shield, cut off her head. He took it with him to the Tuatha Dé Danann.

Caílte spoke:

> Cas Corach of the Hundreds has killed
> the woman, without boasting,
> has left her on the strand,
> washed by the sea's foam.

The host of Lochlann said, You have done a great deed, young man, killing in front of us our champion who used to help us in all our dangers.

Then they inaugurated Eolus, the late king's brother, and came ashore to challenge the Tuatha Dé Danann who said, We accept for we find it more and more easy to fight them.

Early next morning before any one of the host had risen Fer Maise mac Eogabáil got up and took hold of the pronged javelin, so-called because it had five prongs on each side and both edges ornamented with sickle-shaped barbs, every one of which would cut a hair against the stream.

My gods, he said, what kind of man is Eolus?

The most shapely warrior and the finest form in all the world of men, said the man who was with him.

Do not go away from me, said Fer Maise, keep on teaching me knowledge.

After that Eolus put on his battle-garb, seized his weapons, and walked up the ship's gangway.

Young man, that is he, the man said, the man you asked me to point out to you: with a diadem of gold on his head. He carries a red shield and wears a green suit of mail.

Then Fer Maise fixed his foot in a secure position on the ground, put his finger into the thong of the javelin and made a cast at the other that struck the rim of the shield and went through it. It broke his back and, driving his heart out through his mouth in a dark flood of blood, the point of the spear went right through him and lodged in the ship's bulwark.

Caílte said:

The best son fell, Eolus, most dear,
he was left in the wave, a light frigid bed.
That is the story of the strand, although never told,
the loss of a northern host, from proud Lochlann.

But when the host saw those three falling they said they would not continue to fight against the Tuatha Dé Danann and went away to their own land.

Then Caílte said:

Happy those in the fairy mound,
free from tribute over the sea,
escaped from the twisted battle,
without loss, without hurt.

The fall of those three was celebrated throughout Ireland. The Tuatha Dé Danann and the men of Ireland regarded it as a wonderful event that those that had come every seventh year to plunder and pillage them had fallen by these other three.

Where is Eógan, the seer? asked Caílte.

Here I am, said Eógan.

Bring me truth and knowledge about my life for I am a decrepit old man. My end must be near.

Caílte said:

Tell me, seer Eógan, when will Caílte come to the mound?
What life remains to me before I pass over?

Eógan said:

Seventeen years from today, Caílte, of fine fame,
until you fall at Tara's pool, sad for that household.

Victory and blessing on you, Eógan, said Caílte, this prophecy is the same as that made by my lord and chief, Finn, the gentle loving friend.

What length of life, they asked, does Eógan prophesy you will have?

Seventeen years, Caílte replied.

That will be true, they said, for he has never said that someone would have a given life-time but it has happened. For many years he has told us that those three would fall by you with these weapons.

Caílte said:

> I say this to you and what I say is true
> what red Eógan said is not hidden from the host.

People of the fairy mound, it is well, said Caílte to cure and heal me, the reason I came to you. I have given you the fee for my healing. The greatest benefit that was ever done for you I have done it.

It is true what you have done for us, they said. We will change your shape so that you will have agility, full activity, and chief command of young men in the Tuatha Dé Danann.

That, Caílte said, would be pitiful, to take the shape through magic. I will not take any shape except that which my Maker and Creator, the good God, has given me and what the Táilchenn bestows on me in faith and devotion.

The Tuatha Dé Danann said, That is the voice of a true warrior and man of action. What you say is good and we ask for a delay in healing you.

What is the reason for that delay? asked Caílte.

Three ravens from the north that come to us every year and when the boys of the fairy mound are playing the ravens descend on them and carry off one each.

Ilbrec said:

> The three from overseas face the boys at play;
> take three from the field, three horrible disasters.

That is the reason for the delay, Caílte, said the people of the fairy mound.

They remained there for the night until day was come with its full light. Then all the Tuatha Dé Danann went to see the hurling. Every sixth man was given a chess-board, every five a backgammon board, every twenty a lute, every hundred a harp, and every nine shrill dominant flutes. At that time they saw three ravens coming in from the sea to the north. They landed on the sacred tree in the field and gave three harsh gloomy cries. If it were customary for the dead to be raised from the earth or hair taken from human heads those screeches would have done both. They drove the host demented. Cas Corach mac Caincinne took one of the chessmen and cast it at a bird. It entered its mouth and throat and killed him. Fer Maise mac Eogabáil fired at another one and killed it while Caílte cast at the third and killed it.

Caílte said:

> Cas Corach and Fer Maise killed two birds with true shots;
> with skilled hand Caílte killed the third bird on the wing.

All the birds died in this manner.

Caílte said, The birds are destroyed, now make my cure.

But the people of the fairy mound said, Do you not know, Caílte, that the Tuatha Dé Danann have been suffering for a long time.

What suffering is that?

The three sons of the king of Ulster – Conn, Congal, and Colla – have been plundering them, said Ilbrec.

Caílte sang:

> Conn, Congal, and Colla, three unfairly matched,
> travel a great harsh field driven by their grandfather.
> They come at us every year to destroy our rule,
> kill three of our people each time in unequal contest.
> I tell you how it is and what I say is true,
> they will be surrounded, sons of Ulster's king will be scarce.

Those three come to us every year, said Ilbrec, asking for a bloodfine for Eochaid Muinderg, king of Ulster, their grandfather, whom the Tuatha Dé Danann killed in the battle of Baile's Strand. Every year they demand from a fairy mound in Ireland a set combat of three, an unequal contest, for the three of us who are told to take part are killed while the three brothers survive. This year the fight falls to the people of our fairy mound.

After their annual plundering and pillaging of the Tuatha Dé Danann the three sons of the king of Ulster were living in the Mountains of Mourne in the province of Ulster.

One of the sons said, What fairy mound will we attack this year?

The fairy mound of Ilbrec of Assaroe, one of the brothers answered.

But there is a warrior of Finn mac Cumaill's people in the mound with two others whom it would be well to avoid whether they are prepared to fight or are taken by surprise. But if we avoid this mound they will declare it is because we are unwilling to face them on any terms.

The three stayed where they were that night, then they looked to their arms and various edged weapons and early next morning came to Assaroe. The fairy people, Caílte, and his two companions came out onto the green.

Caílte inquired, Are those the three who come to attack you?

They are, the fairy people replied. The men's bodily shape and their equipment are both good.

Caílte said:

> Conn, Congal, and Colla, a fine handsome trio,
> will get a fair contest when they enter the fight.

How long are you fighting against the Tuatha Dé Danann? asked Caílte.

We are at it for a hundred years and every year kill three of them, they replied.

If that is the case, Caílte said, you have avenged your grandfather on them three times over and, if you fight here, you yourselves will fall, for it is you who have an unjust cause.

We will pay you the fine, said Ilbrec.

Out of every fairy mound in Ireland, twenty ounces of gold, twenty ounces of silver, and each side to go free of the other.

Ilbrec said:

> Twenty ounces from each mound for the three equal deeds,
> to be theirs without an affray, a blood-fine for their grandfather.

The brothers said, We will accept that.

It was given to them and they went away taking the blood-fine for their grandfather with them.

Let my cure be done now, said Caílte, for I think it is time.

Where is Bé Binn, daughter of Elcmar? Ilbrec asked.

I am here, the girl replied.

Good daughter, he said, bring Caílte mac Rónaín to some hidden place and see to it that he is cured and looked after since he has turned away plunder and destruction from the Tuatha Dé Danann and from all of Ireland. Have Cas Corach play music and minstrelsy for him and Fer Maise mac Eogabáil keep watch and ward over him and tend to his needs.

Bé Binn and her two sons went to the house of arms where a fine bed was prepared for Caílte's healing and a basin of white gold full of water was brought to the woman.

Taking hold of a crystal pail she put some herbs into it. She broke them into small pieces over the water, gave the pail to Caílte, and he drank a great draught. When he drank the water, he vomited a greenish bile.

Woman, said Caílte, what herb do you have in that?

It is made into a drink from a deadly wind from the waterfall, rivers, inlets and early hunting, said the woman.

Caílte drank and vomited a gush of gory red stuff.

What is that vomit? he asked.

The deadly vomit of spears and javelins that you received in battle and the contests you were ever in.

He took another drink and vomited a jet-black gush.

What caused that vomit?

Grief for your comrades, your foster-brothers, your chief and leader, Finn mac Cumaill.

She gave him another drink, the fourth, and he vomited a yellow substance after it.

What was that gush?

Retention and blood of the poison and deadly pang that you received abroad. I made it into a drink of milk for you, said the woman.

It is a cure for me, said Caílte, for I never found in battle or from a sword anything equal to it that I found more difficult to drink.

She gave him another drink and he vomited a many-coloured gush.

What was that vomit?

A mixture of every race, every strength, and every single feat that you made in a hundred fights and every hill, every rock, and every colour of blood from their upper bodies, a gory bed for their bodies, and your own sleep and they the source of your health.

The woman gave him a can of new milk which he drank but as a result of all that vomiting he was weak and unwell for three days and three nights.

It seems to me, Caílte, said the woman, that you have found relief and comfort.

I have indeed, said Caílte, but the amount of trouble in my head bothers me.

We will give you the washing of Flann, daughter of Flidaisse, said Bé Binn, daughter of Elcmar. Any head that receives it is not affected by pain or baldness or any loss of sight.

They gave him that treatment for a while thereafter.

The people of the fairy mound divided themselves into three to visit and entertain him, one third from their great nobles, a third from their young men and a third from their women, and poets of wisdom and leisure for the period when he would be on his bed of recovery, be it long or short. The people of the fairies also gave Caílte all the special fruits of the hunt or the chase that they secured.

After that the woman, her two sons, Cas Corach and Fer Maise mac Eogabáil, feasted and enjoyed themselves with Caílte.

Before long they heard a sound and strain of such music coming towards them from Assaroe of mac Modairn that anyone would leave the music of the world for the sake of that music. When they heard it they put their harps at the corners of the couches and all came out to listen to the music, much to Caílte's amazement.

He kept it carefully in mind that he was without his agility, handling, and full strength and he said, Great fierce fights and hard conflicts have I gone into, have been at the forefront of battles but today I have not the strength or vigour to go out with the others. Tears fell down his beard.

When the fairy host who had listened to the music outside came back, Caílte sought information from them, saying, What caused the sound of music that we heard?

Uaine Buide from the fairy mound of Dorn Buide of Clídna's Wave in the south and with her the birds of the Land of Promise. She is the woman-minstrel of the whole Land of Promise and this year it is her turn to visit this fairy mound. Every year she chooses a particular mound, this year it is ours.

They came into the mound and all the birds came and sat on the corners and couches. Thirty of them went into the house of arms where Caílte was and began to sing. Cas Corach took hold of his lute and the birds accompanied him in every tune he played.

We have heard a great deal of music, Caílte said, but we have not heard music as good as that.

Then they gave him the washing of Flann, daughter of Flidaisse, with the result that as long as he lived he never suffered from loss of sight, hearing, or hair; he was without scars and whole in body as a result of the healing he received inside the fairy mound.

Caílte said, The reason and cause of my coming, the healing of my foot, let it be done now.

It will be done tomorrow morning, said the woman.

At that time she brought two tubes of Binne, the daughter of Modarn, to Caílte. A woman slave sucked on one tube, a man-slave on the other tube and did not leave in his foot disease, ill-health, or clotted gore that they did not bring out and he was whole in body afterwards. He and his followers remained there for three days and three nights after that healing.

The people of the fairy mound went out to Assaroe. They removed their clothes, went into the waterfall, and began to swim.

Caílte said, Why should I not swim since my health has been restored?

He began to enjoy himself in the water. They then went back into the fairy mound and that night a feasting house was prepared for them. Caílte thanked them for curing him and said, I am whole in body. My blessing on you.

Caílte sang:

> A blessing on the people of the fairy mound, both king and queen,
> health and happiness to the curly-headed band, I have experienced their valour
> My trip to the mound was good, I got there mead and wine,
> excellent men and women there, and sweet song of the birds.
> My trip to the mound was good, I got welcome and healing,
> excellent their men and nobles, and their many-coloured clothes.

My blessing on Bé Binn, daughter of pleasant Elcmar,
excellent her shape, her mind and her advice.
I tell you something, and it is the truth I speak,
although I go away for good, I leave you my blessing.

On our word, said the people of the fairy mound, we have never seen a warrior better than you on the face of the earth, in our opinion Finn himself was not better.

Alas, said Caílte, if you saw Finn you would give up the entire human race and not even mention them. I must leave. Blessing on the people of the mound. The men of Ireland agreed to meet at Tara at the end of a year and I must go there to talk with my comrade and foster-brother Oisín mac Finn. In addition, the Táilchenn has bidden me be there when the nobles of Ireland will be assembled in the one place to relate the great deeds of courage and heroism in arms of the Fian, Finn mac Cumaill, and the other good men of Ireland so that the full story may be redressed and related by poets and writers to the end of time.

We are able to help you, said the girl.

What help is that?

We will bring you at Tara a drink of remembrance so that no waterfall, river, estuary battle or single combat but you will remember.

That is the aid of friends and true kinsmen, said Caílte, and should we have anything you might want I would give it to you.

This is a great favour you have given us, said the girl, for you have saved the Tuatha Dé Danann from the crowd that have plundered and pillaged us every seventh year. I have a ribbed shirt of golden thread for you and while you wear it you will suffer no violation. Also a fringed crimson cloak made of wool from the Land of Promise with a fringe of yellow gold all about it. He who wears it will be the great beauty at all meetings and gatherings. I also have a gift particularly suited for an old man, a fish-hook called Aicill mac Moga, and if you cast it in any waterfall or river you will surely catch something.

What will you do, Fer Maise mac Eogabáil? asked Caílte.

I will remain in this fairy mound, he replied, until the Feis Temrach is held and will bring there all the things that Bé Binn has promised you.

And what will you do, Cas Corach?

I will go with you, replied Cas Corach, to learn knowledge and wisdom until such time as the men of Ireland disperse at Tara.

Then they said goodbye to the people of the fairies and came out to the Hill of the Cry where the people of the fairies made great outcry at being parted from Caílte. It has been called the Hill of the Cry from that day until now.

Caílte spoke: I will not come back to this place from this day until the Day of Judgment.

They came to the Falls of the Kin-Slaying, now called the Falls of Cronán mac Bailb. Once there were seven brothers there. They had a falling out about the Falls and each one killed another with the result that the Falls have been named after them. Their father, Cronán mac Bailb, lived after them and used to lament for his sons here. His heart broke in the middle of the night. From him comes the name the Falls of Cronán.

They were not there long when the clouds of the end of the day arrived. They went from the falls and and saw a big man waiting for them on a hill. They sat down beside him.

Where are you from? he asked.

They told him their names, their family names, and their story.

And who are you? they asked.

I am Blathmac Bóaire, he replied from the borders of Sliab Lug [Slievelowe], from Cúil Radairc, called Cúil Ó bFinn [Coolavin] today.

We would like you to entertain us this night, said Caílte.

As it happened that man excelled all the men in Ireland for inhospitality and niggardliness.

Therefore he said, If you give me a price I will give you service and sustenance for tonight.

What price is that?

There are three standing stones near my place, known as the standing Stones of the Three Men but we do not know why they are called that.

I have it for you, said Caílte, for I remember it. Once there was a good warrior in the Fian of Ireland, Finn Bán, grandson of Bresal, who was also of the Clanna Baíscne and he had three beautiful daughters. Only three in the Clanna Baíscne were his equal: Finn mac Cumaill, Oisín, and Oscar. Finn Bán's three daughters had three perfections of their own to match those of the men: in embroidery and all other skilled handiwork they excelled all the women of Ireland and in the entire island there were no women of finer shape. Everyone who came to the Fair at Teltown, to the great assembly at Uisnech, or to the Festival at Tara wore beautiful elegant clothes and everyone wanted clothes made by those women.

Finn mac Cumaill said to them, Women, do not sleep with any men but men that I and the Fian of Ireland will give you. While waiting word from the Fian-chief, they were at Alma in Leinster for a long time. Three of the Clanna Morna passing by the Rock of Alma saw the women at their embroidery on the rock to the northeast.

Those three warriors – Conán, Art, and Meccon – came there and said, Here is a chance to kill those of Finn and the Clanna Baíscne for, apart from Finn, Oisín, and Oscar, there are not three more valuable than those. They seized the three women and brought them to this hill where Goll and his people were.

Where have you brought those captives from? they asked.

From Alma, said the eldest of the women.

This is a reason to make peace with the Fian, said Goll.

On my word, said Conán, we did not bring them with us to make peace but to kill them in front of you.

Our curse on him who would kill them, said Goll, and as for our being present at their slaughter that certainly will not be.

Then the Clanna Morna left the hill as one man, except for those six. The women asked, Are you going to kill us?

We are, said Conán.

We will give you good favours, the woman said, every evil and every harm you have done to Finn and the Fian to be forgiven and peace made and we ourselves to be your wives.

But these were not given to them, said Caílte. They gave them three blows and cut off their heads. They were buried in the earth here and lie beneath the three standing stones. From them the three stones get their names: Étaín, Aífe, and Aillbe.

Caílte sang:

Three graves are on the hill, the grief is mine,
three dearer than all others under the three stones.
Great the loss of fair Étaín, generous with food and drink,
Aífe there and redhaired Aillbe, famous among the host.
Killed there by the son of Morna, a black deed,
the dear three under the flowers, those three in the grave.

Victory and blessing, said the warrior, you have given good knowledge to me, my son and grandson and we give you welcome for three nights, Caílte, because of the lore you have given me.

They proceeded then to the Mound of Women on Cúil Radairc, called Cúil Ó bFinn today, and entered the fort and the stronghold where they were well served and well looked after that night. They remained there until the following day when morning came with its full brightness. But that day his left leg gave Caílte pain and prevented him from leaving.

A warrior of the house said to him, That leg has shown great vigour although it is sick and unwell tonight.

Caílte spoke this poem:

> I ran from Tara of the troops, it is truth and no lie.
> Thrice I carried off from it three score hundred first bloods.

By virtue of your courage and prowess, king of the Fian, said Blathmac, tell us why you raced against them.

Caílte replied:

> The first run that I made brought many to grief
> when I took, so fair was my run, a couple of every wild animal.
>
> The run that was next thereto, it is truth and no lie,
> I put wild creatures at the cliffs and fords of Ireland.

Your vigour was great, Caílte, said Blathmac.

It was great for from one day to the next I dashed from Tonn Clídna in the south to Tonn Rudraige in the north.

Caílte said:

> This is my run on the third day, 'tis truth and no lie,
> when I released calves to cows in beautiful, chilly Ireland.

And that, Blathmac, is the reason for those runs you asked me about.

Then they heard the clamour of three packs of hounds hunting round the head of Slievelowe with Taidlech mac Ailella, king of the Connaught Leyny.

What is this barking, Caílte? asked Blathmac.

A barking of three packs of hounds with three kinds of animals in front of them.

What are those animals?

The main chase made by these packs, said Caílte, is the chase of very fierce wild stags and very fat hinds.

And this pack after them? asked a warrior.

That is the tuneful chase of dogs in pursuit of swift gentle hares.

And this third pack? asked Blathmac.

That is the furious eager chase, Caílte said, and the slaughter of heavy boars.

And what is this fourth chase? asked Blathmac.

The chase of heavy-sided low-slung badgers.

Behind the hunt they heard the shout of the servants, the swiftest of the boys, and the quickest of the warriors and the men who were the best shots and three strong slaves who bore the greatest burdens. On that day Caílte and Blathmac were at the rear of the hunt but the woman-warrior went out to see the packs and they were just as Caílte had said.

The warrior took the full of a drinking-horn from a vat of mead that she had and gave it to Caílte, saying, The vat is yours, Caílte, and were it a year that you wished to remain here it would still be yours.

Victory and blessing on you, said Caílte, we can only stay one night.

In that case, said the warrior, I want to ask you why this mound is called the Mound of Women?

Nine sisters of the Tuatha Dé Danann came here to meet nine warriors of the Fian but when they got this far the Clanna Morna discovered them and killed them. From them this place has its name, the Mound of the Women.

They remained there for that night, said goodbye next day and gave a blessing.

They went to the Cairn of Fratricide, now called the Mound of Wolfhounds. There as they mounted the hill they saw nine lovely women waiting for them with a queen of excellent shape in their midst. She wore a shirt of royal silk next to her skin, over that a tunic of soft silk, and about her a hooded cloak of crimson fastened across her breast with a golden pin.

When she saw Caílte the woman rose and kissed him three times.

Who are you, woman? Caílte asked.

I am Échna, daughter of Muiredach mac Finnachta, that is, the king of Connaught's daughter.

The women had a chess-board on which they played and a cup of delicious mead that they drank and a polished horn on top of the cup. Every time a game was won or ended they took a drink. They caroused and enjoyed themselves.

That woman had three virtues, she was one of the wisest women in the world, the most beautiful woman in the world, and anyone she advised had both wealth and respect.

Caílte said:

> Échna, daughter of Muiredach, bright radiance above a pool,
> for a month you will give opinions for men alive at this time.

Where were you last night, Caílte? asked the woman.

At the house of Blathmac Bóaire, at Cúil Radairc north in Leyny of Connaught.

Welcome, Caílte, the woman said, you have come in your own way.

She took one end of the chess-board and Caílte the other against his chest saying, I have not played chess for a long time.

When they had played for a while they put the board to one side and observed three forts near them.

Caílte asked the woman, What forts are these?

She replied: I built them.

A good woman made them, he said.

But, Caílte, she asked, what minstrel is that with you?

Cas Corach mac Caincinne, the minstrel of all the Tuatha Dé Danann and the best minstrel in all Ireland and Scotland.

He has a good appearance, said the woman, if only his minstrelsy is good.

On our word, said Caílte, however good his appearance his minstrelsy is better.

Take up your lute, she said.

Cas Corach took his lute, played on it and performed nobly. The woman gave him the two bracelets that were on her arms.

Cas Corach said, Victory and blessing be yours, woman, but I do not need them nor will I ever give them to one I would prefer to you. Take them therefore with my blessing.

Caílte sang:

Échna, daughter of a king, it is time to tell the truth,
I did not see on land or sea an equally pleasant foster-child.
You were the most generous I ever knew, the best for food and drink,
I never saw a better woman in a house in Scotland or Ireland.
She is the most generous I ever saw, the best for food and drink,
she has the best colouring of the western hosts.
I've said it before and what I say is true,
I have never seen anyone alive as beautiful as you, Échna.

It was the end of the day, so they went to the nearest of the three forts where they were placed in a secluded house. Étrom mac Lugair, the woman's guardian, rose and welcomed Caílte. The woman came in after that and they were feasting and enjoying themselves.

Caílte, she asked, why was this cairn called the Cairn of Fratricide and this mound outside the Mound of Wolfhounds?

The Woman of Malice, daughter of Rónán, a sorceress of the Tuatha Dé Danann, fell in love with Finn mac Cumaill. But Finn said that he would never marry a witch so long as he could have any other woman. When Finn released his wolfhounds they came here, one hundred and fifty of them, and the woman to spite Finn put her breath on them and locked them in this mound. And that is why it is called the Mound of the Wolfhounds, answered Caílte.

And the Cairn of Fratricide, said the woman, why was it so named?

Lám Luath son of Cumasc Debtha son of Dénam Comlainn belonged to the people of this country and any occasion of single combat that might happen to the kings of Ireland, to Cormac, Art, or Cairbre Lifechair, it was he, his father and grandfather before him who would undertake them all. At that time in the Duffry in the Dubhfid and in Slievecarbery, now called Slievegorey, there was a warrior named Borbchú mac Trénlámaig, who had a daughter called Niam. Lám Luath had nine brothers and each one of them came separately to ask for Borbchú's daughter.

Each said the same thing to him: We will kill you and all your sons unless you give us your daughter. And Borbchú for fear of being killed used to say to each of them separately: She will be yours in due course.

Then one day on this hill Lám Luath said, Is it true, brothers, that you seek the woman I have sought from Borbchú?

It is true, they replied.

He was seized with a pang of jealousy. He rose up, took his sword, struck the brother next to him and killed him. But seeing this fratricide, the seven brothers that remained put their mouths to the ground and died of grief for their brother. They were buried under this cairn and from them it is known as the Cairn of Fratricide. He who committed the deed submitted to Saint Patrick at Tara and said that if Patrick so instructed he would turn his own sword on himself.

Victory and blessing on you, Caílte, said the woman, you have given us great knowledge. But do you know about a great defect I have for which I cannot find relief?

What defect is that?

A headache but there is no water near us to cool it. I get relief when I put water to my head.

Where is Cas Corach? Caílte asked.

I am here.

Go out to the well, bring this holy water with you and sprinkle it on the well. The magic mist that hangs over it will dissolve and it will serve all men. That well belongs to Cormac's daughter, Aillbe Gruaidbreac.

Cas Corach mac Caincinne got up, took the holy water out with him, shook it on the well and it was visible to all.

The fee of welcome and hospitality is yours, woman, said Caílte, the well will serve you and the people of the territory. The well served everyone until two kings that seized power in Connaught committed fratricide. Their names were

Aed and Eógan. Aed killed Eógan at the pirate's stone, now called Gnáthal's flagstone. On that night the three greatest losses that were ever inflicted on the province of Connaught also took place: the draining away of the falls that flowed out of the Inber na Fer, now known as the Moy; the ebbing of the high tide which used to go up the Gaillim [Galway] river from the main ocean and on which the security of the whole province depended; in addition the running dry of this well, Aillbe's.

We must go away tomorrow, said Caílte. I have never put my head inside the house of a woman better than you.

Before you go, Caílte, she said, I must ask you an urgent question.

What is that?

Who is the minstrel with you and who were his father and mother?

Cas Corach mac Caincinne, the son of the poet of the Tuatha Dé Danann. He, too, is a poet of the Tuatha Dé Danann, his mother is Bé Binn, daughter of Elcmar of the Bruig.

Bad luck indeed, said the woman, that he is not the son of Bodb Derg, or Aengus or Tadg mac Nuadat.

What do you mean? asked Caílte.

I who have never loved any man have fallen deeply in love with him.

None of these, said Caílte, will turn out to be better than him in the long run, since Saint Patrick's promise that in the end he will be the poet of all Ireland. And apart from this minstrel Patrick will consign the Tuatha Dé Danann within the slopes of hills and rocks, except that now and then you may see one of them as ghosts on a transient visit to the earth. And you, Cas Corach, what is in your mind about her?

My mind is this, he replied, that I have never seen in all the women of the world one that pleased me better than that woman.

What then, Caílte asked, prevents you from coming to an agreement?

Let it be according to your will and advice, said the woman.

The men of Ireland, said Caílte, will hold the Feis Temrach and you will be given to Cas Corach there with the rights of a single wife and he will be conferred as the poet of Ireland and Scotland.

When will the Feis Temrach be held? asked Cas Corach.

At the end of the next quarter, Caílte answered.

They said goodbye to the woman and went south to the Hill of the Assembly, now called Carn Fraích meic Fidaig. They found before them on the cairn a man whose hair was rough and very grey. He had a brown cloak with a bronze hollow pin in it. He had a long staff of white hazel in his hand and before him was a herd of cattle in a fenced grassy field.

Caílte sat beside him on the hill. Who are you? he asked.

I am Bairnech mac Cairb, the warrior replied, the steward of Diarmaid mac Cerbaill, king of Ireland. In this district I hold land from the king of Ireland.

Where do you come from?

From Collamair of Brega in the east.

Do you know who was the best that ever came from Collamair? asked Caílte.

I know and the men of Ireland and Scotland know. It is Caílte mac Rónaín. Do you know where that warrior is?

I do, Caílte replied. He is making a circuit of Ireland to wherever his comrades and his foster brothers used to be in his company and I am he. I'm your first cousin for we have the same grandfather.

Caílte kissed him three times with affection and fervour and made him truly welcome.

You have come the right way, Fian-chief, said Bairnech mac Cairb. At the end of the next week Patrick and the nobles of Connaught will come to the Druid's Grave, now called Geidech's Grave. You will stay in your cousin's house, taking food and drink. And were you to come here with the greatest number of Fian and followers you ever had, you would be made welcome until the Adzehead arrives. In this district we have great troubles.

What are they? Caílte asked.

I have many herds of cattle and every year at Hallowe'en a woman comes to us from the fairy mound of Cruachain and takes the nine best cows in every herd and there is no pursuing her so she returns to the fairy mound. Neither myself nor my sons are athletes for our family's share of vigour and might is in you and in your two sons, Colla and Faelán.

Colla's vigour was indeed good, said Caílte.

What vigour had he more than the other son? asked the warrior.

It happened that he played a game of draughts one night on the rampart at Tara because the wife of Binne of the Boyne, the steward of Tara, had fallen in love with him and they, that is Colla and the Fians of Ireland, had a match at running and draught-playing.

How would you like to have the race? the Fian asked Colla.

Let you, the three battalions of the Fian, set your faces in one direction and I will run backwards, Colla answered.

So the race was run and he went over the top of Benn Étair out into the sea and was drowned there, said Caílte.

A pity, the warrior said, it is not he whom I've met, otherwise my cattle would not be stolen without vengeance.

Cas Corach, asked Caílte, do you know which of the Tuatha Dé Danann that woman is?

I know, he replied. She is Scothniam, daughter of the druid Caissirne. She plunders you from the fairy mound of Cruachain. Cathmog mac Firchirp, son of the king of Brega and Mide, killed her father and grandfather and she is taking vengeance on each of you, one after the other.

Then they went on to the stronghold of the warrior, that is, to Lis na Fleide on the western side of Carn Fraích and there were well looked after for three days and three nights.

Well, said Caílte, tonight is Hallowe'en.

If it be so, said the warrior, it is then the woman comes to plunder and pillage us.

Caílte, asked Cas Corach, how would it be if I went tonight to the door of the fairy mound?

Go, take your weapons and throw your spear, said Caílte.

Cas Corach went and not long afterwards saw the woman passing from the fairy mound, a beautiful single-coloured cloak about her with a brooch of gold in it, a shirt of yellow silk next her skin, a knot of the shirt between her legs, two spears in her hands. She had little to fear from the side she faced and little to fear from the side behind her. Cas Corach blew a blast against her, placed his brave forefinger into the thong of his spear, and hurled it at the woman. It lodged in her breast and broke the heart in her chest.

Caílte sang:

> Cas Corach of the melodies killed the furious woman, no bad thing,
> at the door of the mound up north, all at once triumphed over her.

Then Cas Corach cut off her head and brought it back to Bairnech and Caílte.

See, he said, the head of the woman that used to cause plunder and pillage on you.

Afterwards they stayed there for three days and three nights.

Then the same man said, Caílte, do you know of the other persecution that I suffer in this country?

What persecution?

Three she-wolves come every year from the Cave of Cruachain and destroy all our wethers and sheep and we get no chance at them until they go back into the Cave. Blessing on the friend who will drive them from us.

Well, Cas Corach, said Caílte, do you know the three wolves that plunder this warrior?

Indeed I do, Cas Corach replied, three daughters of Airetech from the oppressive group in the Cave of Cruachain. It is easier for them to plunder as wolves than as human beings.

They trust no one? asked Caílte.

They trust only one group, said the warrior.

What group is that?

Were they to see harps and lutes with men of the world they would trust them.

Then they will trust Cas Corach, said Caílte. Where do they usually come to?

Here to Bricriu's Cairn, replied the warrior.

How would it be, said Cas Corach, if I were to go tomorrow and bring my lute to the top of the cairn?

So early next morning he got up and went to the top of the cairn and kept playing and performing until the descent of the clouds of evening. While he was there he saw three wolves approaching. They lay down in front of him listening to his music, but he was unable to attack them. At the end of the day they went north to the cave and Cas Corach returned to Caílte. He told him what had happened.

Go back in the morning, said Caílte. Tell them it would be better to listen to music and minstrelsy in human form rather than as wolves.

Cas Corach went back to the cairn and placed his men around it. The wolves returned and lay as wolves to listen to the music.

Then Cas Corach said to them, If you were humans, listening to the music as humans would be better than listening to it as wolves.

They heard this and threw off the long dark coverings that were round them for the enticing music was as attractive to them as the music of fairies. While they were side by side and elbow by elbow, Caílte observed them. He put his finger of valour into the thong of the spear so that the spear in its deadly flight went through three of the women and stuck into the breast of her that was farthest away from him. They were on the spear like a skein drawn close together.

Caílte said:

> Caílte with his venom killed the strange, unknown trio.
> They fell, a great pity, all at the one time.

Then Cas Corach went to them and cut off their heads. From then until now the Glen of the Wolf-shapes is the name of the glen on the north side of Bricriu's Cairn.

You have performed well, Caílte, said Cas Corach. Today was not the performance of an old man, it was well for your minstrel to be with you.

How was my performance better than that of the minstrel, asked Caílte, for you lured them from the shapes of wolves into the shapes of humans?

They went then to Bairnech's fort bearing with them the heads of those three women as the prize of slaughter and triumph. They remained there for three days and three nights. It was at that time and season that Saint Patrick reached the Druid's Grave, now called the Grave of Geidech, a bishop of Patrick's company who lived there. Or it was Geidech, Maeve, and Ailill's druid, who fell there.

Aed mac Muiredaig, king of Connaught, came to Ráth Chairech Medba, now called the Mairtine of the son of Connra. That night a bad lung-disease afflicted the king of Connaught's wife, Bé Binn, daughter of Eochaid Leithderg, king of Leinster. She died there and was buried in the Hill of the Angels, now called Uarán Garaid, for a thousand angels came there to speak to Patrick three times when he was reciting his hours.

The king of Connaught came to the Druid's Grave where Saint Patrick was. They made a gathering and an assembly of the province of Connaught from Lecc Essa Lomanaig, now called Limerick, to Ess Ruaid mac Modairn, now called Assaroe.

Caílte and his people went on from the Dwelling of the Women to where Patrick was staying with the nobles of Connaught and placed his head on Patrick's chest.

The Connaught nobles welcomed Caílte and Cas Corach.

On our word, they said, never since you left us have we seen a pair that were dearer to us than you.

On my word, said Caílte, I have never since Finn departed seen a company that was dearer to me than you.

Cas Corach rose, placed his head on Patrick's chest, and knelt before him.

The gift of eloquence be yours, my son, said Patrick. Let every third word uttered by men of your art seem musical to every listener and let one of them possessed of your skill always be the bedfellow of a king and the light of every assembly.

As far as Patrick was concerned the arrival of those two was a delight of spirit and mind.

Then Patrick asked Caílte for news from the time they separated until Caílte came to him again. Caílte told him the true story.

Well, Broccán, said Patrick, let Caílte's stories be written down and preserved by you so that they may not be lost and that they may be an entertainment to multitudes and nobles to the end of time.

Holy Patrick, asked Caílte, what are your tales and tidings from the time I left you until today?

Here they are, Patrick replied. Maelán, Mugán, Brothrachán, and Dubchú of the Wiles have been banished from Oenach Derg, now called Aghagower.

Patrick sang:

> The well which I left in the land and my two untroubled salmon
> will remain there till the white Judgment, I tell you, dear Caílte.

Fer Benn, Fer Boga, and Fer Gabla, three brothers who were doing evil and wrong in the west of Ireland and three hundred thousand demons round Cruachán Aigle [the Reek] I drove forth into the sea across Ailén in tSnama since then called the Island of Demons, said Patrick.

Patrick sang:

> My bird, my water, my eagle and my beautiful holy Reek,
> will give protection from me to every one in need.

Holy Patrick, asked Benén Mór mac Aeda, what do you require should be our word for each one who wishes to go to Cruachán Aigle and drink from its well?

Old and young, they will be in your power. I have ensured that the place be a place for holiness and truth. Whoever commits evil or wrong there will experience withering of children, kindred and people. My blessing on him who will honour and defend it. So, Caílte, my friend, said Patrick, these are my tidings and transactions during the year in which you have been away from me.

Victory and blessing be yours, holy Patrick, said Caílte, you have left great benefit in that place for the Irish.

That night they erected his tent over Patrick and the king of Connaught pitched camp for six weeks until the five great provinces of Ireland arrived for the Feis Temrach. They prepared a secret hidden house for Caílte between the king's house and Patrick's tent so that each of the two might have the pleasure of listening to him. Then Cas Corach took his lute and put them into a long sleep and slumber.

They arose next day and a draughtboard was brought to them that they might play on it. Three of the men were found to be missing and the king said that none like them were to be found in Ireland or Scotland.

Then Caílte said, Do not play until I go and find a draughtboard that I saw one time when hiding it.

He went to the top of Sliab Cliathair, now called Slieve Badna, and in front of the fairy mound saw a standing stone. He put his arms around the stone and pulled it from the ground. There was a strong stone lid on a draughtboard in the place of the pillar and a lid under it. He lifted out the Solustairtech, the draughtboard of Goll mac Morna and took three men of gold and three men of silver from it. Then he put the board into the same two compact coverings of stone, came back to the king of Connaught, and placed the men in his hand. Each was as big as the fist of the biggest man in the gathering.

Were there no more than these? asked the king.

Indeed there were, said Caílte, one hundred and fifty men of gold and one hundred and fifty men of silver.

Why did you not bring me the complete set? asked the king.

You did not ask me for a set but three men for playing draughts and I brought you more than you needed. I will not move the board from where the warrior who owned it put it.

So the men were put on the board.

Who owned the board? asked the king.

Goll mac Morna, Caílte replied.

A pity you did not bring it to me.

Do not keep on about it, said Caílte, for I will never give the board to you nor will I bring you any more pieces.

They were not long there when they saw Aillenn Fhialchorcra, daughter of Bodb Derg, son of the Dagda, coming to them with one hundred and fifty women of the Tuatha Dé Danann. The woman sat down on the grass mound with Saint Patrick and the king of Connaught and told them why she had come.

What is your answer for her, king of Connaught? Patrick asked.

I will do whatever you say and wish me to do, said the king of Connaught.

I want to marry her to you for I promised her that you would marry her provided she rejected her false druidic belief and knelt to the Gospel of the King of heaven and earth.

Do you, woman, agree with that? asked the king.

I do, she replied.

So she and her company of women rose and all knelt to Patrick. Patrick joined her and the king in marriage.

Writers believe that was the first marriage the Adzehead performed in Ireland.

And the wedding-fee? asked Benén Mór.

You will have, said the king, the choice of homes of every kingdom from Lecc Lomanaig, now called Limerick, to the Flagstone of Assaroe.

And, Benén said, the fee from you, Patrick, in return to the people of the province?

I will guarantee, Patrick replied, that three kings of their race will rule Ireland and that the prosperity of Ireland will be theirs in perpetuity.

Broccán wrote down these decrees for the province of Connaught and also all that had been given to Patrick. That night after the feast of bedding and hand spreading the couple, Aed mac Muiredaig and Aillenn Fhialchorcra, daughter of Bodb Derg, slept together.

Next day the king got up early. There was a large rock on the hill near them. The king leaned his back against the standing stone and asked Caílte, Why was this stone called The Stone of the Mistake?

One time, said Caílte, when Clanna Morna came to Cuaill Cepáin in Slieve Aughty of Connaught plundering and pillaging Finn and the Fian we three battalions of the Fian marched south to the summit of Slieve Cairn in the district of Corcomroe.

Finn was not sure what the Clanna Morna were doing, that is, he did not know whether they had gone south into Munster or north into the province of Connaught. He ordered his two sons, Uillenn and Caince, to march with their Fian and their people into Munster to get news about Clanna Morna. He sent the two sons of the king of Ulster together with two hundred warriors into the cherished beautiful province of Connaught for the same purpose. There were two sons of the king of Leinster with them named Conla and Cellach. Together with two hundred warriors they followed their foster-brothers and overtook them so that in all there were four hundred warriors.

They came here, continued Caílte, and every day scouted from Áth Colta to Áth Bercha looking for the Clanna Morna and every night they returned here. Finn wondered what his people were doing because no messenger came to him from them.

Then we the three battalions of the Fian rose up and found the track of the host before us. We thought it was the track of the Clanna Morna. So we surrounded them, hand in hand, and quickly killed them, both servant and warrior, the four hundred men that they were. But next day when it was light we recognized our own people. We let out three great cries, lamenting those whom we had killed in error.

Finn ordered a big standing stone to be found for those much-loved four, the two sons of the king of Ulster and the two sons of the king of Leinster. So Oisín and I went to Ráth Medba, now called Ráth Chaerach Medba, and found this stone there. We brought it here and erected it over these men.

Victory and blessing be yours, Caílte, said the entire host. You have given us great lore and disclosure of wisdom on everything that we asked from you.

So this stone is called the Stone of the Mistake from the error of Finn and the Fian when they killed their own people, thinking them to be the Clanna Morna.

Then they went to Tara where Caílte and Oisín told their stories to the men of Ireland and the poets of Ireland preserved everything they said.

Victory and blessing on you, noble men, said the men of Ireland, although there may not be more knowledge and wisdom in all Ireland than you have imparted just now to us it is nevertheless appropriate that they should assemble in one place to receive it.

Then Cas Corach mac Caincinne got up and said, Caílte, my friend, it is now time for me to leave. The blessing of every student be yours.

And the blessing of every guardian on his student be yours, said Caílte, for you excelled the most in art of all those I've seen.

The king of Ireland, Diarmaid mac Cerbaill, said, I make you poet of all Ireland for as long as I reign.

At that time the remaining eighteen of the Fian that had accompanied Caílte came to the hill west of Tara. They bore in mind that since they were without vigour, agility, and full power they were not given that much attention or regard that anyone would even speak to them. They put their mouths to the side of the hill and died. They were buried under that mound which is called the Hill of Nines after them.

This is a wretched business, said Caílte. They were the last survivors of the great and noble people of our chief and leader, Finn mac Cumaill.

That day the old men were burdened with grief for those nines knowing that all that survived of the three battalions of the Fian were Caílte, Oisín, and those eighteen. The men of Ireland were silent, not one of them speaking together, so deeply oppressed were they with the grief that the old men showed for their Fian and their own people.

Then Oisín spoke:

Is there anyone here can tell, though weak or lowly,
where Fian's goblet lies, the Cromglenn, all alone?

Except for this day, said Caílte, there never was a time when I found it hard to speak to you, Oisín.

Caílte spoke:

Is there anyone here can tell where he turned to the right,
to the place in the green glen hidden only by a magic mist?

Oisín asked:

Is there anyone here can tell, though weak or lowly,
who put Curraig's head on the hill over Bodamair?

It was you who took off his head, said Caílte, your father who wounded him first and I who buried him in the hill.

Oisín asked:

> Is there anyone here can tell where he turned to the right,
> there met Finn alone and Oisín leaderless?

Caílte said:

> I took the head with me to the hill over Bodamair.
> It is there since that time at rest inside the hill.

Do you remember, dear friend, said Oisín, who it was that made a cast at Goll mac Morna one morning above Belach Gabráin [Gowran Pass]?

It was I, Caílte answered, that threw the spear at him. It knocked the golden helmet off his head and carried off a piece as thick as its own shaft from his flesh.

He took that proudly, said Oisín. Although it was a bad wound he put the helmet on again, took his weapons in his hand and called out to his people that he did not feel harmed in the least.

Then Oisín spoke:

> Is there anyone here can tell, though weak or lowly,
> who wounded brave Goll one morning above Belach Gabráin?

Caílte said:

> It was I struck the king, a gallant deed, Oisín,
> with a true javelin cast at the hardy son of Morna.

The king of Ireland asked them, Who killed Cairbre Lifechair in the Battle of Gabair?

It was Oisín's son, Oscar, who killed him, said Caílte.

It is best to tell the truth, dear friend, said Oisín.

Who was it then who destroyed him? asked the king.

Orlám, king of Fotharta in the south, said Oisín, a favourite warrior I had and my father before me.

Oisín said:

> Orlám son of the king of Fotharta, not a vainglorious man,
> a brother of Brónach, no lie, killed Cairbre Lifechair.

And Oscar? the king asked. Who killed him?

A single cast by Cormac's son, Cairbre Lifechair, killed him.

And Mac Lugach. Who killed him in the same battle?

Bresal mac Éirge, son of the Norse-Gaels' king from Inse Gall [Hebrides] far away, who was captain of the king of Ireland's household.

This was the last night of the Feis Temrach. They spent that night feasting and enjoying themselves. Next morning the entire host got up. The men of Ireland divided up according to their provinces, their own territories, and places of origin.

The king of Ireland came early next morning to the flagstone of the druids northeast of Tara. His wife was Bé Binn, daughter of Alasc mac Aengusa, king of Scotland. He spoke to her as follows: I want to go on a great circuit of Ireland and I want you to remain in Tara attending to the old men so that no disgrace or reproach shall come to me from the men of Ireland.

The queen replied, As you will decide and as they will request so will their happiness be achieved.

The king and the queen entered the house together where the old men, Oisín and Caílte, were and the king told them this. But Oisín was the most modest man in Ireland and said, King, it will not be done like that. Take your wife along with you and leave us to the chief steward.

Well, said the king, bring the chief steward to us.

He and his wife were brought in and the king said to them, This is the way I want you to feed the old men: put seven score cows into a fenced field and milk them for them every night, the men of Ireland must provide rations for a thousand for them every other day, they must have liquor and milk also in Tara to bathe in every other day and a layer of fresh rushes strewn in their beds. And this: they must not have drunk the last of their liquor before fresh liquor is ready to hand. And you, steward, said the king, have seven sons. I will have you and them killed should the old men be short in any item of all this.

Oisín said, The dwarf's lair in Tara that all of Ireland used to try was not more wonderful than ourselves being entrusted to Mael Muirir mac Dubáin, Tara's chief steward, and to Cuarnait, his wife, daughter of Becán, the stockowner.

What wonder was attached to the stone of destiny? asked Diarmaid mac Cerbaill.

Anyone accused by the men of Ireland was placed on that stone. If he were innocent he would turn white and red but, if not, a black spot would appear on him in some obvious place. In addition when Ireland's king stepped on to it the stone would cry out under him and her three chief waves boom in answer, the wave of Clídna, the wave of Tuad, and the wave of Rudraige. When a provincial king went onto it, the stone would rumble under him. When a barren woman stepped on it, a dew of black blood broke out of it. When one that would bear children did so, it sweated a nursing drop.

Diarmaid mac Cerbaill asked, And who was it lifted the stone or that carried it out of Ireland?

A warrior of great spirit, said Oisín.

EXPLANATORY NOTES

The Fian were described as a band (also bands) of skilled, professional warriors who defended the sovereignty of Ireland and guarded the land. They were also hunters who moved freely across the countryside, outside the bounds of organized society, enjoying the pleasures of the chase and the beauty of the natural world. They had a close relationship with the supernatural world of the Tuatha Dé Danann, who were thought to live in caves, under mounds, or on islands. Their dwellings were known as *sid*, translated here as 'fairy mound' and they are distinguished by their beautiful appearance and beautiful clothes. The result of this affinity with the supernatural brings the cycle of tales associated with Finn mac Cumaill, the leader of the Fian, into the romantic-mythological tradition widely known later in European literature and in Arthurian romance. Fian tales were very popular in Irish tradition. In Irish belief it was easy to pass from the real, transitory and mortal world into the timeless, supernatural world, the place of the immortals who were forever young. The Otherworld had various names including The Land of Promise in this text.

Finn mac Cumaill belonged to the Clanna Baíscne whose main rivals were the Clanna Morna led by Goll mac Morna. Finn was not only a warrior but had the gift of prophecy since the time he burned his thumb on the Salmon of Wisdom which he was cooking. The tooth he touched when trying to cool his thumb became known as the Tooth of Wisdom; by touching it he could discover truth. Finn's main followers in this text are Caílte and Oisín. Their survival from the third century to the fifth is a convenient fiction. Caílte's stories about various places belong to the tradition of *Dinnshenchas* (the lore of place-names) which was deeply imbedded in Irish culture.

Patrick, also known as the Adzehead (Irish Táilchenn), is credited with bringing Christianity to Ireland in the fifth century. In the course of the *Dialogue* he engages in missionary activity, going to each of the four provinces to convert the provincial kings and their followers. This part of the work is based on the various lives of Patrick which are found in the corpus of Patrician hagiography.

Since this translation does not always give English equivalents of personal names or of place-names it may be useful to provide some of the basic words. The word 'mac' means 'son,' 'meic' means 'of the son'. Thus Caílte mac Rónaín means Caílte son of Rónán, with the family name in the genitive or possessive form. Mac Tomaltaig means son of Tomaltach. Similarly Clanna Morna means 'the family of Morna'.

The following are some of the words found in various names:

Árd=height
Áth=ford
Baile=homestead or residence
Bán=white
Buide=yellow
Caill=wood
Carn=cairn
Carraig=rock
Cell=church
Cét=hundred
Cluain=meadow
Cnoc=hill
Crob=hand
Dá=two
Derg=red
Druim=ridge or back
Dub=black, dark
Dún=fort, fortress or dwelling
Finn=white
Folt=hair
Garb=rough
Inver=estuary
Leth=half
Mag=plain
Mór=great or large
Ruad=red
Sliab=mountain
Tír=country, territory
Tonn=wave
Tráig=strand
Tulach=hill
Ucht=breast